A
Threat to the Republic

The Secret of the Lincoln Assassination that Preserved the Union

Jerrod Madonna

A Threat to the Republic

Copyright 2006 by Jerrod J. Madonna. All rights reserved. Printed in the United States of America. No part of this book may be used or reproduced in any manner without written permission except in the case of brief quotations embodied in critical articles and reviews.

Acknowledgments

My gratitude and thanks to Stephen Wilensky and Annelise Finegan for their kind reviews and support. To the Surratt Society members particularly Laurie Verge, Joan Chaconas and Sandra Walia for their tireless work and research on my behalf. To my friends and family who had to put up with me through this effort. Thank you one and all.

To my wife Marianne,

Whose patience and encouragement on this adventure of discovery made the journey possible.

Preface

Most Americans know the story of John Wilkes Booth and the assassination of Abraham Lincoln, but many do not know that it was a hastily assembled plot constructed from two separate missions launched by the Confederate government in the waning days of the civil war. The first mission was a plot to kidnap the president in order to exchange him for Confederate prisoners of war. That plot failed due to the unpredictability of the president's schedule and the playboy lifestyle of the mission's leader, John Wilkes Booth.

The failure of this operation forced a more desperate decision upon rebel leaders. They launched a new mission shortly before the fall of the Confederate capitol at Richmond. The goal of this plot was to detonate a bomb in the White House and initiate a new phase of the conflict, guerilla warfare. This operation also failed with the capture of the men responsible for carrying out the mission. At this point Booth, determined to redeem himself for his previous failure, completed the task.

Preface

In the view of many, the assassination of Abraham Lincoln was the final act of the Civil War, one that accomplished nothing but the murder of America's greatest president. In reality, the assassination was greatly beneficial to the post war southern states. The reconstructed Confederacy contained far more of the white supremacist vision of John Wilkes Booth than it did of the Union victors. The Lincoln assassination began a chain of events that widened the schism between North and South and led to another form of enslavement for blacks that endured for one hundred years.

The assassination occurred at a critical point in American history. After four long years, the shooting war was over but the political divisions that caused the conflict had yet to be resolved. Lincoln understood that the coming reconstruction would be a difficult and dangerous task that was necessary to prevent a future civil war from re-igniting. The timing of his murder brought about a renewed thirst for revenge by many northerners. To quell these feelings the government moved quickly to apprehend and bring the conspirators to justice.

The speed at which the arrests, trial and executions occurred was astounding compared to modern times. In a mere twelve weeks from Lincoln's death, four accused conspirators were hanged in the nation's capital.

Secretary of War Edwin Stanton argued that Lincoln's assassination and the attempted assassination of Secretary of State Seward were acts of war committed during an armed rebellion and that a military tribunal should decide the fate of the conspirators. The attorney general agreed, and a tribunal was set up under the guidance of the war secretary. The evidence presented at this trial became the official government position as to the assassination of Abraham Lincoln

Preface

Tribunals were a political weapon used throughout the war. Under the rules of a tribunal, conviction needed only a majority opinion rather than a unanimous verdict. In addition, a tribunal could keep testimony secret by not opening the proceedings to the public. The administration's rush to prosecute gave Confederate operatives an opportunity to derail the government's case against the Confederate hierarchy by providing false witnesses and testimony. At the conclusion of the trial, evidence became scattered and stories of conspiracies began to take root.

The man closest to the evidence in the case, Secretary Stanton, firmly believed that Lincoln was a victim of a plot by the Confederate government. Continually briefed by agents in the field, he was keenly aware of the threats to Lincoln's life and did all he could to protect the president. Due to planted testimony, Stanton was unable to prove his assertion that the Confederate government was responsible to the tribunal hearing the case.

After his death in 1869, Stanton became the victim of character assassination by Confederate sympathizers due in large part to his successful prosecution of the war and his reconstruction efforts. The campaign reached it's logical conclusion in 1937 when Otto Eisenschiml wrote that Stanton colluded with Radical Republicans to have Lincoln killed. Eisenschiml's thesis struck a chord with his audience. By 1937, most of the Civil War generation had passed on, but the horror stories of the Radical Republicans and the reconstruction era continued to be resurrected and exaggerated in the segregated South.

Preface

Columbia University's William Dunning perpetuated the view of Reconstruction that the former slaves proved to be incapable of self-government necessitating segregation. His school gave academic respectability to the viewpoints of segregationists and slavery apologists who cast the Radical Republicans as the sole villains of the era. This viewpoint commonly called the 'Dunning Effect' was prevalent from the early years of the twentieth century until the Civil Rights era of the 1960's.

Recent research has continued to unravel the incongruities concerning the assassination and the reconstruction period that followed. In 1977, a search of the files of General W.E. Doster, defense attorney for conspirators Lewis Powell and George Atzerodt, produced a long missing statement of George Atzerodt, the man accused of attempting to murder Vice-President Andrew Johnson. This 'lost confession' was, made on May 1, 1865 and while parts of it, favorable to the government's case, were 'leaked' to the press and published in various newspapers at the time, the complete statement was not published until October 1988 in the Surratt Courier.

The document was a key element of authors Tidwell, Hall and Gaddy in their groundbreaking work *Come Retribution.* In his statement to police, Atzerodt revealed the follow-up mission to Booth's kidnapping scheme, a project to blow up the White House and kill Lincoln. The research verified Stanton's suspicions that Confederate leaders were involved in the plot against Lincoln. The authors documented the South's Grand Conspiracy to decapitate the leadership of the North by mining the White House. When a small group of cavalry thwarted this attempt, Booth took it upon himself to complete the mission with his small cell of conspirators. The 'Tidwell thesis' brought into question the long held assertion that Booth's actions were that of a small group and not a wider conspiracy.

Preface

The story of the assassination as presented at the trial has numerous gaps in the official and unofficial records. Many of the gaps were due to the explosive political situation under which Union prosecutors' worked. Their resultant actions left many questions unanswered and many answers unquestioned.

At the conclusion of the trial, the government dropped a curtain of silence on the case. Unlike the Kennedy assassination a century later, there was no official commission set up to review the facts and document them. Thus, it became the challenge of numerous minds to find the 'truth'.

Historians know that when reconstructing the past, large portions of the truth are available in many books and libraries. However, it is the small details of the account, the gaps of knowledge that obscure the complete picture of the story and prevent the full truth from being known. In the case of the Lincoln assassination, second hand information, educated guesses and political spin began to fill many gaps in the story.

One part of the assassination story that has helped to obscure the events of that evening was the claims of the assassin himself. Hiding in a swamp, Booth was stunned to read of the vilification of his act by Southern leaders and newspapers. With pen in hand, he began to write his own account of the assassination, twisting the facts to make him the hero of the narrative. Even though the many eyewitnesses to the event and the known evidence contradict Booth's version of the story, Booth's account has been accepted to many as gospel

Another gap was Booth's method of escape over the Navy Yard Bridge into the Maryland countryside. The sentry at the bridge took responsibility for letting Booth pass but never explained his reasoning. It seems inconceivable that an experienced sentry, whose sole purpose was to prevent people without proper authorization from crossing a bridge, would allow not one but two men to talk their way across in a time of war. If it did, logic would dictate that the sentry be court-martialed considering that his lapse contributed to the escape of his commander in chief's assassin. Yet in this case, the sentry did not even receive an official reprimand. What really happened at the bridge and why this seeming lapse of security was never addressed can be pieced together from the statements of the government's prime source of information, convicted conspirator George Atzerodt.

Successful interrogators will tell you that obtaining the truth depends upon an atmosphere of dependency and trust between the subject and the interrogator. The prisoner must realize that his welfare is wholly in the hands of his interrogators and believe that his only hope is to cooperate completely.

The historical record is clear that this was the case with George Atzerodt. The foreign-born Atzerodt derided in history as an ignorant drunkard and coward, had also proved himself a reliable source. In an attempt to save his life, he told authorities all he knew about John Wilkes Booth, the plots against President Lincoln, and the people he knew to be involved. Atzerodt gave his interrogators an inside look at the structure of Booth's group. With Atzerodt's statements in hand the government was able to quickly find witnesses who could confirm the facts as Atzerodt related them.

Preface

However, the prosecution was selective in what parts of Atzerodt's deposition they used. There was no follow-up on his assertion that the White House was a target for a mine, most probably because it was not essential to the prosecution's case. They chose not to investigate the role of Richard Smoot in the Lincoln kidnapping scheme because they did not want to believe that the kidnapping and assassination were separate plots. Later examination and revelations showed Atzerodt was truthful in these uninvestigated statements.

The 'mosaic theory' of intelligence gathering, works by gleaning little tidbits of knowledge from people and placing them together into a coherent picture. Investigators know that the process of gathering and culling bits and pieces of information that may seem innocuous at first glance could take months, if not years to come into focus.

In Atzerodt's case the information the government placed in the official record and what they chose to ignore had interesting consequences. For example, Atzerodt asserted that he refused to be part of a murder and that fellow conspirator Davy Herold was actually the man assigned the task of killing Andrew Johnson. This statement did not fit nor assist in the case the government was building against him so the prosecution chose to ignore it even though the evidence suggests that his claim had far more merit than the government's assertion that 'Atzerodt was lying in wait' to kill the vice-president. Atzerodt's statement that Herold was to be the designated assassin was withheld from the public until January 1869, **after** Atzerodt was hanged and Andrew Johnson was out of office.

Preface

Another innocuous statement made by Atzerodt and disregarded by the government proved very revealing. While being held prisoner aboard the *Montauk*, he told his interrogator that Booth and Herold had seen Andrew Johnson. If the two men had indeed made a previous contact with the vice-president, it would have had truly far reaching implications If Atzerodt was telling the truth, many anomalies of the case, the mosaic we were viewing, begin to fall into place. Clearly, the implication of this one allegation would have created a political crisis so extensive that it would have plunged the then fragile and divided U.S. government into anarchy.

Many times in history, we often find instances of small isolated events that combine to become a tipping point with consequences nobody could foresee and become a force impossible to forestall. While investigating the assassination of Lincoln, it became apparent that Stanton recognized the destructive power of an innocent favor by Andrew Johnson and realized that it had to remain secret. To Stanton revelation of this event represented, 'a threat to the republic'. Atzerodt's confession of the events leading to the assassination was promptly lost for the next 112 years.

To many Americans the issue of national security and the need for keeping secrets has been an abused trust by our political leaders. So much so, that the thought of the government of the United States crumbling into anarchy seems a remote and ridiculous proposition. However, during the Civil War, many loyal groups and individuals, some with the best of intentions, were actively destroying the fabric of the country. Lincoln was walking a fine line trying to keep all factions satisfied while fighting the bloodiest contest of all time.

Preface

American politics is supposedly a bloodless battleground but in the 1860's the rules had changed. The Lincoln assassination began one of the most critical and hate filled eras of American politics. Radicals in the legislature demanded retribution for the war and felt that only Negro suffrage would prevent another war. Lincoln's successor, Andrew Johnson managed to alienate so much of the country with his incompetence, vindictiveness and demagoguery that his impeachment came within one vote of conviction. The loss of Lincoln's political shrewdness at that critical juncture of our history still echo throughout the country. Every time we hear 'the race card' played for political gain, it illustrates the failure of the post war reconstruction.

There have been many false conspiracy theories with regard to Lincoln's assassination. Over time, Northern industrialists, the Catholic Church, Rothschild bankers, Abolitionists, Cabinet members and secret American societies have all taken turns of being the power behind the plot.

However, the pieces of the puzzle point to the conclusion that there were four separate conspiracies activated during the spring and summer of 1865. The failure of the kidnapping conspiracy set in motion the 'torpedo plot' to blow up the White House. The failure of this operation led to Booth's successful assassination plot, which necessitated a government conspiracy of silence on critical details of the plot.

This final conspiracy was successful. It was initiated not for the financial or political gain of any group or individual but to preserve the government in a time of crisis. Unfortunately, the man who benefited most from this strategy proved to be unworthy of his position and set the nation's race relations back one hundred years in a vain effort to consolidate his power.

Preface

The conclusions in this book are based upon the credibility of the government's primary informer, George Atzerodt and the historical record of the time.

*From the cowardice that dare not face the new truth,
from the laziness that is contented with half truth,
from the arrogance that thinks it knows all truth,
good Lord, deliver us.*

..... *a Kenyan prayer*

Contents

1. The Indispensible Man — 21
2. Enter the Paladin — 45
3. Kidnapping Lincoln — 77
4. The Plot Unfolds — 109
5. The Great Manhunt — 149
6. The Secrets of Mars — 189
7. Trial and Cover-up — 213
8. A Critical Rupture -1865 — 247
9. The Counter-Revolution of 1866 — 279
10. The Implosion of 1867 — 313
11. Epilogue — 349
12. Afterward — 381

Chapter 1

The Indispensible Man

The Winter of Secession

On December 20, 1860, the galleries of St. Andrews Hall in Charleston, South Carolina were stacked with onlookers as 169 delegates wearing somber clothes and an air of pride, rose one by one and voted "aye" in favor of the Ordinance of Secession. The document, unanimously approved, and read to the delegation, received punctuated applause from the standing-room-only crowd of witnesses. When the speaker read the final paragraph formally dissolving the union between South Carolina and the United States, the galleries burst into wild celebration with hats thrown in the air and women waving their handkerchiefs in approval. To Robert Barnwell Rhett, the hungriest of the fire-eating secessionists, this moment was the culmination of his personal thirty-year quest. Rhett, took the floor and implored the other slaveholding states to join South Carolina in the forming a confederacy. And so it began: America's second revolution was launched, not with a shot but with a shout.

On the same day in Washington, a short, energetic, bespectacled man became the new attorney general. Edwin McMasters Stanton, the person who ultimately would be most responsible for the reunification of the country, quietly entered public service.

Stanton was born in Steubenville Ohio, and suffered in his early years from asthma. Unable to participate in the activities of normal boys, he learned to hide his handicap behind a curt attitude.

22 A Threat to the Republic

Forced to leave school at thirteen following the death of his father, he obtained an apprenticeship to a bookseller in order to help with the financial needs of his family. At sixteen, he was able to obtain a series of loans through the family lawyer and attended Kenyon College. Upon graduation, he married his sweetheart Mary Lamson and began to practice law in Ohio.

As he started to build his reputation as a lawyer, he participated in the Ohio Democratic Party and worked successfully in the campaigns of Martin Van Buren, Lewis Cass, and James Polk. While engaged in these activities, he met fellow Ohioan and anti-slave advocate Salmon Chase. Chase was a religious, self-righteous man who tried hard to recruit Stanton to his newly formed Liberty Party. Chase fervently believed that slavery was the central problem facing the nation and had to be resolved before addressing any other political issue. Stanton backed Chase behind the scenes whenever he could, but he chose not to publicly announce his support. The abolition of slavery was a lightning-rod issue, and Stanton had enough political acumen to avoid being pigeonholed on a single emotional topic.

Between 1844 and 1846, three tragedies befell Stanton, leaving him extremely depressed. During that period his wife, infant daughter, and brother all died. He wrote to Chase, "Events of the past summer have broken my spirits, crushed my hopes, careless of the future – in a state of bewilderment the end of which is hidden."[1]

The abrupt loss of those he loved threw him into a deep state of hopelessness. He suddenly became the sole support of his son Edward, his mother, and his brother's wife and three children. He also became withdrawn and miserable, declining social gatherings and political discussions.

In order to work his way out of his depression, Stanton turned his full energies to his law practice. He turned down an opportunity to run for governor of Ohio and dedicated himself to building his professional career and income. He established a law practice in the booming town of Pittsburgh in Pennsylvania and soon built a reputation for thoroughness, effectiveness, and – most importantly – success in the courtroom. His reputation as a winner brought him important clients from his home state of Ohio along with cases from Philadelphia, Harrisburg, and Washington.

Stanton's courtroom style was often quarrelsome and intimidating. He was always a serious combatant, and resolutely kept his focus on his task. He attacked cases with his full soul and passion, and supported his positions with painstaking research. He was haughty and rude to fellow lawyers in the courtroom, but his skills soon gained him enormous respect within the legal community. In private life, he hid behind his stern mask to avoid the pain of intimate relationships, but was always warm and generous to those allowed into his circle.

By the mid-1850's he felt strong enough to mingle again in social affairs. He met and fell in love with Ellen Hutchison whose family owned the church pew in front of his. Ellen, as Stanton was to discover, had a strong will of her own. She brought him happiness and a common sense approach that balanced his natural urge to excitability. They were married in 1856.

Before he was summoned to Washington, Stanton's successful legal pleadings led to the establishment of national sovereignty over all internal navigable waters; the right of the people to control methods of public transportation; and the first successful use of the temporary insanity plea.

24 A Threat to the Republic

He was now about to enter a hornet's nest of trouble. The Democrats had just lost the 1860 election due to a split in the party initiated six years earlier by Senator Steven A. Douglas of Illinois and the passage of his Kansas-Nebraska act. The act effectively repealed the Missouri Compromise of 1820 and threw the question of slavery in the Western territories into the hands of the territorial legislatures. Among the fallout from this act was a minor civil war that erupted in the territory of Kansas between slavery and antislavery forces that resulted in a complete realignment of the major political parties. The Whig Party died and the Democratic Party lost influence in the North. The newly formed Republican Party became a new force combining the Whigs and anti-slavery Democrats.

President James Buchanan, during his lame duck term in office, was desperately trying to appease the secessionists in his party who were beleaguering him with demands. When Stanton took his seat in the cabinet, he was appalled to learn that Buchanan had given verbal assurances to the congressional representatives from South Carolina that he did not intend to reinforce the forts in Charleston while the State prepared for secession.

This status-quo arrangement changed early on the morning of December 27, 1860, when Major Robert Anderson, commander of the Federal garrison at Fort Moultrie in Charleston, determined that the fort was militarily indefensible. With daily mob tensions rising in the area, the safety of his troops was in jeopardy. On his own initiative, he ordered his officers and soldiers to the newer, safer fortifications of Fort Sumter, which was still under construction in Charleston Harbor.

The South Carolina delegation immediately howled that Buchanan had violated his pledge. They demanded that the president countermand Anderson's action and abandon Fort Sumter. Other Southerners in the cabinet viciously condemned Anderson's act and the spiritless Buchanan was ready to accede to their demands.

Stanton vigorously protested the president's pending action. He sternly informed Buchanan: "Mr. President, it is my duty as your legal advisor to say that you have no right to give up the property of the Government, or abandon its soldiers to its enemies; and the course proposed is treason and if followed, will involve you and all concerned in treason."

Buchanan was shocked by Stanton's threat, but soon realized that if he did not hold firm against Southerners' demands, his planned retirement in Pennsylvania would be anything but peaceful. Although he continued to waver, he ultimately decided not to abandon Fort Sumter. If war was to come over this issue, he was content to leave the consequences of that decision to his successor.

Stanton also witnessed first-hand the traitors in Buchanan's cabinet who had initially persuaded the vacillating president to side with them in the dispute. Among the leaders in this effort was Secretary of the Interior Jacob Thompson.

"That man from Mississippi is betraying us," Stanton confided to Secretary of War Holt. He was correct.

Thompson had been sending information to his secessionist friends in the South. When General Scott dispatched the supply ship *Star of the West* to reinforce Fort Sumter, Thompson secretly sent advanced word to South Carolina. Their pre-warned militia spoiled Scott's surprise move and fired a cannon shot across the ship's bow forcing it to retreat. Thompson then traveled to North Carolina to urge the State to secede, with the apparent blessing of Buchanan himself.[2]

But, the Attorney General's showdown with Buchanan changed the momentum of the Union's impending disintegration. Stanton rallied Northern leaders such as Benjamin Butler, Charles Winters Davis, and Thurlow Weed. Members of Congress freely discussed talk of impeaching the president. Stanton also opened an informal channel of communication with the incoming Secretary of State William Seward and warned him of decisions made by traitors in the government.

The *New York Tribune* wrote, "The marked change of policy is felt in the very air. It is Stanton."

This change of direction by Buchanan infuriated the extremist Senator from Texas, Louis Wigfall. Born and educated in South Carolina, Wigfall launched a plot to kidnap Buchanan and install Vice-President Breckenridge as the *ad term* executive until the achievement of a compromise between conservative Democrats and Republicans. The scheme fell apart when Secretary of War Floyd refused to join the coup d'état.[3]

At the attorney general's urging, the House of Representatives launched an investigation to uncover subversion within the government. At the time, only 300 – 400 marines stationed at the Washington Arsenal were available to defend a city whose mayor and chief of police were secessionists.

The Indispensible Man

Washington was rife with rumors and plots in the spring of 1861. Stanton revealed to his friend, incoming treasury secretary, Chase, that he believed an attempt to set up a provisional Confederate government in Washington would occur before Lincoln took office unless the city received military reinforcements. He was convinced that the secessionists were not only forming their own country but were also plotting to take-over the Northern states. He realized that if they could seize the public buildings and records of Washington, they could easily gain foreign recognition as the legitimate government of the United States.

As he continued trying to appease the secessionists, President Buchanan refused to see the imminent peril of the situation and declined to ask the states for additional troops. General-in-Chief, Winfield Scott, pleaded unsuccessfully with Buchanan to reinforce the Southern forts and armories against possible seizure.

A veteran and hero of the War of 1812, the Seminole War, and the War with Mexico, Scott had been an advisor to every president since Thomas Jefferson and America's most successful general since George Washington. England's Duke of Wellington, the victor of Napoleon at Waterloo, declared Scott "the greatest living soldier" and urged young English officers to study his Mexican campaign as one "unsurpassed in military annals."

A Threat to the Republic

Although Scott was now well past his prime at seventy-four years old, his reputation and loyalty to the Union rather than his native state of Virginia would prove crucial to stemming the gathering secession movement. When approached to lead Virginia's forces he boldly declared, "I have served my country under the flag of the Union for more than fifty years and as long as God permits me to live I will defend that flag with my sword, even if my own native State assails it."

Stanton's department uncovered a plot to disrupt the official electoral count of the votes on February 15. The scheme was an effort to prevent the constitutional declaration of Lincoln's election victory. If successful, it would throw the election of president into the House of Representatives. When he heard of the plan, Scott declared emphatically.

"I have said that any man who attempted by force or unparliamentary disorder to obstruct or interfere with the lawful count of the electoral vote should be lashed to the muzzle of a twelve-pounder gun and fired out of a window of the Capitol. I would manure the hills of Arlington with fragments of his body, were he a senator or a chief magistrate of my native state! It is my duty to suppress insurrection – my duty!"

When challenged by the secessionist Senator from Texas Louis Wigfall as to whether he would dare to arrest a senator of the United States for an overt act of treason, he answered emphatically, "No ..... I will blow him to hell!"

The battle-worn lion may have been old but he still had a mighty roar and no one within earshot dared to test his resolve. Under Scott's tightened security the counting of the electoral votes was properly completed while agitators hurled insults from the streets outside the capitol building.

The Indispensible Man

With Lincoln's election officially confirmed there was no legal way the secessionists could prevent him from assuming office. At this point, Southern senators decided it was best to form a new government in Montgomery, Alabama, and hand the incoming president a *fait accompli*. Scott and Stanton's actions stemmed a rapidly deteriorating situation. To prevent political interference, Stanton avoided President Buchanan and worked directly with General Scott arranging with the Governor of Massachusetts to have troops available if needed.

Due to the many death threats received, Scott advised against an inauguration parade. When he was overruled, Scott stationed artillery at every cross street and sharpshooters on top of every building on the route. He also managed to muster enough members of the weak regular army into the capital to defend the city and discourage any disruption. When viewing the unprecedented display of strength, *The New York Times* coined a catch phrase by describing this army as a "gathering host of loyal freemen, under the command of the _Great Scott_!"

On March 5th 1861, Abraham Lincoln became president over a divided country, and Edwin Stanton resumed life as a private citizen.

President James Buchanan

During the secession crisis in 1860, President James Buchanan appointed Edwin Stanton as Attorney General. Stanton's uncompromising legal positions put an end to Buchanan's appeasement policy towards the South.

Buchanan believed that he would be the last American President and later remarked that he didn't want to go home by the "burning light of hanging effigies". He retired after Lincoln's inauguration and stayed largely out of public life from that point on. He spent several years writing a book to explain and defend his administration's policies.

The Indispensible Man

Organizing the War Machine

The United States was in no shape to fight the war that started in April 1861. Realizing that the cupboard was bare, Secretary of War Simon Cameron began purchasing supplies from whoever would promise to provide them. Cameron, formerly a powerful senator from Pennsylvania, had been the political lynchpin of the iron and railroad interests. Lincoln named him as his secretary of war because he desperately needed the support of these industries in order to cope with the national emergency Cameron, as it turned out, proved to be overmatched for the position. Allegations of corruption and fraud by the contractors and the War Secretary were plentiful.

Representative Albert Riddle of Ohio said, "In any official matter he would ask you to give its status and what he had last said about it." Once informed, Cameron "would look about for a scrap of paper, borrow your pencil, make a note, put the paper in his trousers and your pencil in the other,"

Republican floor leader Thaddeus Stevens warned Lincoln that Cameron, a fellow Pennsylvanian, might not have been above temptation in the War Office.

Lincoln, conscious of Stevens' insinuation, asked him point-blank, "You don't mean you think Cameron would steal?"

"Well," said Stevens dryly, "I don't think he'd steal a red-hot stove."

When Cameron heard about the conversation, he demanded that Stevens retract the remark. Stevens dutifully went back to Lincoln to fulfill his promise to Cameron. "Mr. Lincoln", he said somberly, "I believe I told you that Cameron would *not* steal a red-hot stove. I now take that back."

32 A Threat to the Republic

One victim of Cameron's ineptitude was General William T. Sherman then head of the Department of the Cumberland. Cameron insisted that a friend of his should sit in on their military discussion. The unidentified man was a newspaper reporter.

Sherman stated he needed 60,000 troops to drive the enemy from Kentucky, and 200,000 to carry the war to the Gulf of Mexico. Cameron could not comprehend the breadth of Sherman's strategy and thought he was crazy.

The *New York Tribune* printed Sherman's entire report and insinuated that his mind was unstable and he should not be trusted with any important command. Sherman was relieved of duty and given a leave of absence.

By December, Lincoln realized that "the bottom was out of the tub". The misconduct in the war department was preventing Treasury Secretary Chase from raising the capital needed to keep the war funded. Wall Street financiers were no longer interested in buying government bonds for what looked like a long, mismanaged war. In a face-saving move for the ineffectual Cameron, Lincoln appointed him as the Minister to Russia. This position was the Siberia for failed bureaucrats. When President Andrew Jackson was asked why he appointed the ineffectual James Buchanan to the post he answered, "Because I couldn't find anyplace further away."

Seward, Chase and Lieutenant-General Scott pushed Lincoln for the nomination of Edwin Stanton to fill the vacant post. He was a firm Unionist, and it was felt that his Democratic Party membership would help heal the political rift caused by the war. It was also important to assure the nation that the war was not a Republican Party war but one conducted by a united North.

Lincoln favored Joseph Holt for the position but gave the appointment to Stanton based upon both recommendation and reputation. The two men had met professionally when Stanton was the lead attorney working on the famous McCormick Reaper case with Lincoln. As a country lawyer from Illinois, Lincoln had been given the full Stanton treatment of rudeness and contempt for his limited legal abilities. Driven to the sidelines on the case, Lincoln watched as Stanton provided him with an education on how to prepare cases for a large legal action.

Impressed with the energy and research Stanton used to present his case, Lincoln realized that he needed to improve his own competency if his law practice was to retain important cases. Although knowing firsthand that Stanton could be difficult to work with, he was equally aware that the war department badly needed Stanton's energy, honesty and competency.

Lincoln confided to George Harding, a fellow attorney on the McCormick case, "I am about to do an act for which I owe no explanation to any man, woman or child in the United States except you. You know the war department has demonstrated the great necessity for a secretary of Mr. Stanton's great ability, and I have made up my mind to sit down on all my pride, and maybe a portion of my self respect and appoint him to the place."

Massachusetts Congressman Henry Dawes dropped in on the president after the announcement of the appointment to congratulate him on getting a man like Stanton for his cabinet. He then warned him that the new secretary of war might "run away with the whole concern."

Lincoln acknowledged Stanton's traits of relentless drive coupled with a state of high anxiety and said, "We may have to treat him as they are sometimes obliged to treat a Methodist minister I know of out West. He gets wrought to so high a pitch of excitement in his prayers and exhortations that they are obliged to put bricks in his pockets to keep him down. We may be obliged to serve Stanton in the same way, but I guess we'll let him jump a while first. Besides, bricks in his pockets would be better than bricks in his hat." [4]

On January 15, 1862, Stanton became secretary of war. He would have just three months to get the armed forces ready for the spring campaign. He quickly realized the enormity of the crisis and pledged his unrelenting drive to preserving the nation. In addition to the normal duties of the war department, Lincoln's suspension of the writ of *habeas corpus* gave more power to Stanton's department than at any other time in the nation's history.

The writ guarantees a prompt hearing in court to determine the legality of the arrest. With the writ suspended, Stanton could jail anyone at anytime for any reason. He had a large force of detectives who oversaw the arrests of suspected rebels and were in charge of the prisons that housed them.

The problems Stanton inherited were enormous. Washington was full of army officers looking to advance their careers thru political connections rather than competency on the battlefield. The government's payroll included people who were aiding and abetting the secessionists while some army divisions went unpaid for weeks.

Contractors fraudulently looted the treasury and expenditures spiraled out of control. England and France watched the developments from overseas eagerly supplying both sides in the conflict. Most of the cloth used to make uniforms for both the North and South came from abroad. Although the South was able to get credit from European banks, the North paid for their supplies with the gold from California's mines.

By the end of January, Stanton was ready to invoke measures to end these problems. He ordered that the war department would not award contracts to foreign suppliers for any article that was producible in the United States; he then cancelled all outstanding orders with those suppliers. Lincoln and Seward initially opposed this move thinking that it would "complicate the foreign situation" and force one of the European powers to ally themselves with the rebels. Stanton argued that it would keep gold within the country and make the United States a self-supporting nation. Besides, he said, "If the order was not issued, there would very soon be no situation to complicate."

This order, it turns out, would have far-reaching effects on the struggling nation. It would boost the burgeoning industrial age in America by making it self sufficient in many areas. The growth of the Union Army that took farmers from the fields resulted in the replacement of their labor with the McCormick Reaper. Singer's sewing machines replaced much of the manual labor needed to make uniforms and the North's rapidly escalating ability to replace destroyed locomotives and tracks ultimately led to the construction of the transcontinental railroad and the opening of the West after the war ended.

36 A Threat to the Republic

Stanton then revamped the procedure for contractors by requiring them to have all contracts submitted in writing to the head of the proper bureau. Any deal that was not written and properly authorized was considered fraudulent and not to be paid. This brought about howls of protest and enormous political pressure on Stanton, but the cantankerous secretary stubbornly held his ground and saved the Treasury millions of dollars.

His first military crisis occurred on March 9, 1862, when Navy Secretary Gideon Welles informed the president that the ironclad *Merrimac* had left port in Norfolk and had destroyed the warship *Cumberland* and the frigate *Congress* off Hampton Roads with a loss of more than 300 men. The presence of the ironclad seriously jeopardized General McClellan's newly launched Peninsular Campaign by placing his starting point, Fort Monroe located at the tip of the peninsula, in imminent danger.

Welles tried to calm the situation by saying that the *Monitor*, the Union ironclad, was ready to engage the *Merrimac*, but Stanton was not reassured and began to cross examine Welles:

"How many guns did the *Monitor* have against the six-gun *Merrimac*?"

"Two," was the reply.

"And what precautions have you issued if the *Monitor* loses the battle? Why is it not unlikely that we shall have from one of her guns a cannon ball in this room before we leave it?"

Welles, taken aback by this challenge, weakly replied that he had confidence in the *Monitor*, a ship that had never had a sea trial and had just left her dry dock to do battle for the first time.

Stanton quickly dispatched telegrams to the governors of the East Coast States to be ready to obstruct their major harbors with wrecks and chains.

"The president himself was so excited that he could not deliberate or be satisfied with the opinions of non-professional men, but ordered his carriage and drove to the navy yard to see and consult with Admiral John Dahlgren and other naval officers, who might be there. Dahlgren, always attentive and much of a courtier had, to a great extent, the president's regard and confidence; but in this instance Dahlgren, who did not know of the preparation or what had been the purposes of the Department, could give the president no advice or opinion, but referred him to me (Welles)." [5]

Stanton ordered Dahlgren to load sixty canal boats with rocks in order to obstruct the Merrimac should she steam up the Potomac. This order produced an inter-department conflict with the Navy since the order did not come from the navy secretary. When Welles went to the president, he found that the order from Stanton had Lincoln's approval. Lincoln felt that the precaution was warranted but if not needed could do no harm. Welles, a political insider, was upset that Stanton, the newcomer had assumed responsibility and upstaged him in front of the president. After the *Monitor* fought the *Merrimac* to a draw and relieved the crisis, Welles scornfully called the rock-filled boats *Stanton's Navy*.

The *Merrimac* incident drew a line between Welles and Stanton. When Stanton later asked him for help in securing the Mississippi and its tributaries from the rebels Welles turned him down.

38   A Threat to the Republic

Welles was primarily concerned with ocean-going vessels, which could blockade the South. He was not interested in building river craft. The resourceful Stanton then called upon his former legal clients in the shipping industry who sold him inland riverboats and had them rebuilt as rams and gunboats. In perhaps the greatest achievement of the war, within 60 days Stanton had not only built and equipped a river navy but had captured the city of Memphis and cleared the Mississippi up to Vicksburg. Combined with this feat was his personal leadership of the land and naval victory at Norfolk, which forced the scuttling of the *Merrimac*. Stanton's victorious campaign was a source of great embarrassment and irritation to Welles. Stanton never visited the Navy Department and Welles never visited the war department. He felt that Stanton had showed him up, and he never wasted an opportunity to criticize him.

As he became more familiar with his position, Stanton began to put his stamp on the department. He announced that only the merit criteria would produce military promotions, the dismissal of all "neutral" and disloyal employees and the imprisonment of military personnel who looted or stole. He organized the Military Telegraph and Railway Systems bringing them under his command. He armed the slaves of rebel masters to serve in the Union Army and lobbied hard for the Emancipation Proclamation. Most important of all, however, he took many arrows of criticism for Lincoln.

In an effort to have the remaining part of his day free from interruptions, Stanton gave the morning hours to the public. At 9:00 every morning, he slipped into his "suit of armor" and went to the head of the long line of people waiting to see him in his reception room. He never sat during these meetings; instead, he stood at a high desk and listened to people from all walks in life that had waited to talk with him.

Contractors, politicians, schemers, soldiers, mothers, and office seekers typically asked for favors. In an attempt to visit with as many people as possible, Stanton was quick, curt, and direct. He had devised a rule or procedure to handle each situation. Those who followed the rules typically received their favor, those who did not found him to be mean-spirited and dictatorial.

One who found this out quite early was Mary Lincoln who had sent to him a man requesting a commissary appointment. Stanton tore up the card and told him," If you have to have a card from the First Lady, you're obviously not capable." The next day the man returned with a formal request from Mrs. Lincoln. Stanton tore that up as well. Then he called on Mrs. Lincoln and gave her a lecture on her duties to the nation and her husband. She apologized and promised never to bother him with such requests again. Mary Lincoln had a long list of people whom she disliked, including Stanton's wife Ellen; but she always respected her husband's war secretary.

During this daily routine, he was intensely earnest with all who came to him no matter what their positions were. The interests of the government were always his paramount concern.

John Hay, Lincoln's secretary once remarked that he thought it preferable to "make a tour of a smallpox hospital than to ask Stanton for special favors."

Even friends of Abraham Lincoln found this to be true. A man, who had once befriended Lincoln early in his life, asked for an appointment for his son. Congressional representatives Lovejoy of Illinois and Julian of Indiana met with Lincoln, who endorsed the application and sent them to see Stanton. Stanton refused the application and did not have the time to argue the point. "The position is of high importance, and I have in mind a man of suitable experience and capacity to fill it. I do not care what the president wants, the country wants the very best it can get. I am serving the country, regardless of individuals."

When the congressmen returned to Lincoln and related their experience, Lincoln shook his head apologetically and replied, "Gentlemen, it is my duty to submit. I cannot add to Mr. Stanton's troubles. His position is one of the most difficult in the world. Thousands in the army blame him because they are not promoted and other thousands blame him because they are not appointed. The pressure on him is immeasurable and unending. He is the rock on the beach of our national ocean against which the breakers dash and roar without ceasing. He fights back the angry waters and prevents them from undermining and overwhelming the land. Gentlemen, I do not see how he survives, why he is not crushed and torn to pieces. Without him, I should be destroyed. He performs his task superhumanly. Now do not mind this matter, for Mr. Stanton is right and I cannot wrongly interfere with him."[6]

The more Stanton accomplished the more he became indispensable to Lincoln. His handling of the war enabled Lincoln to address the numerous political problems facing the administration. Lincoln affectionately nicknamed him "Old Mars" after the Roman god of war and took care not to make too many suggestions that compromised his authority. Stanton gave no indication of displeasure at the title Lincoln had bestowed upon him, but neither did he give Lincoln the satisfaction of knowing that he enjoyed the nickname.

Once when complying with a petitioner, Lincoln sent a written order to Stanton who, not only refused to execute the order but blurted out, "If the president wrote this then he's a damn fool!"

When the startled petitioner returned to Lincoln and told him of Stanton's statement; Lincoln, in mock astonishment asked, "Did Stanton really call me a damn fool?" When assured that he did, Lincoln replied, "Well, I guess I had better see Mr. Stanton about this. Stanton is usually right."

While Lincoln showed great deference to the arrogant General George McClellan, Stanton quickly grew tired of his haughty attitude, lack of progress, and personal snubs. Convinced that McClellan was editing field reports to his personal advantage, Stanton ordered the telegraph office transferred from McClellan's headquarters to an office in the war department. This order gave Stanton control over all military communications. The move heralded the beginning of the end of McClellan's career and made Lincoln a frequent visitor to the war department.

Gideon Welles groused about this in his diary. "Stanton does not care usually to come [to the White House], for the president is much of his time at the war department, and what is said or done is communicated by the president, who is fond of telling as well as of hearing what is new. Three or four times daily the president goes to the war department and into the telegraph office to look over communications."[7]

A Threat to the Republic

Over time, Lincoln and Stanton developed a deep and abiding friendship. Stanton, like many others in the country, realized his first impression of Lincoln and his abilities had been shortsighted. Both men spent their summers in adjoining cottages at the Soldiers Home north of the city to escape the summer heat. Lincoln's self-effacing character broke down the walls that the volcanic Stanton had built around himself. Lincoln spent more time with Stanton than any other member of his cabinet. Whenever there was an impasse between them, Stanton would argue passionately but would ultimately yield to Lincoln's judgment. Stanton's sharp mind and attention to details frequently saved Lincoln from error. Lincoln's humor, firm support, and lack of pretentiousness saved Stanton from the outrages of partisan politics. The two of them recognized and appreciated each other's strengths; together they counterbalanced each other's faults.

Even though their personalities seemed to be polar opposites, they shared the same philosophy of democracy. They understood why the enormous effort the nation was undergoing was necessary to preserve democratic principles. Slavery was not only a moral problem but also an economic, religious, and political one. Even though the North was fighting to end the rebellion and preserve the Union, many were not necessarily fighting to end slavery. However, both men knew that the slavery issue drove everything. Due to the politics of the time and the fragile coalition that Lincoln was trying to maintain between the northern and border states, the issue was initially framed into how best to use it to win the war. Once the war was over, it would need to be re-addressed on a more permanent basis otherwise a future conflict would be inevitable.

The rapport between the two men engendered hard feelings among cabinet members Montgomery Blair, Gideon Welles, and Salmon Chase, as they vied for Lincoln's attention. In the case of Chase, who had ambitions to succeed Lincoln as president, the relationship between Lincoln and Stanton eventually caused an irreparable split in Stanton's and Chase's long friendship late in Lincoln's term.

The issue of Lincoln's security caused a major disagreement between the secretary of war and the president that was never resolved. Within the White House itself, all the doors to the Pennsylvania Avenue side of the mansion were open throughout the day and late into the evening. There were two officers assigned during the day, one guarding the outer door and one guarding Lincoln's office.

His private secretary John Nicolay wrote: "From the very beginning of his presidency, Mr. Lincoln had been constantly subject to the threats of his enemies. His mail was infested with brutal and vulgar menace, and warnings of all sorts came to him from zealous or nervous friends. Most of these communications received no notice. In cases where there seemed a ground for inquiry, it was made as carefully as possible, by the president's private secretary, or by the war department; but always without substantial result. Warnings that appeared most definite, when examined, proved too vague and confused for further attention. The president was too intelligent not to know that he was in some danger. Madmen frequently made their way to the very door of the executive office, and sometimes into Mr. Lincoln's presence. But he had himself so sane a mind and a heart so kindly, even to his enemies that it was hard for him to believe in political hatred so deadly as to lead to murder." [8]

Newspapers lampooned Lincoln for sneaking into Washington to foil an assassination attempt before his first inaugural. Stung by this criticism, Lincoln protested the presence of armed guards as imperialism not worthy of a democracy. Stanton using his own authority ordered a cavalry detail to protect him on trips between the White House and the Soldiers Home; he also placed an infantry company on the grounds of the White House and had a member of the Metropolitan Police Force accompany him whenever he left the Executive Mansion.

Lincoln did not like these arrangements. He hated being on his guard and having to distrust any man who approached him. Mary Lincoln also worried about his carelessness. "Mother has got a notion into her head that I shall be assassinated, and to please her I take a cane when I go over to the war department at nights – when I don't forget it."

Oftentimes, Lincoln would get so involved in whatever subject he was thinking about that he would forget his vulnerability and not wait for his guards. Eager to escape the realities of the war, his trips to the theatre became more frequent and noted by one of the most famous actors of the day.

Chapter 2

Enter the Paladin

A Star is Born

John Wilkes Booth was a charming, intelligent, and charismatic man who was well liked and admired by everyone who knew him. Engaging and appealing both on and off the stage, his action on April 12, 1865, was a complete shock to those who befriended and worked with him. When friends recalled their memories of him, they often spoke of his generosity and magnetic personality. He seemed to be able to draw to him people of all stripes, and all enjoyed his company. How he came to be Lincoln's assassin is a story of how deeply the Civil War affected the thinking and actions of the people of that era.

Booth was born the ninth of ten children on his family's farm outside of Baltimore in 1838. His father Junius was one of the most famous actors on the American stage known for the power of his performances and his problems with alcohol. He named his last son after the famous English Parliamentary radical John Wilkes with whom he claimed a family connection. Wilkes known in England as "the agitator", published attacks on King George III in the 1770s and supported the rights of the American colonists.

The boy grew up to be the family favorite. Spoiled by both parents they allowed him to do pretty much as he pleased. His father was a pacifist who forbade his sons to hunt. He believed that the sanctity of life extended to animals and taught his sons never to kill any living thing; even the rattlesnakes on the farm were off limits. He also refused to own slaves hiring free blacks to help on the farm he named Tudor Hill.

But with his father away acting most of the time, his favorite son proved to be the rebellious sort who enjoyed challenging the rules. As a young boy, he took pleasure in shooting his mother's tomcats or the slaves' dogs. His punishment was never more than a mild reprimand.

His brother Edwin described his brother's maturation process as harmless fun. "He would charge on horseback through the woods on the Maryland farm, spouting heroic speeches, holding in his hand a lance, a relic of the Mexican War."

As a young man, John Wilkes attended the Milton Academy, a college preparatory school near Baltimore where he developed a tenacious rather than intuitive intelligence. He had a great power of concentration and never let go of a subject until he had it mastered. From early boyhood, he was argumentative and fervid in debate bringing more energy to his schoolwork than his brothers. [9]

It was near that campus that a farmer named Edward Gorsuch asked for federal assistance under the new Fugitive Slave law in arresting some escaped slaves. When they approached the town of Christiana, Pennsylvania, they met with armed resistance by abolitionists and former slaves. In the ensuing fight, Gorsuch was killed and his son wounded. The result of this tragedy personally affected the young Booth a friend of the wounded son. To him the abolitionist cause was lost forever.

Booth's sister Asia recalled that as a lad of twelve, he had met a gypsy who offered to read his fortune for a fee. Legends, ill omens, and superstitions were prevalent parts in people's lives during that time. The young Booth gave her the palm of one hand as he wrote what she told him with the other.

"Ah, you've a bad hand; the lines are all cris-cras. It's full of sorrow, Full of trouble, Trouble in plenty, everywhere I look. You'll break hearts; they'll be nothing to you. You'll die young, and leave many to mourn you, many to love you too, but you'll be rich, generous, and free with your money. You're born under an unlucky star. You've got in your hand a thundering crowd of enemies-not one friend- you'll make a bad end, and have plenty to love you afterwards. You'll have a fast life-short, but a grand one. Now, young sir, I've never seen a worse hand, and I wish I hadn't seen it, but every word I've told is true by the signs. You'd best turn a missionary or a priest and try to escape it."[10]

Throughout his life, whenever misfortune came upon him, he remembered the words of the gypsy. Her predictions would haunt him until the end of his days.

After the Milton Academy, Booth attended St. Timothy's Hall, an Episcopalian military academy in Catonsville, Maryland. St. Timothy's was a school that stressed discipline and military order, and attracted many sons of the finest families in Baltimore. It is here Booth met his future co-conspirator Sam Arnold and became an expert at horsemanship and pistol shooting.

Although his father preferred that his children become farmers or learn a trade skill, he also encouraged their interest in literature and the arts. When he was home, he would entertain them by reading books from his extensive library or telling them stories of his acting travels on the road.

As Junius Sr. aged, his dependency upon alcohol became greater. His oldest son June began accompanying him on his tours to keep watch on him. After four years, June gave way to Edwin. Both sons began to earn their spurs on the stage while keeping their father away from the bottle.

When their father died in 1852, Edwin was ready to give up acting, return home and run the family farm. However, his mother told him that young Johnnie and the rest of the children could manage without him. Edwin toured the West with a troupe that included a talented actress named Laura Keene and began to develop his craft.

Unfortunately, young Johnnie's heart was not in farming. As overseer of the farm, he looked down upon the hired help and kept his distance from people of color. The notion of rank instilled by his military education brought out his elitist feelings towards those who worked the land.

He was little help to his mother and refused his brother June's advice to return to school. He was headstrong and undisciplined but his mother refused to try to control him fearing that he would become even harder to handle.

When Edwin and June successfully followed their famous father's footsteps onto the stage, the Booth name became America's first family of actors. To their precocious little brother, it was only a question of time before he surpassed them as the brightest star of the family. Booth confided to his sister Asia, 'I must have fame, fame!'

The 1850s was a period of political instability in the country. The passage of the Kansas-Nebraska Act brought the slavery issue into the forefront and eventually the disintegration of the Whig party. During this time, Booth became more politically aware and opinionated on the issues facing the country. He and his sister Asia attended rallies of the nativist Know-Nothing Party. The party was both anti-Catholic and anti-immigrant. It championed the so-called rights of Protestant, American-born, male voters.

The party began as a secret society getting its informal name from its members replying, "I know nothing," when asked about their role in the organization. The Know-Nothings alleged that

Pope Pius IX was an opponent of liberty, democracy and Protestantism. They fanned the fears about the new waves of immigration as a plot to subjugate the United States through a continuing influx of Catholics controlled by Irish bishops obedient to and personally selected by the Pope. With the dissolution of the Whigs, membership in the new third party soared. By 1854, the Know-Nothings formed the American Party and won state and city offices nationwide in that year's election.

However, winning elections through demagoguery and initiating changes to meet these imagined fears are two different things. The early enthusiasm for the party of fear and rage wore thin. In the 1856 election, former President Millard Fillmore, the Know-Nothing candidate, carried only Booth's state of Maryland before the party dissolved.

When he turned seventeen Booth decided, against his mother's wishes, that it was time to join his brothers in the family business. He began his stage career at the St. Charles Theatre in Baltimore at the urging of his future brother-in-law, John Sleeper Clarke. Clarke was a schoolmate of Edwin Booth and worked with him on amateur productions. Clarke later became Asia's husband, a famous comedian and an astute theatrical impresario working with the Booths on many successful ventures

The next season Booth became a stock company member at the Arch Street Theatre in Philadelphia where he struggled to learn his lines and perfect his technique. The spoiled Booth believed that his mere appearance on stage would win him acclaim. As a result he failed to properly learn his lines and had a disastrous year. The embarrassment of his failure caused him to move on to other cities and audiences using the stage name J.B. Wilkes in order to avoid comparisons with his famous father.

Not until the 1858 season at the Marshall Theatre in Richmond did Booth begin to hit his stride as a stock actor. He still flubbed his lines on occasion but learned to disguise his mistakes with dramatic rhetoric or acrobatic choreography. In October, Edwin came to Richmond to perform Hamlet and cast John as his friend Horatio. At the end of the play he took his brother aside and announced to the audience, "I think he's done well, don't you?" The audience responded enthusiastically.

The handsome young man began to give a spark to the characters he played, and started to gain favorable comparisons to the performances of his father and brothers. Southern society was more accepting of actors than the North. In Richmond he was socially accepted, and began to enjoy the attention and adulation of the Southern aristocrats. His education at St. Timothy gave him the skills of an expert fencer, a great horseman, and a crack shot with a pistol. These valued talents allowed him to ingratiate himself with the southern society of Richmond. His elegant manners, attentive personality, strong physique, black wavy hair, and dark lustrous eyes charmed the Southern belles.

Booth's idyllic life changed one year later when abolitionist John Brown and eighteen of his followers raided the town of Harpers Ferry, Virginia, taking control of the federal arsenal. Brown intended to use the armaments seized to free all the slaves in Virginia. The reaction to the raid was electric. An armed slave rebellion had long been the nightmare that Southerners most feared.

Southern secessionists, a very vocal minority, did everything possible to play on Southern fears and transform Southern anger into an anti-Northern fever pitch. Democrat Party newspapers anxious for a political angle to the raid, played into the secessionists hands by turning the incident into a plot sponsored by the newly formed Republican Party. The long fuse to war lit by Brown was fanned immeasurably by partisan hatred.

One of the main casualties of this hatred was Senator William H. Seward. Seward was widely regarded as the lead Republican and its probable presidential candidate in 1860. Even though he condemned the raid, Southerners and Democrats raged that his speeches against slavery inspired Brown's attack.

From the floor of the U.S. Senate, future Confederate President Jefferson Davis declared: "We have been invaded and that invasion and the facts connected with it show Mr. Seward to be a traitor and deserving of the gallows!" These unremitting attacks had a dampening effect on Seward's political career as party leaders began to look more favorably towards the moderate dark horse candidacy of Abraham Lincoln.

Two weeks before Brown's execution, Virginia's Governor Henry A. Wise fearing a plot by abolitionists to rescue Brown at Charlestown, called out the city militia Richmond Grays to provide security. To Booth the adventure of the moment appealed to the heroic figure he longed to become. Watching the Grays assemble on the train he impulsively signed on. He purchased a uniform and boarded the train. The two men who would change America's destiny would come together.

As the Grays kept their vigil over Brown, John would entertain them with readings from Shakespeare. A reporter from a Richmond newspaper saw the performance and wrote: "Amongst them [the soldiers] I notice Mr. J. Wilkes Booth, a son of Junius Brutus Booth, who though not a member[of the troop], as soon as he heard the trap of the drum, threw down the sock and buskin [his job as an actor], and shouldered his musket with the Grays to the scene of the deadly conflict".[11]

Brown approached his execution as a foretold date with destiny. Conscious of his impending martyrdom Brown addressed the crowd with his prophetic vision.

"I, John Brown am now quite certain that the crimes of this guilty land will never be purged away; but with blood. I had as I now think: vainly flattered myself that without very much bloodshed; it might be done."

The manner by which Brown approached his death deeply affected Booth. His prophecy and the manner in which he faced the gallows harkened him back to the little boy charging on horseback with a lance and fiery speeches. Brown died a hero to his cause and his name became celebrated in history and song. "John Brown was man inspired," Booth admitted later, "a brave old man."

Booth witnessed Brown's devotion and longed for his fame but the price of fame was sacrifice and his immaturity prevented it. Even as an actor, he resented his brother Edwin's dedication to his craft. He could not discipline himself to learn his lines correctly, often covering his errors with histrionics. He could shoot small animals without fear of retaliation but could never put himself in harms way for a cause. The uniform he wore was merely an actor's costume. As he removed it for the last time, he understood that he would have to gain the notoriety he desired in another way.

The War Years

After the execution of Brown, Booth returned to Richmond to learn that he had been fired for leaving his job without giving any notice. Many playgoers wrote letters of objection to the theatre manager and his fellow militiamen marched to the theatre in protest. The groundswell of support and publicity gave the actor newfound fame.

Edwin's fiancée Mary Devlin wrote, "Your news concerning the mad step John has taken I confess does not surprise me. 'Tis a great pity he had not more sense but time will teach him…I hope nothing serious will occur there, for it would frighten your mother so."[12]

As Booth continued his tour below the Mason-Dixon Line, he exaggerated his role in witnessing the hanging of John Brown into his participation in Brown's capture at Harpers Ferry. The story took on a life of its own, and the publicity it generated helped to make Booth a favorite in the South. Booth learned that reality was any story that he could twist to his benefit. John Wilkes Booth became not only a star of the stage but a Southern patriot as well, mesmerizing his fans with talk of 'rebel heroism'.

When the shooting war began, the fiery Southern patriot hastily retreated to Baltimore. He told his friends that a pistol had exploded accidentally wounding him in the foot and he needed to recover at home. The timing of this 'accident' provided a convenient excuse to avoid putting his words into action.

At the end of the 1859 theatrical season Booth learned that a new touring company was gearing up for the 1860 season. A touring group provided the stars for the plays in out-of-town venues while the local theatres provided the stock company of actors. To become a touring star was the highest rung of the ladder, and with Edwin's help, John Wilkes Booth became a leading man.

Throughout the war years, Booth played to some outstanding reviews in the North. However, like so many families during the war that pitted brother against brother, his support of the Southern position was contrary to the rest of his family. Because his sympathies toward the South combined with his sibling rivalry with Edwin was so virulent, Edwin refused to discuss the issue with him. To keep peace, Booth promised his mother that he would not cause a split in the family by actively supporting the Southern cause although he told his sister that he regretted doing so.

During the 1862 to 1863 season, Booth's sympathies for the Confederates led to his arrest in St. Louis for making anti-government statements. After paying the fine and taking the oath of allegiance, he continued his tour. In July of 1863, he told his entourage, "What a glorious opportunity there is for a man to immortalize himself by killing Lincoln."[13] Many thought of him as a blustering coward but sometime during this period, he became involved in clandestine operations with Southern agents. He told his sister Asia,

> "I have only an arm to give; my brains are worth twenty men, my money worth a hundred. I have free pass everywhere. My profession, my name is my passport. My knowledge of drugs is valuable, my beloved precious money – is the means, one of the means by which I serve the South."[14]

Booth told Asia that he was smuggling precious drugs to the Confederates, particularly quinine. Blockade running was a dangerous but highly profitable operation, and quinine was a most desired commodity. It is unknown if Booth profited by this activity or did it solely for patriotic reasons.

What we can conclude from this insight is that the actor knew how to lie effectively to high placed officials, gain their trust, and obtain passes for covert purposes. Booth acknowledged to his sister that he had obtained a pass that 'has given me freedom of range'. The news that her brother and hero was a spy shocked Asia. "I found myself trying to think with less detestation of those two despicable characters in history, Major Andre and Benedict Arnold.'[15]

Successes on the stage led the restless Booth into another risky venture. He decided to go into the oil business and drill in the fields near Franklin, Pennsylvania. He formed a partnership with John Ellsler and Thomas Mears called the Dramatic Oil Company where Booth furnished most of the capital. He planned to join his partners in Pennsylvania as soon as the 1863 to 1864 season had finished; until that time he had important engagements to complete.

Among these was an appearance at the brand new Ford's Theatre in Washington where he portrayed the double roles of Phidias and Raphael in *The Marble Heart* before President and Mrs. Lincoln. His performance that night must not have been up to his usual high energy standards. John Hay, the president's secretary, described the play as, "rather tame". However, the president sent word backstage that he would like to meet the actor, but Booth declined the invitation. On February 1, 1864, Booth began a two-week run as Richard III in Nashville, Tennessee where he met Military Governor Andrew Johnson and spent time with his secretary William Browning.

During an engagement in New Orleans, Booth began to have problems with his voice. His constant run from one theatrical engagement to another was making him a great deal of money but the constant toil was having an effect. Booth had little time or use for vocal exercises and now he began to pay a price. Doctors told him that he had been misusing his voice, prescribed rest, and vocal exercises.

After a three-week hiatus, he returned to the stage with a four-week engagement in Boston beginning on April 25. Booth struggled through his problems with the hoarse voice but it would be the last major engagement of his career. His voice needed rest.

As the summer progressed and the oil drilling began, Booth became involved with another activity. On July 26, 1864, he registered at the Parker House in Boston along with three men from Canada. One of these men was a frequent occupant at the St. Lawrence Hall in Montreal, the headquarters of the Confederate Secret Service. Based upon his actions after this meeting, it is apparent that Booth changed his plans from becoming an "oil man" to becoming an active operative in the Confederate Secret Service.

The war was going badly for the Confederates that summer as Grant continued to wage a fierce war of attrition with the Army of Northern Virginia. As he moved his army closer to Richmond, Lee attempted to relieve the pressure on his defenders by sending General Jubal Early up the Shenandoah Valley to liberate prisoner of war camps, and, if possible, take Washington. Lee hoped that this movement would be a replay of Stonewall Jackson's Shenandoah Operation that Lee had used so effectively to stymie McClellan's Peninsular Campaign in 1862.

Enter the Paladin

Jubal Early was arguably the Confederacy's most aggressive general. In a message to Lee he promised that he would "threaten Washington, and if I find an opportunity, to take it". As he approached the city, Col. Bradley Johnson suggested a lightening cavalry strike to capture Lincoln and bring him to Richmond as a prisoner of war. The plan sounded feasible to General Wade Hampton but Early demurred.

Fort Stevens guarded the city and Early expected it to be lightly manned. As he looked at the parapets through his field glasses, he could see that they were heavily lined with troops. Grant had sent his Sixth Corps to block Early's advance. Realizing the heavy stakes involved he decided to forgo an attack on Washington and send Johnson's cavalry to free the twelve thousand prisoners residing in Point Lookout prison on the peninsula between the Chesapeake and Potomac.

Unfortunately, Grant sent enough reinforcements to blunt both advances. As Early retreated, Grant launched General Philip Sheridan on a scorched earth campaign after him through the Shenandoah Valley. Although Early and Johnson failed, they passed along the idea of kidnapping Lincoln to the Confederate hierarchy where it began to take root.

In September, Confederate agents were given the task to determine the feasibility of abducting Lincoln through a clandestine operation. The man heading this mission was Thomas Nelson Conrad.

Conrad began the war as headmaster of Georgetown College. He was a frequent guest of President and Mrs. Davis whenever he was in Richmond.[16] Conrad knew Washington very well and stayed undercover at the Van Ness mansion near the White House. The house was one of the first mansions built in Washington. John Peter Van Ness, the previous owner was famous for the lavish entertainment he provided Washington lawmakers at the home.[17] After his death in 1847, Virginian and Confederate sympathizer Thomas Greene purchased the house. It's location at the foot of Seventeenth Avenue and bordering the White House grounds it gave Conrad an uninhibited view of the rear of the White House.

For this mission he reported directly to Secretary of War James Seddon and drew his funds from Secretary of State Judah Benjamin. His cell of agents kept a vigilant watch on Lincoln's comings and goings from across the street at Lafayette Square.

The plan Conrad developed was to capture Lincoln on his way to his summer residence at the Soldiers Home north of the city. He wrote that we: " … determined at what point it would be most expedient to capture the carriage and take possession of Mr. Lincoln and then … to move him through (southern) Maryland to the lower Potomac (Charles County) … and deliver the prisoner to Mosby's (Rangers) for transportation to Richmond." [18] Conrad's plan and escape route would later become Booth's blueprint.

Lincoln abhorred a military guard, which made the plan feasible. However, the day Conrad was ready to strike; he was shocked to see Lincoln's carriage accompanied by a cavalry detachment. Believing his effort had been compromised he abandoned the attempt. He wrote, "Having sent a lengthy communication to Richmond in which I recited *in detail* our efforts to capture the president and our humiliating failure, and stating that I did not see any use of staying any longer"[19].

Enter the Paladin 59

Conrad wrote that he later learned that some of Mosby's Rangers were drinking in a tavern and bragging about the plan. He concluded that this indiscretion probably tipped federal authorities.

While the Confederates continued to grasp for a lightning-in-a-bottle solution to their rapidly depleting resources, the abduction plan was revived. It would be an operation that would carried out by the Confederate Secret Service based in Montreal under the direction of George Nicholas Sanders.

Thomas Nelson Conrad

Thomas Nelson Conrad was a chaplain and a rebel spy in the Washington area. He proposed the assassination of General Winfield Scott in 1861 and later formulated the Lincoln kidnapping plan for Confederate Secretary of War Seddon in September 1864.

After he failed to accomplish the task, he recommended that Richmond abandon the plan. Instead, the plan was passed along to Booth.

He later wrote two books about his adventures.

The Canadian Spymaster

Long before the war began, George Nicholas Sanders was a dangerous rebel to both his friends and foes. Born in Kentucky in 1812, he moved to New York City in 1852 determined to become a political operative in the Democratic Party. He established the publication *Democratic Review* in January 1853. Its primary objective was to infuse younger blood into the party and to help him establish his own political society that he termed "Young Americans".

The paper began as a supporter of Stephen Douglas. However, Sander's slurs on Douglas's opponents were so virulent that he created a powerful backlash against the candidate. Douglas asked him to stop his support after one issue but the unstable Sanders thoroughly enjoyed the havoc he caused and ignored Douglas's pleas. Sanders interpreted political opposition as a slight upon his personal honor. He continued his unabated attacks on the 'old fogies' of the party single-handedly dooming Douglas's campaign.

The focus of "The Young Americans" was to attack the tyrannical dictatorships of Europe and exploit the character weaknesses of Jews, Blacks, and American Indians. They stood for expanding America's territorial acquisitions at the expense of Europe's decaying powers. Jefferson Davis, a disciple of what was then called Manifest Destiny, saw in Sanders a manipulator of the highest rank. While serving as secretary of war under Franklin Pierce, Davis had him appointed as Consul to London to accompany the weak-minded, easily manipulated Ambassador to England, James Buchanan.

The European Revolution of 1848 – the "springtime of the peoples" -- was still in full swing. Revolutions broke out in France, the German principalities, the Italian states, and the Austrian empire.

Small revolts fueled by contempt and despair were occurring all through Europe and put down just as quickly. The fear of spreading chaos throughout the continent dampened these rebellions from scattering beyond their local sources. Many of these troubled places later became prime emigration areas for the work force that contributed to the United States westward expansion after the Civil War.

At this time, London was a safe haven for noted revolutionaries such as Karl Marx, Victor Hugo, Louis Kossuth, Giuseppe Garibaldi, Giuseppe Mazzini, Louis Blanc, and Ledru-Rollin. Sanders befriended them all, giving the appearance that the U.S. supported revolutions throughout Europe. His activities soon came under the surveillance of Napoleon III's secret service. They learned that Sanders issued a passport to Victor Fronde, who was part of a plot to assassinate Napoleon. Sanders followed this up with a letter addressed to the "People of France" urging a violent overthrow of their government and implying support for the assassination of Napoleon III. It seems clear that Sanders was not afraid of assassination as an acceptable tool.[20]

In 1854, the United States' ministers to England, France, and Spain met at the request of the president to determine how best to persuade Spain to sell Cuba to the United States. Cuba was a strategic piece in the political confrontation embroiling the North and South. Due to its location, if it would enter the Union as a slave state if it was obtainable. Sanders advocated, "to work with a strong determination to take over Cuba at all hazards, regardless of International law, Monroe Doctrine or anything else that might appear in their way". Sanders' utterances became the backbone of the official response when Pierre Soule, minister to Spain, issued the Ostend Manifesto, threatening Spain with invasion if they were unwilling to sell Cuba. This threat of a war without presidential knowledge greatly embarrassed the State Department forcing the resignation of Soule and the recall of Sanders.

Coming home and seeing civil war as inevitable, Sanders was determined to help the South succeed and to turn a profit for himself. At the outbreak of the war in 1861, he was busy trying to get the split state of Kentucky to join the Confederacy while at the same time promoting the manufacture of artillery shells and ordnance in Nashville, Tennessee.

In spring 1862, he spoke to his old friend Jefferson Davis about letting him use his contacts in England to propose a contract between the Confederate government and the British business house of *Fraser, Trenholm & Company* for six armed iron-plated merchant vessels to break the Federal blockade of Confederate ports.

The primary partner in the company was George Alfred Trenholm, who had made a fortune in the cotton trade. The company owned plantations, banks, steamships, and railroads and became the overseas financier for the Confederate government.

However, Union spies caught wind of Sanders activities and set out to intercept him with the contracts. If successful, their efforts would net them a very dangerous man and keep England neutral in the war. Sanders escaped the trap, but his son Reid and the contracts did not. England remained neutral, and Reid Sanders later died in prison further fuelling Sanders resolve.[21]

In 1863, Sanders approached Davis with the idea of creating an operational base in Canada and working with the Peace Party (Copperheads) in the North to disrupt the Union from behind the lines. It was not until 1864 that Davis was ready to go ahead with the operation after receiving money from the Confederate Congress.

Jacob Thompson, the insidious former U.S. Secretary of the Interior and long-time associate of Davis was selected to head the operation along with former U.S. Senator Clement Clay.

When Sanders, who was in Europe at the time, heard the news, he quickly set sail for Montreal arriving on June 1, 1864 and immediately began to alienate all around him.

On June 9, Thompson in a letter to Clay wrote that he had learned that Sanders was on his way to see Clement C. Vallandigham, the noted Copperhead leader in Windsor: "George Sanders has come to see Vallandigham. He has come from abroad Europe to do what he says he did not know we intended to do, and has gone on to do it. There is such a thing as spoiling the broth by having too many hands in it." [22]

On June 17, Clay in a letter to Secretary of State Benjamin complained, "George N. Sanders is at Niagara Falls, representing himself as sent by our government to encourage peace and meeting citizens of the US and CS to devise a joint action for that end. I hope he will not do so silly a thing, but I wish he were in Europe, Asia or Africa." [23]

The Niagara Falls peace initiative was a political gambit by Sanders. The goal was to paint Lincoln as an aggressive warmonger immediately before the 1864 election. He wrote to *New York Tribune* editor Horace Greeley and offered the services of Clement Clay, Robert Holcombe, and himself to negotiate a peace settlement. Copperheads often used these false olive branches to weaken Northern support for the war. They were designed to encourage the hopes of the citizenry that Lincoln was the only obstacle to peace and reunion. However, to Davis and the Confederates peace without independence was impossible.

Predictably, Lincoln's response included terms that were unacceptable giving Sanders his propaganda victory. The public was war weary and Sanders Niagara initiative contributed to Lincoln's re-election woes. It was not until the fall of Atlanta in September did public opinion revert to Lincoln's favor.

Unfortunately, Sanders did not realize that his scheme was working at cross-purposes with those of Thompson, who was intending to launch an armed revolt in the North with the Copperheads. It's a difficult task to rouse citizens to leave the safety of their homes and take up arms against the government, when at the same time their side is negotiating for peace. The revolt, for which Thompson was working, never occurred.

Booth received a briefing on his mission at the St. Lawrence Hall in Montreal during the last half of October. St. Lawrence Hall was Sander's headquarters. The Confederate commissioners in Canada, Clement Clay and Jacob Thompson, did not reside in Montreal. Clay lived in a borrowed house in St. Catharine, and Thompson made his headquarters in the Queens Hotel, Toronto.

Records show that Booth's room was next to Sanders for his ten-day stay. During this time, it is likely that Sanders regaled Booth with his stories of political radicals, clandestine operations, and assassination of political tyrants. Sanders believed in the radical cliché that chaos and disorder could topple governments. He was the sort of idealist who felt that his righteousness principles entitled him to impose his views on others. In Booth he found an able and willing disciple.[24] To Booth, these were the plots and intrigues that he gave life to on the stage. Sanders gave him the chance to play the role in real life, and he relished the opportunity.

It is also likely that Sanders told Booth of the five million dollars that the Confederate Congress had behind closed doors appropriated for the secret service. The promise of fame AND fortune for kidnapping Lincoln proved irresistible. All the people Booth recruited or tried to recruit spoke of Booth's promise of riches that awaited them after completion of the deed.

Enter the Paladin

In many ways, Booth was the perfect man for the mission. He was suave, debonair, and adept at smuggling and ad-libbing his way out of situations. He was independently wealthy with no immediate family ties. His business allowed him to move from place to place without attracting attention, and if recognized, he would attract hero worship rather than mistrust. John Wilkes Booth accepted the mission of kidnapping the President of the United States.

George N. Sanders

A born revolutionary with very few scruples, George Sanders had little regard for right and wrong and frequently worked at cross-purposes with his superiors. He was a fanatical elitist preaching liberty- equality – fraternity in Europe, but believed slaves should be handled with a whip and a gun.

Operating in Canada he pushed his 'electoral chaos' plan amongst Confederate reps and Copperheads and was in frequent consultation with Jefferson Davis, Judah Benjamin and Beverly Tucker.

His successful propaganda campaign deflected blame for the assassination from Southern leaders and changed American history.

Desperate Times

During the winter of 1863, Southern leaders took stock of their situation. The repulse at Gettysburg and the taking of Vicksburg had effectively cut the Confederacy in half and forced them into a defensive posture. All commerce that traveled down the Mississippi was now in control of the Union. Lee's defeat at Gettysburg scuttled their strategy of gaining a peace settlement by extending the conflict to Northern cities. The South was fighting a defensive war on all fronts.

By this time, the Confederacy was robbing the cradle and the grave for men. The conscription roles had run dry and desertions were growing steadily. Many rebels began to secede from the war because their farms were failing and their families starving. To speed up this process of bleeding the South white, Grant put an end to the custom of exchanging prisoners.

Facing up to the resource limitations before them, the Southern strategy for 1864 was to fight the Northern armies at least to a draw and instigate enough political unrest to either defeat Lincoln in the upcoming elections or force him into a negotiated settlement.

To enable this plan the Confederates decided to take advantage of the laxity of Canadian neutrality and upgrade their underground activities in the country. The Confederate Congress voted to fund the project with a budget of one million dollars in gold.

Enter the Paladin

Their objective was to create fear and instability in the North and force the Union to disengage troops who were besieging the South. To do this they planned guerilla raids against Northern cities and prisoner of war camps, organize anti-Lincoln movements, sabotage railroads, disrupt shipping, start yellow fever epidemics, and create general terror throughout the Union.

The political strategy to unseat Lincoln fell apart when Sherman took Atlanta in early September 1864 and began his march to the sea. War weary Northern voters began to see victory in sight and felt no need to remove Lincoln from office. Sherman's march to Savannah cut the main railroads carrying the food that fed Lee's army. The manpower that the South needed to continue the war began to reach the critical stage. U.S. Grant was extending his lines around Richmond, forcing Lee to spread his army so thinly that eventually he would not have sufficient reserves to counter a Union breakthrough. Desperate times called for desperate measures. Lincoln's re-election in November pushed rebel leaders to green light Booth's mission.

Before Booth could assume his duties, he had one more performance to give. His brother Edwin wanted to help a commission to build a statue of Shakespeare in the newly developed Central Park in New York. For this cause he proposed a benefit performance of *Julius Caesar* with all proceeds going towards erection of the statue. To assure a sellout he asked his brothers John and June to join him on the stage. This benefit was the only time the three brothers performed together.

The one time performance was a rousing success raising over $4,000. Unfortunately, the play occurred on the same night that Confederate raiders tried to burn the city by lighting fires in various sections of town. At the beginning of the second act, the smell of burning from the hotel next door caused a near panic in the theatre. Edwin stopped the show and calmed the audience telling them that there was nothing to fear, firefighters had the blaze next door under control.

At Edwin's house, the next morning the breakfast conversation was about the fires. Edwin blamed them on the war and hoped that Lincoln's re-election would finally bring about peace. John exploded with a diatribe against Lincoln, saying that the South was justified in burning New York as retaliation for Sherman's burning of Atlanta. The conversation became so heated and John so passionate for rebel success that Edwin told him to take his comments to people who supported them, not in the "house of a Union supporter!" The hotheaded John had broken his promise to his mother not to cause a split in the family. With Edwin's condemnation still ringing in his ears, the banished brother began his new life.

Shortly after arriving in Washington, Booth sought out two boyhood friends from Baltimore, Sam Arnold and Michael O'Laughlin. Both men served in the same Confederate regiment early in the war, returned home, and were depressed about the South's dwindling fortunes. At a meeting at the Barnum Hotel in Baltimore, Booth made his first contact with the pair in over thirteen years. They talked about their schoolboy days current events, and drank a good deal of whiskey. After determining that both men were trustworthy compatriots, Booth outlined the plan.

He informed them that Lincoln made the Soldiers Home just outside of Washington, his summer residence. On the journeys Booth explained, no one accompanied him other than his carriage driver. They could take him and rush him to lower Maryland. With a boat already moored and a boatman at the ready, they could get him to Richmond in less than a day. With Lincoln a prisoner, the Confederacy would force the North to resume the prisoner exchanges suspended by Grant when he took command. Nationalistic glory would shower the kidnappers and best of all, no one would be hurt. Arnold and O'Laughlin patriotically and drunkenly agreed to the scheme and pledged themselves to secrecy. They then returned home to wait for further details from Booth.

Armed with a letter of introduction supplied by operatives in Montreal, Booth travelled to southern Maryland to meet with important members of the Confederate underground operating in the area. Secessionists made up the vast majority in Maryland's lower counties. In the election of 1860, Lincoln received fewer than five votes from Charles County. Booth surveyed the area posing as an interested land buyer. His contact with Dr. Samuel Mudd got him an introduction to the most important member of his crew, John Surratt.

Surratt was a twenty-year-old Confederate agent living with his widowed mother at her boarding house on H Street in Washington. His expertise was gathering intelligence on troop movements in the Washington area and carrying dispatches to Confederate ships on the Potomac by agents as far away as Richmond. His father, John Harrison Surratt, Sr., owned a tavern and boarding house twelve miles outside the city. The tavern served as the local post office, which had given the name to the town on which it sat as Surrattsville[25], Maryland. When his father died, John briefly took over the duties as postmaster giving him the opportunity to make many underground contacts in the Southern Maryland area.

The Surratt tavern was a frequent rest stop for Confederate agents working "The Secret Line" of underground communications in the area. This line was so efficient that newspapers printed in New York could be in Richmond within 24 to 48 hours. However, with the recent abolition of slavery in Maryland, John's mother Mary Surratt found that she could no longer make a profit on the tavern. She leased the facility to John Lloyd, a former police officer, so that she could run the boarding house on H street fulltime. When the famous actor John Wilkes Booth became her son's new friend a strange new assortment of individuals suddenly began frequenting her H Street home.

John Surratt became part of Booth's plot on December 23, 1864. He was one of the most trusted couriers in the Confederate Secret Service. Surratt had delivered messages between Richmond and all points north. Since he was the only unmarried man among the messengers, he ran most of the dangerous missions. He managed to carry important dispatches on his person or in his buggy through federal checkpoints without ever being caught or arrested. He knew the routes and the people who could best give assistance. With Surratt's commitment, Booth could concentrate on the financing and planning. Surratt would be in charge of recruitment and logistics.

Within a few weeks, the able Surratt accomplished the following tasks:

- He recruited George Atzerodt to be the boatman. Atzerodt frequently moved Surratt, mail, and other Confederate spies and couriers across the Potomac at Port Tobacco. George's expertise was his knowledge of the river in that area, especially the creeks and other small hiding places.

- With the help of Thomas Harbin, another Confederate agent, Surratt purchased a flat-bottomed boat from Richard Smoot. The boat had the capacity and the capability of carrying the entire party across the river. Atzerodt would conceal the boat until needed.

- He recruited Davy Herold, an unemployed pharmacy clerk. Herold was a frequent visitor at the Surrattsville tavern, used as a safe house for Confederate agents.

Enter the Paladin

Herold was an adept bird hunter and knew the unmapped roads within the area.

Once they assembled their action team, Booth and Surratt decided they needed some muscle for the job. They wanted a strong and fearless professional with experience in taking prisoners. Out of the backwoods came Lewis Thornton Powell. Powell was from the Forty-Third Battalion of Virginia Cavalry also known as Mosby's Rangers, the group assigned to work with Conrad on the original kidnap plan. The Rangers conducted intelligence and hit-and-run operations in the rear of Union armies before melting into the countryside. They operated in Northern Virginia supported by the local population, stayed away from well-travelled routes, and stole along unmarked paths behind enemy lines forcing the Union to commit thousands of troops to defend against their raids

Powell "deserted" from the Rangers and sought out the provost marshal of Fauquier County for help as a civilian refugee. The marshal sent him to Alexandria where he took his oath of allegiance as Lewis Payne, sold his horse, and proceeded to Baltimore where he met up with Surratt and quickly became the final part of the team.

At the end of January of 1865, Surratt reported to Confederate Secretary of State Judah Benjamin and Colonel John Mosby in Richmond to discuss the plan. Mosby's Rangers would be an integral part of the plan to intercept any pursuit and to receive the hostage.[26]

John Loved Lucy

One of the best-kept secrets of the assassination story was John Wilkes Booth's relationship with his fiancé, Lucy Lambert Hale. Booth was a notorious womanizer. In 1861 actress, Henrietta Irving slashed him with a knife when she discovered that she was not the only woman in his life and he did not intend to marry her.

Booth recovered from this incident and was seen frequently in the company of many women, most of them actresses in the stock companies of the cities where he played. Booth was one of the first action stars of the stage. His forte was playing roles with energy and passion. Offstage he used his charm and good looks to seduce many young women while his on-stage persona invoked hero worship in many female fans.

In one case, a beautiful young girl from Philadelphia pursued him so intently that he warned her: "*beware of actors. They are to be seen and not known.*" This advice intensified her persistence until she became another one of his conquests. When Booth made the National Hotel in Washington his headquarters in November of 1864, his frequent consort was a pretty, nineteen year-old redhead from Baltimore named Ella Starr Turner.

The National Hotel was the top hotel in Washington until a number of guests died from an outbreak of virulent dysentery on the eve of James Buchanan's presidential inauguration. Southerners were the primary patrons of the hotel. They blamed the outbreak on a Republican plot to wipe out Democrats rather than the sewage backup that contaminated the hotel's kitchen. After that episode the Willard Hotel quickly became the city's eminent hotel functioning as the crossroads of Washington society and politics.

While John Surratt was recruiting conspirators for the plot, Sam Arnold was still waiting for news from Booth. He saw at least

Enter the Paladin

two good opportunities to kidnap Lincoln go to waste. Twice Lincoln crossed the Eastern Branch Bridge accompanied only by a coachman and a guest but Booth let the opportunities pass. As Arnold wrote in his memoirs:

> "The month of January had passed and as yet nothing had been accomplished. February ushered itself in, only to be a repetition of the former month; as Booth through riotous living and dissipation, was compelled to visit the City of New York for the purpose of replenishing his squandered means."[27]

The riotous living that Booth was experiencing in January and February was the romance he was pursuing with Lucy Hale.

Lucy was the younger daughter of John Parker Hale, a former senator from New Hampshire. Senator Hale was one of the nation's leading abolitionists taking his first stand by refusing to vote for the annexation of Texas, because it would extend the institution of slavery. After twenty years in Congress, he was finally defeated in the November 1864 elections. He and his family moved into the National Hotel while he served the final session of his term from December to March. During this time, Hale was lobbying Lincoln for the recently opened position of Minister to Spain. While the Senator worked towards his next assignment, daughters Lucy and Lizzie worked as volunteers with the Sanitary Committee during the day and attended dances at night.

Lucy was an alluring twenty-three year old beauty with large blue eyes, dark hair and a striking figure. She had a soul that reflected the sweetness and goodness of her character as well as a charm that beguiled many a young man. Lucy was one of the most sought-after young ladies in the Washington social circle. Her charm, intelligence, and wit attracted the interest of some of Washington's most eligible bachelors. Among these was future chief justice Oliver Wendell Holmes, Jr., son of the famous poet-physician Oliver Wendell Homes Sr. Holmes met her in 1858, and continued his acquaintance while stationed as a Captain in the army defending Washington.

John Hay, the president's personal secretary and future secretary of state, was also an admirer. He wrote; " I came back from the station wondering if there were anyone else in the world just like you; one of equal charm, equal power of gaining hearts, and equal disdain for the hearts you gain. The last glance of those mysterious blue-grey eyes fell upon a dozen or so of us and everybody but me thought the last glance was for him…You know how I love and admire you. I do not understand you, nor hope to, nor even wish to. You would lose to me some of your indefinable fascination if I knew exactly what you mean."

The president's eldest son, Robert Lincoln, had met her in Boston when he was a student at Harvard and sent her flowers from the White House conservatory. This acquaintance greatly pleased her father. Abraham Lincoln had been a friend of Senator Hale since Lincoln's term in Congress in the 1840's. Robert was himself a very impressive young man whose future seemed bright. [28]

Booth met Lucy during one of the many dances held at the hotel for their guests and soon fell under her spell. His sister Asia reported that Johnnie had become enraged at the sight of Lucy dancing with Robert Lincoln. He decided to take on the challenge with his usual intensity and with a distinct advantage. He was available to Lucy at anytime while her other suitors were either working or serving in the army.

Senator Hale was not approving of this new devotee for his daughter's affections. He preferred she used her charisma on Robert Lincoln or one of her other suitors. Marriage to an actor would have been a social step backwards. However, the Senator took solace, in that his upcoming assignment to Spain would probably cool his daughter's ardour.

Lucy was a devoted daughter and she firmly shared her father's abolitionist views. Although Booth was ready to turn against his own blood relations on this issue, he managed to put aside his politics for the love of a woman. It was a tribute to her charm and allures that for two full months she managed to turn Booth's attention away from his kidnapping plot in order to concentrate his time on her. During this 'romantic period' of Booth's life, he went through the motions of working on his scheme in order to keep his cabal together but made no effort to carry it out.

It is possible that his initial motivation with Lucy was to use her to gain information or access to important people, but the relationship developed into more than Booth expected. As he confessed to his sister, he "undesignedly fell in love with a senator's daughter". By February, he was so smitten that he spent most of a night with his brother June in New York working on a poetic valentine for her. June was amused to see his brother, so knowledgeable of the great poems in literature, labor so intently to create a poem that he could normally write in minutes. To June this was a revelation. "John sat up all Monday night to get Miss H's Valentine in the mail, and slept on the sofa to be up early; kept me awake by every now and then using me as a dictionary". [29]

According to Booth's sister Asia, they were to be married within a year when Lucy promised to return from Spain "either with her father or without him". That decision made secretly between the two of them occurred only a few days before the assassination.[30]

A Threat to the Republic

Lucy Hale

Booth's engagement to Lucy Hale was not a secret to Booth's family. Booth's mother advised "- you are aware that the woman you make your wife you must love and respect beyond all others – if the lady in question is all you desire- I see no cause why you should not try to secure her – her father has his appointment, would he give his consent?"

After Booth's death, his brother Edwin released a letter from her where she avowed that she would have gladly married Booth on the gallows. This photograph of her was found on his body.

Chapter 3

Kidnapping Lincoln

The Hampton Roads Conference

While Judah Benjamin met with Surratt and Mosby in late January, Francis P. Blair, patriarch of the influential Blair family met with Jefferson Davis with a plan for peace. He proposed that the North and South use the Monroe Doctrine to unite and throw the French out of Mexico through a joint campaign. Lincoln thought the scheme ridiculous, but he could not afford to alienate the powerful editor and patron, so he allowed him to go to Richmond to see what might develop.

Davis was feeling pressure from the Confederate Senate for ending the war. He rightly believed that nothing would come of the negotiations other than the demands for "unconditional submission". He saw the conference, however, as an opportunity to discredit the growing peace movement in the South by distorting the surrender terms and relighting the fires of Southern patriotism. With this in mind, he authorized Blair to inform Lincoln that he was ready to "enter into conference with a view to secure peace to the *two countries*". Lincoln responded that he was ready to receive overtures "with the view of securing peace to the people of *our one common country*".

Secretary Benjamin immediately saw the conflict that would occur between the one-country/two-country viewpoints and sought in his instructions to give his commissioners some leeway in their discussions. Davis refused. He corrected the instructions and made certain that unless Lincoln viewed the South as a separate country there would be no peace.

The conference took place February 3 on the Union steamer *River Queen*. Secretary Seward presented the North's terms:

1. The restoration of the National authority throughout all the States.

2. No receding by the Executive of the United States on the slavery question.

3. No cessation of hostilities short of an end to the war and the disbanding of all forces hostile to the government.

Lincoln promised generous treatment towards rebel leaders and the confiscation of their property, based upon his pardon power. On the question of slavery, he suggested the possibility of compensating slave owners $400 million for their loss, but there would be no turning back on emancipation. Seward informed them that the House of Representatives had just passed the Thirteenth Amendment, and its ratification would make all other legal questions on the subject moot.

In any case, remarked Lincoln, slavery as well as the rebellion was doomed. There would be no armistice; surrender was the only means of stopping the war. He advised that the South cut their losses, return to the old allegiance, and save the bloodshed of their young men. Since, the commissioners had no power to negotiate surrender terms they dejectedly returned home.

In the wake of this failure, Robert E. Lee received a letter from his principal spy, Benjamin Franklin Stringfellow.[31]

Richmond Feb. 24th 1865

Genl R.E. Lee;

Genl, I think that Genl. Grant can be captured – it will take <u>time</u> and <u>means</u>. I have no positive plan, beyond the determination to succeed or perish. I only desire to know that it will meet with the approbation of those most deeply concerned with the welfare of our country and that precursory aid will be given. I expect to be able to return the money borrowed from the government. If I fail to accomplish great good, I bind myself to return the amount borrowed out of my own funds.   *Your Obt. Servant*

B.F. Stringfellow

Kidnapping Lincoln

If any Southerner was capable of capturing Grant, Stringfellow was the man. During the previous year, he managed to penetrate the Union lines for information and had the chance to shoot the General in the back. Being a religious man, he declined the opportunity but was now willing to try to kidnap him if the government would approve. Lee sent Stringfellow's letter on to Davis.

On the same day that Stringfellow was proposing to kidnap Grant, Andrew Johnson was sidestepping a kidnap attempt in Louisville. Confederate agents were ready to capture him in his hotel room, but Johnson unexpectedly took a boat to Cincinnati.[32]

Davis was in the process of taking political advantage of the failed Hampton Road talks to exhort the Confederacy into a greater commitment. As Virginia legislators met to adopt resolutions condemning Lincoln and reaffirming their independence, Davis addressed them. He told them that they "stood upon the verge of success, which would teach the insolent enemy who had treated our propositions with contumely, that in that conference which he plumed himself with arrogance, he was indeed talking to his masters". He predicted that by the end of June the North would come to him asking for peace.

Vice-President Stephens later remarked that he thought Davis's performance was "brilliant" and that his were speeches bold, but he also thought the president was demented. He wondered what Davis could have been thinking when he predicted bringing the Union to its knees by June. He wondered if Davis was "relying on something I and the world knew nothing about".

On March 1, Davis met with Franklin Stringfellow. His purpose was to promote him and to give him a new assignment. A desperate covert mission to Washington was about to be launched and the beginning of a new phase of the war.

Lieutenant Benjamin Franklin Stringfellow

Benjamin Franklin Stringfellow was perhaps the most dangerous and daring spy in the Confederate army with a reward of $10,000 offered for his capture.

Stringfellow served as Jeb Stuart's personal scout and chief spy. Upon Stuart's death he reported directly to Lee but during the month of March 1865 he infiltrated Washington on a special mission for Jefferson Davis.

After the war he became an Episcopalian minister and at the age of 57, served as a U.S. Army chaplain in the Spanish-American war. He died in 1913.

Lincoln's Second Inaugural

March 4, 1865, Inauguration Day was wet and windy. Rain had been falling for a week and the streets were a sea of muck. Women in long formal dresses were no match for the weather. Most were soaked to the skin and splattered with mud. Remembering the lessons learned from the last inauguration security was extremely tight. Lincoln continued to receive threats worrying everybody but the president.

Abolitionist Frederick Douglass caught perhaps a glimpse of things to come when he observed the vice-president-elect "On this inauguration day, while waiting for the opening of the ceremonies, I made a discovery in regard to the vice-president — Andrew Johnson. There are moments in the lives of most men, when the doors of their souls are open, and unconsciously to themselves, their true characters may be read by the observant eye. It was at such an instant I caught a glimpse of the real nature of this man, which all subsequent developments proved true.

I was standing in the crowd by the side of Mrs. Thomas J. Dorsey, when Mr. Lincoln touched Mr. Johnson, and pointed me out to him. The first expression which came to his face, and which I think was the true index of his heart, was one of bitter contempt and aversion. Seeing that I observed him, he tried to assume a more friendly appearance; but it was too late; it was useless to close the door when all within had been seen. His first glance was the frown of the man, the second was the bland and sickly smile of the demagogue. I turned to Mrs. Dorsey and said, 'Whatever Andrew Johnson may be, he certainly is no friend of our race'."[33]

Taking place in the senate chamber, the inauguration of the vice-president was the first formal procedure of the day. Before entering the assembly room, Johnson asked the man he was replacing, Vice-President Hannibal Hamlin, if there was any whiskey available to help him through the ceremony. Johnson needed a 'hair of the dog' treatment; he had celebrated his new office the night before with Senate aide John W. Forney and downed quite a few tumblers of whiskey[34]. Johnson filled a large glass from the bottle offered by Hamlin, drank it down in one gulp and then repeated the operation. The effect was almost immediate.

As Johnson took his place and began his address, he slurred his words and rambled. He boasted about his humble plebian origins and glorified himself as *"one who claims no high descent, one who comes from the ranks of the people"*. This was a favorite topic of Johnson's, striking out against the aristocracy and publicizing his own lowly background. Jefferson Davis once described him as a man who took a great deal of pride in claiming he had no pride. Repeatedly he returned to the theme of his humble origins. *"Humble as I am, plebian as I may be deemed…."* He then proceeded to lecture the assembly of Senators, Congressmen, Supreme Court Justices as well as the members of the Diplomatic Corps on the subject. As they sat there *"with all their fine feathers and gewgaws as well as Mr. Secretary Seward, Mr. Secretary Stanton and Mr. Secretary – who is the Secretary of the Navy? – And to you Mr. Secretary Welles – that you derive all your power from the people!"*

Joshua Speed, the new Attorney-General, shook his head and whispered to Gideon Welles, 'This is in wretched bad taste." As Johnson droned on, he then exclaimed, "The man is deranged!"

Welles then whispered to Stanton, "Johnson is either drunk or crazy!"

Stanton nodded, acutely observing, "There is evidently something wrong."

Republican senators hid their faces in their hands. Even some members of the press corps were too ashamed to write the news. "The second official of the nation – drunk, drunk! when taking the oath of his office, bellowing and ranting and shaking his fists at Judges, Cabinet and Diplomats, and making such a fool of himself that indignation is almost compelled to pity," privately wrote reporter Charles Dudley. He added that he felt such revulsion that he could not write it.[35]

While the audience watched stunned and horrified at the performance, Lincoln closed his eyes, dropped his head in humiliation, and waited. Hamlin kept nudging Johnson from behind to signal him that he was holding up the inauguration ceremony, but that only prompted Johnson to orate even louder and return to his theme. "… *I'm a-going to tell you – here today-yes, I am a-going to tell you all that I am a plebian! I glory in it! I am a pull-E-bian! The people-yes, the people of the United States, the great people have made me what I am….*"

Supreme Court Justice Nelson looked on with his lower jaw dropped in blank horror. Chief Justice Chase's expression was one of granite until Johnson finally stopped and turned to take the oath. Chase exchanged glances with Nelson who was finally able to close his mouth.

After taking his oath, Johnson in a final theatrical gesture removed his hand from the bible, kissed it, held it up to the shell-shocked audience and announced, "*I kiss this Book in the face of my nation of the United States!*"

Lincoln leaned over and whispered to the parade marshal, "Do not let Johnson speak outside."

The president then moved outside to the platform on the eastern front of the Capitol. As he appeared, the band began to play and the cheers from the crowd became overwhelming. As Lincoln unfolded his speech, the sun burst through the clouds and flooded the Capitol steps with light. Chief Justice Chase saw it as "an auspicious omen of the dispersion of the clouds of war and the restoration of the clear sun light of prosperous peace".

The president gazed into the illuminated faces of his audience and said, *"With malice towards none, with charity for all, with firmness in the right as God gives us to see the right, let us strive to finish the work we are in; to bind up the nation's wounds; to care for him who has borne the battle, and for his widow and his orphans; to do all which may achieve and cherish a just and a lasting peace among ourselves and with all nations."*

Journalist Noah Brooks wrote; "Among the memories of a lifetime, doubtless there were none more fondly cherished by those who were so fortunate as to stand near Lincoln at that historic moment than the recollection of the beautiful solemnity, the tender sympathy of those inspired utterances and the rapt silence of the multitudes."[36]

Among those in the crowd who were not impressed was John Wilkes Booth. Booth was the guest of Lucy Hale that day and had a grandstand position behind the speaker's platform. Booth was within shooting range of the president but did not strike. In early March, Lincoln was far more valuable alive and in the hands of the Confederacy than he was dead. The situation would be different one month later.

Kidnapping Lincoln

John Wilkes Booth observes Lincoln's second inaugural speech from the balcony above.

Dinner at Gautiers

On the evening of March 15, the play *The Tragedy of Jane Shore* was playing at the Ford's Theatre. Booth rented the presidential box for Powell, Surratt, Nora Fitzpatrick, and ten-year-old Apollonia Dean for an evening out. The ladies were residents of the Surratt boarding house and were used to cover Booth's true intentions. Booth's purpose was to familiarize Powell and Surratt with the box and theatre layout. As the play was going on, Booth went backstage to talk with the cast and crew. At midnight, the men dropped the ladies off at the boarding house and went to a private meeting.

Booth had rented a private room at Gautier's Restaurant, near Twelfth Street and Pennsylvania Avenue.[37] The room stocked with liquor, steamed oysters, and cigars for the conspirators' private meeting. Arnold and O'Laughlin were completely in the dark about the meeting until Herold came to get them. They had never before met the other conspirators or even knew of their existence. Once all were together, Booth took center stage and explained the plan.

The kidnapping was to take place at Ford's Theatre as Lincoln watched a play. He had rented a stable behind the theatre and told them all about the back exits. At a given signal, Herold and O'Laughlin would turn out the gaslights, and Arnold, Booth and Atzerodt would rush the box, handcuff the president and lower him to Powell on the stage. A carriage would be waiting in back for a quick dash to the bridge where a waiting Surratt would facilitate the escape.

Kidnapping Lincoln

After capturing the president, they would out run their pursuers by having fresh horses available to them along the way. They calculated that racing the animals at top speed they could cover the thirty-seven mile distance to Port Tobacco in seven hours. Once there they would cross the Potomac River in the boat Surratt purchased and be in Virginia in about half an hour. [38]

Booth the dramatist thought this was a sound plan but his boyhood pal Sam Arnold did not. He had been waiting months and turning down employment opportunities for Booth to finalize his plan. He had agreed to help capture Lincoln somewhere on a country road, not in a crowded theatre. He did not believe there was any way for the plan to succeed without someone sending up an alarm. Besides, he pointed out; the purpose of the plan was to force the Union to resume the prisoner exchange program. Grant had resumed the exchange in mid-January. The newspapers were already running stories about prisoners returning home.

Booth taken aback by Arnold's response realized that he now had a potential mutiny on his hands. To answer this challenge he responded with his usual stage dramatics. He assured his men that capturing Lincoln was still in the best interests of the Confederacy for negotiations of independence or a fair peace. Then he angrily reminded Arnold of the oath he had taken and said, "Do you know you are liable to be shot?"

Arnold, a war veteran and the man who knew Booth for the longest time, was not intimidated by the actor's foolhardy bravado. As far as he was concerned, Booth had broken the compact. He replied, "If you feel inclined to shoot me, you have no farther to go. I shall defend myself."[39]

With his bluff called, Booth promptly relented and agreed to go back to the original plan of abducting Lincoln on a country road. However, Arnold was tired of waiting for Booth. He had lined up a job for himself to begin the following week. "Gentlemen," he announced, "if this is not accomplished by the end of this week I forever withdraw from it."

Booth was incensed at Arnold's audacity but could not be sure if he was speaking only for himself or if other members of the group agreed with him. It was now Thursday morning, and Arnold's threat gave him a mere three days to put his plot into action or risk the disintegration of his cabal. All agreed that nothing more could be accomplished that night, so the meeting ended. Booth would take care of Arnold later, in his own way.

Sam Arnold

Like Michael O'Laughlin, Arnold was a boyhood friend of Booth's and was recruited at the same time. He left the conspiracy after the failure to capture Lincoln on March 17th and implored Booth in a letter to give up his kidnapping plan.

Booth saved the letter in his hotel room which led to his capture as a conspirator. He was convicted of being part of the conspiracy and sentenced to life.

Kidnapping Lincoln

Fiasco!

On March 17th Booth supposedly received word from an actor friend that Lincoln was going to attend a matinee performance of *Still Waters Run Deep* for the wounded soldiers at the Campbell Hospital. He immediately assembled the conspirators in front of Mrs. Surratt's boarding house and told them the time to strike was at hand. The Campbell Hospital was located on Seventh Street near the Soldiers Home so he put the original plan into action. They would stop Lincoln's carriage as he returned from the play, overpower the coachman, and handcuff the president. The hijacked carriage would then make a mad dash across the Bennings Bridge into southern Maryland. Herold would join them with two contraband Spencer repeating rifles. They would change horses in the little village called T.B. and take the boat from Nanjemoy.

Booth rode up to the hospital to do some reconnaissance, and learned that Lincoln had changed plans and was not in attendance. As if to rub salt in the wound, Lincoln was at Booth's hotel attending an impromptu ceremony regarding a captured battle flag. Upon hearing the news, the team dispersed and quickly went their separate ways.

Arnold and O'Laughlin returned to Baltimore. Surratt was convinced that the Federals got wind of the plot and were after them. He hid the illegal carbines between the walls of the Surrattsville tavern and began a search for legitimate work. He returned to the boarding house and asked his roommate Louis Weichmann if he could get him a clerkship somewhere. Davy Herold received a clerkship at a hospital for the Army of the James and was going to report April 1.

Atzerodt had nowhere to go, so he decided to stick around. As long as Booth was paying his room and board, he would stay as long as he was welcomed.

It's not known whether Lincoln actually changed his plans that day or the entire scenario was a complete fabrication foisted by Booth. It's entirely possible that additional pressure to complete his mission came from the Confederate hierarchy. Lee could not keep Mosby's troops stationed in the Northern neck forever and Booth had a cipher key for messages sent in the Confederate code, so he could have been in contact with his sponsors.

The entire incident could have been Booth's way of throwing in the towel and allowing him to save face as a loyal patriot. Once again, he could charge on horseback through the woods spouting heroic speeches, and fight an imaginary foe.

Booth took Powell and headed for New York. The city had scores of Confederate sympathizers; many were financiers who were losing money on the embargoed cotton trade. "It is one of the minor ironies of history that when cannon fire at Fort Sumter began the Civil War, the loyalty of America's biggest city was much in doubt," wrote historian George J. Lankevich. "In the 1860 presidential campaign, Manhattan did not support Abraham Lincoln for president, and on January 7, 1861, Mayor Fernando Wood, a Peace Democrat, proposed that to protect its commercial predominance and their excellent trading relationships with the Southern states, the city withdraw from the Union and declare itself a free city."[40] Exactly to whom Booth was reporting and financing his activities are unknown.

When Booth returned to Washington on March 25, he and Atzerodt called on Mrs. Surratt at her request. At this meeting, he learned that Confederate agent Augustus Howell had been arrested at the Surrattsville tavern. His arrest forced her son John to replace him on his mission to escort Sarah Slater (a.k.a. Kate Thompson), the primary courier of the Confederate Secret Service, from Montreal to Richmond.

With Surratt gone, Booth tried to bring Arnold and O'Laughlin back from Baltimore. He had intelligence that Lincoln invited Senator Charles Sumner to Ford's Theatre to see Verdi's opera *Ernani*, but neither man was interested in rejoining the group. Arnold then made the mistake of writing Booth a letter imploring his old friend to give up his plan. Rather than taking it in the spirit in which it was given and destroy it, Booth kept it stored it in his trunk. Lincoln who was visiting Grant at City Point inadvertently sidestepped the entire situation by deciding to extend his visit in order to witness the assault on Richmond. He cancelled the invitation to Sumner.

By this time, events and plans were changing in Richmond. With Grant tightening the noose on the city, evacuation was imminent. With Richmond in Union hands, there would be no place to move a kidnapped president. Realizing that the kidnapping plan was no longer feasible, General Lee informed Colonel Mosby on March 27, "If any of your command is in the Northern Neck, call it to you." Mosby abandoned the corridor he was guarding to intercept any pursuers of the kidnapped president. [41]

As the military situation worsened, Confederate agent Franklin Stringfellow was busy gathering intelligence in Washington. Stringfellow had established a number of intelligence cells throughout the war and earned a much-respected reputation for success, disguises and narrow escapes. In March, he was sent back into Washington specifically by Jefferson Davis. Although Stringfellow did deliver a message to a foreign embassy in Washington, he never revealed the entire purpose of his mission at this late date in the war. Most of what we know comes from bits and pieces of lectures he gave after the war along with a vague letter he wrote to Jefferson Davis at the former president's request to help him in the writing of his memoirs. We do know that he was a marked man in the North and took a great risk to himself by operating in Washington

Among the places he stayed at this time was the Kirkwood House, because that was where the vice-president was residing. It is not known if they ever had contact with each other, but the comings and goings of important people to Andrew Johnson's door was an opportunity for a spy to learn a great deal.[42] Stringfellow also reported that he was "in constant communication with an officer occupying an important position about Mr. Lincoln. I made him a proposition which he said he would consider, then he thought that he would accept it, but would answer me in a few days".[43]

On March 29, Surratt and Slater arrived in Richmond along with dispatches from Jacob Thompson in Montreal for Secretary Benjamin. At that point, it was likely that Booth's credibility was deemed worthless. Surratt surely had nothing good to say about his leadership skills since he wasted three months of time, ran up expenses, and his master plan to abduct the president in a crowded theatre nearly caused an internal revolt. At this meeting, it was probably revealed that a contingency plan was being launched. Slater and Surratt were to pass the word to operatives in New York and Canada.

The Confederate Torpedo Bureau was the Manhattan Project of its era. The bureau contained creative people who experimented with munitions and fuses. Developing reliable fuses that could set off charges from a distance was a new technology, and the bureau created them for both sea and land mines. Their most spectacular success came in August 1864 when a twelve pound mine equipped with a timing device was smuggled on board a ship carrying armaments for Grant's army at City Point. The explosion blew up the ordnance depot killing more than two hundred people and destroying more than $2,000,000 of equipment. After meeting with Surratt and Slater, Benjamin assigned explosive expert Sergeant Thomas F. Harney from the Bureau and a small action team to Mosby's raiders. He also withdrew fifteen hundred dollars in gold "for Secret Service" without specifying its usage. Mosby was assigned to infiltrate the team along with their fuses and detonators into Washington where Harney would mine the White House.

On April 1, Stringfellow's luck ran out. His cover as a dentist who could travel throughout Maryland was exposed, and he sought to escape the city. He wrote that he relied upon "a person whose name is linked in the history of those dark days, I went some twelve miles that first evening".[44]

Twelve miles was the exact distance to the Surrattsville tavern. Since Booth and John Surratt were not in Washington that day, the person who most likely aided his escape was Mary Surratt.

We know from boarder Lewis Weichmann's memoirs that on April 1 she left the boarding house sometime after breakfast. She returned in the evening from Surrattsville with her brother and asked Weichmann to return the horse and buggy to Howard's livery stable. Stranded without return transportation, her brother walked home to Surrattsville the next day. Since women simply did not travel alone in those days (especially during wartime), it appears she was the one who accompanied Stringfellow out of Washington and then had her brother escort her back home.

Despite these efforts, Union cavalry captured and arrested Stringfellow the following day. Although he managed to destroy most of the incriminating evidence against him by eating it, he was unable to digest a report on the defenses of Washington sewn into his coat. [45] From this information, it seems obvious that Stringfellow's assignment was to lay the groundwork for Harney's mission.

Slipping a man into a guarded city was one thing, but bringing along enough ordnances to blow up a building as big as the White House was a tougher task. Black powder would have to be obtained and secured somewhere in Washington. There was not enough time to bring in the equipment piecemeal, and with cavalry increasing their patrols in the Virginia countryside looking for Mosby's raiders, Stringfellow needed to find a blind spot. There could be no other reason for Stringfellow to require information on Washington's defenses. The Confederacy certainly had no army at this point in the war to exploit any weaknesses that he may have uncovered. Stringfellow's failure in his last mission sealed the fate of Harney's.

As the month ended, Booth met for the last time with O'Laughlin and Arnold. O'Laughlin had loaned Booth $500 and was looking for its return. Arnold asked if Booth had received the letter he had written him imploring him to give up the kidnapping plot, and Booth told him that he had not. Arnold then asked him to destroy it when it arrived, and Booth promised that he would.

Booth told them that Lincoln had changed his plans and stayed in City Point, so his last ditch attempt to kidnap the president was over. He assured them that he abandoned the entire enterprise, and that he was returning to the stage. The weapons he had bought for them could be kept, sold, or do with them whatever they desired. The next day, Booth took the evening train back to New York a very depressed man. His dreams of fame and military glory were shattered. He had experienced failure, and it grated on him.

Time was also running out on John and Lucy's relationship. Senator John Hale's appointment to become Minister to Spain became official on March 10, and his lame-duck session in the Senate was finished. Lucy would soon be sailing with her father to Spain. She and Booth were together in Newport Rhode Island at the Aquidneck Hotel when Richmond fell on April 3. Booth signed the register as "J.W. Booth and Lady, Boston" but they never used the room. Apparently, Booth's dark mood was so gloomy that it depressed Lucy. They took the next train to Boston most likely to visit Booth's brother, Edwin, who was playing an engagement there. It would have been a good time to tell the family of his engagement and seek reconciliation with his brother.

From Boston, Booth returned to New York and learned of the Torpedo Bureau plot to blow up the White House by use of a mine. There was no time left for a kidnapping. Decapitating the Union government was the South's last chance to give their troops a chance to regroup. During his final visit to New York, he met up with his long-time friend actor Samuel Chester.

Samuel (Knapp) Chester started his career in Baltimore at the same time as Booth and they had been friends for some time. Booth trusted him enough to include him in his kidnapping scheme telling him about it on Christmas evening 1864. Booth told him that his part would be easy. All he had to do was open the back door of Ford's theatre on a pre-arranged signal. He told Chester, "there was plenty of money in the affair; that if I would do it, I would not want again for as long as I lived; that I would never want for money." Chester, a family man, turned him down wanting no part of it. Chester thought the scheme a complete fantasy and felt his friend was playing a cruel game with him.[46]

During this visit, Booth was drinking heavily and in a combative mood when they sat down together. With the new directive to decapitate the government playing heavily on his mind, he burst out to Chester: "What an excellent chance I had to kill the president, if I had wished on Inauguration day" he cried. "I was on the stand, as close to him nearly as I am to you!"

Chester was shocked and tried to calm him down before his intoxicated friend got them both arrested. Booth started to ramble. His continued talk of kidnapping or killing the president unnerved Chester. Booth stopped his rant and repeated to him what he told Arnold, that the scheme had been completely abandoned. He told him that he had spent a fortune on the plot and now was selling his horses to recover some of his losses.

Kidnapping Lincoln

This assurance seemed to relieve Chester's apprehensions, and he decided to change the subject. He asked Booth about the ring on his little finger. He couldn't help but notice that Booth kept kissing it as he paused between sentences. Booth smiled and explained that he was engaged to be married and was deeply in love with the lady. She came from an excellent family. Her only objection to Booth was that he was an actor. His only objection to her was that she was an abolitionist. Chester was glad to hear of it hoping, no doubt, that she could sooth his friend's political passions. Generous as always, Booth then insisted on picking up their bill. He returned to Washington on the night of April 9.

Booth's mood had not improved upon his arrival back in Washington. He told Atzerodt of the torpedo plot that he had heard about in New York. It is unknown if Booth had any assigned role in this project but he confided to Atzerodt "if he did not get him quick the New York crowd would". According to Atzerodt, Booth interviewed a new conspirator two days before the assassination and Atzerodt was told to get travel papers to Richmond from the vice-president. "Booth," he said, "would get his papers out of the theatre."

John Wilkes Booth

Booth was a Southern sympathizer often making the argument for the Southern cause. Although a friend of the South for smuggling quinine through the lines it's not clear he was an active Confederate agent until the summer of 1864.

His sister Asia described him as "a man so single in his devotion, so unswerving in his principles that he would yield everything for the cause he espoused."

Lincoln's proposal to extend voting rights to emancipated slaves turned a kidnapping plot into murder.

A Hopeful Spring

During the latter part of March, Washington became infested with hungry and demoralized deserters from the Confederate Army. Washington alone took in over three thousand while others were deserting to Fort Monroe, Annapolis, and all around the lines. With the obvious signs of a rebel collapse, sympathetic Northern newspapers increased their demands that the administration negotiate with the Southerners for an end to the war. Anticipating the fall of Richmond, Lincoln left for Grant's headquarters at City Point, Virginia[47], over Stanton's protests. When he heard that Lincoln planned to go to Richmond, Stanton wrote:

> "Allow me respectfully to ask you to consider whether you ought to expose the nation to the consequence of any disaster to yourself in the pursuit of a treacherous and dangerous enemy like the rebel army. Commanding generals are in the line of their duty in running such risks, but is the political head of a nation in the same condition?"

Meanwhile, Grant's army had enveloped Petersburg on March 28. Believing that Lee would try retreating to the South where he could merge with General Joseph Johnston's army in North Carolina, he sent Phil Sheridan's cavalry to block the way. General George Pickett beat back Sheridan at Five Forks, but when the Southern officers left the field at the end of the day for a fish fry, Sheridan counterattacked and won the battle. Lee's line of retreat towards Johnston was closed as well as his access to the rations he stored along the way. When the beleaguered Lee heard the details of the battle, he furiously relieved Pickett of his command. The defeat forced him to disengage from his trenches and retreat before he was ready.

Kidnapping Lincoln

Desperate now to save his army and knowing he could no longer stop Grant, Lee realized that he must abandon Richmond. On Sunday, April 2, he sent a message to Davis that he would abandon the city that night. Davis received the message while he was attending Sunday services. The congregation seemed to know what the message contained as Davis hurriedly left the church. As one described it, the news "fell upon them like a thunder-clap from clear skies, and smote the community as a knell of death". From this point on, the war became a footrace with Lee short of rations trying to outrun his pursuers.

On the morning of April 4, Lincoln left his ship at City Point and took a walk with his son Tad through the streets of smoldering Richmond. To the former slaves of the Confederacy, it was the coming of the Messiah as they cheered and knelt before him for his blessing. Lincoln told them, "Don't kneel to me. You must kneel to God only and thank Him for the liberty you will hereafter enjoy."

Lincoln enters Richmond. April 4, 1856

Guarded by a small detail of ten sailors and four officers he toured the city by carriage. The tobacco and cotton barns burned by the fleeing Confederate leaders were still smoldering as Lincoln inspected the liberated Castle Thunder and Libby prisons. He interrupted his tour to stop at the home of General Pickett, the officer he once recommended for cadetship at West Point. In her account, Mrs. Pickett greeted the president at the door and briefly exchanged pleasantries about friends they had in common. Lincoln, she said, admired her new baby, and planted it with a kiss. He then went to the Confederate White House, where the housekeeper showed him Jefferson Davis' office. Told that Judge Campbell and others were asking for an interview he sat at Davis' desk and talked to his Confederate callers.

Unknown to Lincoln, was that a few hours before his arrival at Davis' house the Union guard took from Davis' writing desk a symbolic present left by the fleeing rebel leader to his occupiers. It was a torpedo bomb in the shape of an imitation lump of coal used to throw in the coalbunkers of Union war-ships and blow them up. Terror and guerilla warfare would now take the place of Lee and his soldiers.[48]

As Lincoln toured Richmond, a Confederate enlisted man named Snyder from the Confederate Torpedo Bureau entered the headquarters of Brigadier General Edward Hastings Ripley, commander at the occupation with a story to tell. He informed Ripley that a party had been dispatched from the Bureau with a secret mission to strike at the head of the Yankee government. He wanted to put Lincoln on his guard believing him to be in great danger and warned him to take greater care of himself.

Ripley put Snyder under oath as his adjutant took down the statement. The next morning at 9:00, Ripley went to see Lincoln on his ship the *Malvern* and read the statement to him. He asked the president to talk to Snyder but he refused. Lincoln was still feeling the rush of walking through the streets of Richmond. He told Ripley "I can't bring myself to believe that any human being lives that would do me harm."

As Lincoln was dismissing the warnings of Snyder, Colonel John Mosby was hastily assembling Company "H" under the command of Captain George Baylor. They were to link up with Stringfellow who would supply the explosives. Sergeant Harney carried the fuses and timing devices on his person. If intercepted, he would tell his captors that he was bringing the ordnance to Mosby.

The next day, a carriage accident involving Secretary of State Seward caused him to suffer multiple contusions and a broken jaw. Stanton telegraphed Lincoln, telling him that the bedridden Seward was not in mortal danger. However, he did use the accident it as a pretext to urge the president to stop exposing himself to danger and come home. Lincoln had hoped to witness the end of the war before returning, but on April 8, he ordered the *River Queen* to sail for Washington.

On the following day April 9, it ended. Ulysses S. Grant rode up to Wilmer McLean's home in Appomattox Court House to meet with Robert E. Lee. For almost a year, he had pounded away at the Army of Northern Virginia trying to make it yield. He had come to hate the war, hoping that he could out flank Lee and end the bloody business sooner but Lee countered him at every move.

As Lincoln instructed both Grant and Sherman on the *River Queen*, the surrender terms were both simple and generous. After exchanging pleasantries, Grant looked at Lee's handsome sword that hung at his side. Trying to make the process as painless as possible, he decided that to require officers to surrender their swords would be an unnecessary humiliation.

Grant silently wrote out the terms and handed the document to Lee. Enlisted men would surrender their arms, but the officers could retain theirs. Once completed, all would get individual paroles if they promised not to take up arms against the government. Government authorities would not disturb them so long as they observe their paroles and the laws in force where they may reside.

After reviewing it, Lee informed Grant that the cavalrymen and artillerymen in the Confederate Army owned their horses and asked that they keep them. Grant agreed. It was the planting season; most of the privates in Lee's army were small farmers and needed their horses and mules.

Lee then whispered to Grant that his army had eaten nothing but some parched corn since leaving Richmond. Grant turned to Sheridan and ordered 40,000 rations given to Lee's starving army.

As Lee signed the surrender, he told Grant, "This will have the best possible effect upon the men. It will be very gratifying and will do much towards conciliating our people."

Conciliating the country was Lincoln's goal.

Since the beginning of the war, the Radicals in Lincoln's party demanded that officers resigning their Federal commissions to go south, should be hanged or exiled when captured for violating their oaths of allegiance to the country. Secessionists in the south used this rhetoric to push their armies to fight to the end, since there would be no mercy from the Yankees.

The paroles given helped to silence the politician's thirst for blood. The entire surrender was a quiet one Grant told his army there would be no celebration of victory. "The rebels are our countrymen again; the best sign of rejoicing after the victory will be to abstain from all demonstrations on the field." There would be no humiliation of the vanquished foe. They could go back to their homes farms and sweethearts as free men and rebuild their lives.

Before evacuating Richmond, the Confederate Congress ordered all the cotton, tobacco, and other property burned to prevent it falling into the hands of the Union. Richmond burned while Davis and his cabinet fled the city.

A Triumphant Return

When Lincoln returned from City Point on April 10, crowds gathered on the lawn to catch a glimpse of him and entice him to give an impromptu speech. Lincoln was finally a hero. For four arduous years, critics deemed his attitude towards the South as too soft. At every misstep in the campaign, they abused and ridiculed him. Now in the glow of victory they knew the critics had misjudged him. Old Abe was the people's champion and the swarm of admirers could not get enough of him. Several times, he sent out word to dispense the crowds, but they returned repeatedly. "Speech! Speech!" they cried until finally the fatigued Lincoln asked them to return the following night so that he could prepare some appropriate remarks.

Upon Lincoln's return to Washington, he received a letter of resignation from his weary secretary of war. Stanton had promised himself that he would resign when Richmond fell and retire to private life. It had been a long, arduous assignment and he had fulfilled it admirably. Resigning now would give his replacement nearly a full term to put his stamp on the war department. Lincoln read it with tears filling his eyes. He tore it in two and placed his hands on Stanton's shoulders.

"Stanton," he said, "you cannot go. Reconstruction is more difficult and dangerous than construction or destruction. You have been our main reliance; you must help us through the final act. The bag is filled. It must be tied and tied securely. Some knots slip, yours do not. You understand the situation better than anybody else, and it is my wish and the country's that you remain."

Stanton begged the president to understand that he had not proposed to leave him with any tasks not provided for. He had made an outline of a plan for reconstruction explaining what Congress must provide for all of the Southern states with explanations of various circumstances that to consider. He gave instructions to the quarter-master general on how to turn over property seized to their rightful owners, he made memorandums on re-establishing national post offices, federal courts, revenue service, and made preparations to reopen commerce and social intercourse between the sections. He had also suspended the draft, stopped buying ordnances for the army, and made plans for the discharge of army veterans back into civilian life.

Lincoln listened, smiled, again put his hand on his shoulder, and said triumphantly, "Stanton, you give the very reason why you should not resign. You admit that you have looked into the future, foreseen troubles there, and tried to prepare in advance for my relief and benefit of the nation. Your recitation sustains me exactly. You must stay."

Stanton understood and returned to his desk without a word. He could not over rule Lincoln's appeal. The shooting war between the states was over, but the political war that began it was far from finished.[49]

On that same day in Fairfax County, Virginia, the Eighth Illinois Cavalry had a running fight with a group of Mosby's raiders. Col William Gamble reported the capture of two rebels Sergeant William Francis Harney from the Torpedo Bureau and his guide Thomas Franklin Summers from the 35th Virginia cavalry on the banks of the Potomac. The prisoners were sent to the Old Capitol Prison in Washington. [50]

A Threat to the Republic

This skirmish foiled the Confederate Government's Torpedo Plot to blow up the White House, though no one outside of a select few of Confederates knew the full extent of the consequences. The triggerman in the Confederacy's last-ditch effort was now in custody. News of his capture appeared in the *Washington Daily Morning Chronicle* the next day as a filler item in the paper.[*]

On Tuesday night April 11, government buildings were illuminated and torchlight parades lit up the city as Lincoln stepped to the window to give his promised speech. Rather than feed the frenzy of the crowd with a victory speech, Lincoln chose to speak of the new relationship between the Union and the Southern states. If a fair and lasting peace was to be fashioned from the spoils of war, the country would have to forgive and forget. Lincoln would need the support of the people and he determined that now was the appropriate time to ask for it:

> "We meet this evening, not in sorrow, but in gladness of heart. The evacuation of Petersburg and Richmond, and the surrender of the principal insurgent army, give hope of a righteous and speedy peace whose joyous expression cannot be restrained. In the midst of this, however, He from whom all blessings flow must not be forgotten. A call for a national thanksgiving is being prepared, and will be duly promulgated. Nor must those whose harder part gives us the cause of rejoicing, be overlooked. Their honors must not be parceled out with others. I myself was near the front, and had the high pleasure of transmitting much of the good news to you; but no part of the honor, for plan or execution, is mine. To Gen. Grant his skilful officers, and brave men, all belongs...."

---

[*] Thomas F. Harney took the oath of allegiance to the United States on July 7, 1865 and became a free man. On the same day, George Atzerodt, Louis Payne, Davy Herold and Mary Surratt were hanged at the Washington arsenal.

Among the crowd, that evening was perhaps the bitterest man in Washington. John Wilkes Booth listened intently to Lincoln's words. For eight months, he had been preparing for his starring role in this war. He had assembled a crew and planned the kidnapping of the president. Less than a month ago, he put the scheme into action, only to be foiled by Lincoln's last minute change of plans. After all the time and money he invested, he had been tossed aside by those he hoped to please. So Booth stared, glared, and listened to the hated tyrant who upstaged him, as he discussed the reconstruction effort in Louisiana.

> "... It is also unsatisfactory to some that the elective franchise is not given to the colored man. I would myself prefer that it were now conferred on the very intelligent, and on those who serve our cause as soldiers...."

Lincoln's words hit Booth like a slap in the face. The idea that a colored man could stand on equal ground with a white man was immediately abhorrent to him. "Nigger Citizenship" would never happen no matter what they accomplished or how intelligent they were. This could not and would not ever happen if he had breath in him. His hands clenched in a rage, Booth turned and ordered Lewis Powell shoot Lincoln immediately. Powell refused. Booth urged him again telling him the crowd was so great he could avoid detection but again Powell refused. Booth turned away in disgust vowing, "That will be the last speech he will ever make."[51]

A Threat to the Republic

President Abraham Lincoln

On April 11, Lincoln told his wife and a few friends about a dream he had: "There seemed to be a death-like stillness about me. Then I heard subdued sobs, as if a number of people were weeping. I left my bed and wandered downstairs…until I arrived at the East Room... Before me was a catafalque, on which rested a corpse wrapped in funeral vestments. 'Who is dead in the White House?' I demanded of one of the soldiers. 'The president was the answer, 'he was killed by an assassin!' Then came a loud burst of grief from the crowd, which awoke me from my dream. I slept no more that night."

Chapter 4

The Plot Unfolds

Ominous Warnings

Throughout his life, Abraham Lincoln suffered from serious bouts of depression. Friends noted that he could turn his emotional state from joke telling and mirth to sadness and self-persecution in a very short time. The perpetual look of sadness was his most prominent feature and created a great deal of sympathy for him. William Herndon, Lincoln's law partner wrote:

> Mr. Lincoln was a kind of fatalist in some aspects of his philosophy, and skeptical in his religion. He was a sad man, a terribly gloomy one—a man of sorrow, if not of agony. This, his state, may have arisen from a defective physical organization, or it may have arisen from some fatalistic idea, that he was to die a sudden and a terrible death. Some unknown power seemed to buzz about his consciousness, his being, his mind, that whispered in his ear. "Look out for danger ahead!" This peculiarity in Mr. Lincoln I had noticed for years, and it is no secret in this city. He has said to me more than once, "Billy, I feel as if I shall meet with some terrible end." He did not know what would strike him, nor when, nor where, nor how hard; he was a blind intellectual Sampson, struggling and fighting in the dark against the fates. I say on my own personal observation that he felt this for years. Often and often I have resolved to make or get him to reveal the causes of his misery, but I had not the courage nor the impertinence to do it. [52]

One method Lincoln used to overcome his fatalistic feelings of impending doom was to tempt fate and take chances that a cautious man would avoid. His tour of Richmond the day after its fall was typical of the reckless disregard of his own safety. During Jubal Early's attack on Washington in July 1864, Lincoln stood tall on the parapets of Fort Stevens, watching the battle when a Confederate sniper shot the officer standing next to him in the thigh.

After the incident, John Hay recorded in his diary that, "The president is in very good feather this evening. He seems not in the least concerned about the safety of Washington. With him the only concern seems to be whether we can bag or destroy this force in our front."

One month later an assassin attempted to murder the president. Lincoln related this story to his chief of security, Ward Hill Lamon:

> "Last night about eleven o'clock, I went to the Soldiers' Home alone, riding *Old Abe*, as you call him (a horse he delighted in riding), and when I arrived at the foot of the hill on the road leading to the entrance to the Home grounds, I was jogging along at a slow gait, immersed in deep thought, contemplating what was next to happen in the unsettled state of affairs, when suddenly I was aroused–I may say the arousement lifted me out of my saddle as well as out of my wits–by the report of a rifle, and seemingly the gunner was not fifty yards from where my contemplations ended and my accelerated transit began. My erratic namesake, with little warning, gave proof of decided dissatisfaction at the racket, and with one reckless bound he unceremoniously separated me from my eight-dollar plug hat, with which I parted company without any assent, express or implied, upon my part. At a break-neck speed we soon arrived in a haven of safety. Meanwhile I was left in doubt whether death was more desirable from being thrown from a runaway federal horse, or as the tragic result of a rifle-ball fired by a disloyal bushwhacker in the middle of the night."[53]

This incident appalled Lamon, but Lincoln remained convinced that the bullet was merely a stray shot from a hunter. However, Lamon decided in the Fall of 1864, to patrol the grounds of the White House every night in case the 'hunter' returned. On one of these patrols he found a man skulking in the White House shrubbery where with one powerful punch between the eyes he sent the trespasser to Valhalla. A search of the body by the secret service found him to be a Southerner in possession of two pistols and two knives.[54]

Lamon had been part of Lincoln's entourage from the beginning, escorting him safely through the Baltimore train station plot in 1861. He understood that Lincoln was in constant danger and often resigned his position in frustration over Lincoln's seemingly indifference to threats and warnings of death. Lincoln always convinced him to stay on, with a promise to be more careful. However, it seems that his melancholy pushed him to welcome the stimulus of danger. He continued to expose himself irresponsibly.

Lincoln was well aware of the rumors surrounding the death of his predecessor Zachary Taylor. The land acquired from the War with Mexico was the issue of hot debate in 1850. Southern slaveholders believed that their class system was doomed if it remained an isolated southeastern enclave while free states were allowed to spread across the entire continent. The right to extend slavery into the newly acquired territories was a necessity if the institution was to survive. Taylor a war hero, himself a southerner and a slaveholder was emerging as a pivotal player and taking a surprisingly tough stance against the slaveholding interests. When threats of secession filled the air, Taylor let it be known that he personally would lead troops against any "traitors," and hang secessionists "with less reluctance than I hanged spies and deserters in Mexico."[55]

Henry Clay proposed a compromise in the Senate to try to avoid a conflict but Taylor adamantly opposed the bill. Taylor's Vice President Millard Fillmore then informed the president that in the event of a tie in the Senate on Clay's compromise bill, he as presiding officer, would cast the deciding vote in its favor.

On July 4, 1850, Zachary Taylor attended the laying of the cornerstone of the Washington Monument. That evening after dinner, he suddenly took ill. Five days later, the healthy and hardy president was dead. Before dying, Taylor may have suspected foul play. He told his doctor: *"I should not be surprised if this were to terminate in my death. I did not expect to encounter what has beset me since my elevation to the presidency. God knows I have endeavored to fulfill what I conceived to be an honest duty. But I have been mistaken. My motives have been misconstrued, and my feelings most grossly outraged."* [56]

Taylor's fortuitous death marked a sudden shift in the political climate. Clay's 'Compromise of 1850' passed, postponing the Civil War for eleven years. However, at the time many believed it occurred because the 'slavocracy' poisoned Zachary Taylor. [57]

Shortly after Booth's death the *Pittsburgh Chronicle* reported the following;

> On the 4th of June, 1864, Booth registered his name, took a room, and remained a short time at the McHenry House, Meadville. While there he wrote with his diamond ring, upon the glass in the window of his room, this sentence:
>
> "Abe Lincoln departed this life Aug'st 13th, 1864. By poison."
>
> The plate of glass on which the sentence quoted was written, has been carefully removed from the window and framed for preservation.

Whether Booth was given information relating to another Confederate plot or the window was etched by a resourceful hotel entrepreneur after the fact, is not known.

The thought that poison might be used against him as a weapon had to have crossed Lincoln's mind in early 1862, with the sudden death of his son Willie. Willie's death was a devastating blow to his parents, sending them both into a deep depression. Even Jefferson Davis sent his condolences. For Willie's father it was probably the most intense personal crisis of his life. Combined with the constant bad news from the war front, Lincoln needed all the fortitude he could muster to continue functioning. Like many grieving families, the Lincolns turned to the growing spiritualist movement seeking comfort through mediums that seemed to spring up in the Northern cities.

The Plot Unfolds

To cope with her grief, Mary Lincoln began attending séances at the home of Cranston Laurie in Georgetown. The Lauries' home was the center of spiritualist activity in Washington where many mediums came to help people in need. At one particular séance, a particular young medium impressed her so much that she invited her to the White House to conduct a séance in the Red Room with her husband.

Nettie Colburn was a twenty-year-old trance medium who had the ability to link with a spirit that foretold of future events. She accepted no money for her talent feeling that it was wrong to profit on her gift from God. Lincoln, who had his own prophetic visions, was impressed with her talent and invited her back for other readings.

Aware of the political implications, Lincoln avoided the spiritualists in public but Mary openly welcomed them. Her grief was so great that she wore mourning clothes for almost three years and never re-entered the room where Willie died. Spiritualist Margaret Laurie became her close friend and confidante introducing her to many mediums who conducted séances for her and the president at the White House.

Nettie Colburn's last visit with the president occurred shortly before his second inauguration. At this meeting, she reminded him that her "friends" had foretold him that in spite of his doubts, he would win a second term. However, they also reaffirmed that the shadow they have spoken of still hung over him.

Lincoln acknowledged the admonition saying that he had received warnings from other mediums that his life was in danger but could not believe that anyone wanted to harm him. Colburn cautioned him that his danger lay in his over-confidence in his fellow man. Lincoln sadly replied that he would live until his work was done and after then it wouldn't matter. Lincoln then extended his hand saying that he hoped to see her in the Fall. She promised she would come *'if you were here'*.

Ward Hill Lamon

A physically imposing man Ward Lamon acted as a self-appointed bodyguard to President Lincoln. Once when walking with Lincoln a Confederate sympathizer stopped them and shook the President's hand, wringing it till he cried out with pain. A powerful blow from Lamon's gigantic fist sent the assailant crumbling to the ground. Standing over the prostrate man Lincoln told his friend: "For God's sake, Ward, The next time you hit a man, strike him with a club or crowbar or something that won't kill him!"

Lamon was on an assignment for Lincoln in Richmond on the night of the assassination. Before he left, he implored the president not to "go out at night while he was gone, *particularly to the theatre.*"

The Plot Unfolds

Setting the Stage

John Deery ran a billiards saloon located above the lobby of Grover's theatre. A cordial host and a good friend of Booth, he shook his head in despair as he watched his friend consume glass after glass of brandy at his bar on Wednesday, April 12. The next day Booth returned and asked Deery for a favor. Could he reserve the right hand box at Grover's for him on Friday night? It was to be the opening of the exciting new play, *Aladdin*. The amiable Deery asked Booth why he didn't do it himself, and Booth replied, "If I try to buy a ticket, Mr. Hess, the manager would insist on giving me the box, and I prefer to pay for it." The box he requested was next to the president's box, a perfect spot for an ambush. Deery agreed to the favor.

Friday night was the one night of the week that Lincoln preferred to relax by attending the theatre when possible. Knowing Lincoln's routine, Booth was guessing that this new play, with all of its favorable pre-publicity would be the one Lincoln would attend. To hedge his bet he had already talked to Dwight Hess about his plans for the evening. Hess told him that not only was he going to illuminate the theatre but was also going to present a spectacular production commemorating the fall of Fort Sumter exactly four years ago. "Are you going to invite the president?" Booth asked. "Yes," said Hess, and then he thanked him for reminding him to send the invitation. The White House accepted Hess's invitation on behalf of Lincoln's son Tad and their doorkeeper Alphonso Dunn. They watched *Aladdin* that night while the Lincolns went to Ford's Theatre.

Booth had already staked out Seward's house, charming a chambermaid for information. She gave him the layout of the house, where the bedroom was located, and how many people resided there. As Booth busily went about his business that day, he ran into a friend Edward Person. In a brief conversation, Booth and told him that he had "the biggest thing on his hands that had ever turned up, and that there was a great deal of money in it."[58]

Grant arrived in Washington late on April 13. Secretary Stanton invited him to his home for a fireworks illumination party. At that time, Grant told Stanton that President and Mrs. Lincoln had invited him to the theatre the following night. Stanton scowled and told him that Washington was filled with people who would do the president harm. He advised him to turn down the invitation and asked him to urge the president not to attend. He had done so himself many times, but Lincoln ignored his pleas. Grant needed no arm-twisting. He was looking for a reason to turn down the president. He would make his excuses after the cabinet meeting late the next day. Hopefully, the president would find it inconvenient to ask someone else at such a late date and forgo the theatre.

That night military bands played on Franklin Square, and Stanton's party stood on the front porch to watch the fireworks. A man in a dark suit approached the house and asked Major Kilburn Knox, a war department employee, "Is Stanton in?"

"I suppose you mean the Secretary?" said Knox.

"Yes," said the man. "I am a lawyer in town. I know him very well."

When Knox told him that he should not disturb the Secretary, the man went to the other side of the steps for five minutes saying nothing. Then he came back to Knox and said again, "Is Stanton in?"

Knox convinced that the man was intoxicated ignored him.

"Excuse me," he said. "I thought you were the officer on duty here."

"There is no officer on duty here," replied Knox.

With this information, the man stepped back and then walked into the house. Within a few minutes, he was asked to leave.

During the trial both Hatter and Knox identified the man as Michael O'Laughlin. This identification was faulty due to other eyewitnesses who were able to account for O'Laughlin's activities that night and the fact that O'Laughlin was not wearing a dark suit but a plaid one. The identity of this mysterious man in the dark suit and his role in the assassination plot has never been determined.[59]

By the night of Thursday April 13, Booth had put his players into place. Herold spent the night in the village of T.B at the house of a distant cousin Joseph Eli Huntt.[60] Huntt's home was where Booth planned to get fresh horses for his kidnapping attempt[61]. It's probable that Herold was attempting to make certain that a fresh pair of horses were ready for the next night.

Powell was staying at the Herndon House, and Booth moved the slovenly dressed Atzerodt from the Pennsylvania House on C Street to the first-class Kirkwood House, where the vice-president was staying. By moving Atzerodt to the red-carpeted Kirkwood, Booth knew that old George would stand out like a sore thumb. The weakest member of the group, by Thursday night Booth probably envisioned him as nothing more than a sacrificial lamb. It is unknown where Booth spent that night. When called upon on the morning of April 14, the bed in his room had not been touched.

The fourteenth of April was a beautiful spring day with sunshine, warmth, calm, and the promise of peaceful days ahead. Around 10:30, a messenger from the White House arrived at Ford's Theatre to reserve the state box for the Lincolns that night. When Mrs. Lincoln, heard that it was actress Laura Keene's benefit and farewell performance for her play *Our American Cousin*, she decided to attend.[62]

Booth and Lucy were seen together at the hotel at around 10:00. Shortly before noon, Lucy left to spend the afternoon with John Hay, who was helping her study Spanish, while Booth walked from his hotel to Ford's Theatre. He stopped in front talking with stagehands when one of the crew, Thomas Raybold, told him that he had mail. In the process of this conversation, he heard something that set him back. The president and General Grant were coming to the theatre that night. "Here?" said Booth, "to see *Our American Cousin?*" Henry Ford, brother and acting manager of the theatre confirmed the rumor. "That's right," he said. "Maybe the stale old comedy will do some business; it will be a whale of an attraction." Booth was familiar with the play. His brother-in-law John Sleeper Clarke had produced it in Richmond when Booth was a stock actor.[63]

Until that moment, it was doubtful that Booth even knew Grant was in Washington since he had only arrived late Thursday evening, but this news was too good to be true. Ford's Theatre was where Booth had planned to kidnap Lincoln only the month before. He knew every room, door, and passageway in the place. He expected Lincoln to attend the new play at Grover's but he was ready for him in either theatre. Not only would he get the president, but he would get a bonus by getting Grant at the same time!

Raybold handed Booth his correspondence as he continued his talk with Ford. He then sat down on the front steps of the theatre digesting this new information. He slowly opened the envelope and began to read his mail. Ford remembered that he laughed as he read his letter, shaking his head, obviously amused by what was inside. He sat on the steps for nearly half an hour. Undoubtedly, he was mulling over the chess pieces he would have to move on his board and contemplating the good fortune that had just come his way.

Ford was convinced that it was not until this moment that Booth decided to kill the president. However, the evidence shows that he had already begun maneuvering to make his strike. He already knew the location of each of his intended victims and Herold already performed his route reconnaissance mission to T.B.. Ford's news merely changed Lincoln's location.

Booth then entered the theatre and watched the actors run through their lines in an abbreviated rehearsal. Laura Keene was making her one thousandth performance that night as the play's star. She was to lead the audience and cast in singing orchestra leader William Withers' tribute anthem "Honor to Our Soldiers". Due to the president's attendance, a sellout crowd was expected and they were tightening up their timing. Finally, Harry Hawk stood on stage alone and delivered the funniest line in the play:

> 'Don't know the manners of good society eh? Well I guess I know enough to turn you inside out, old gal - you sockdologizing old man trap!'

Booth saw his opportunity. This was the play's biggest punch line. The audience would be laughing and the stage practically bare. This was the time to strike the blow.

About 2:00, Booth arrived at Mrs. Surratt's boarding house to ask her for a favor. Would she deliver a package and a message to her tavern keeper in Surrattsville for him? The message was important and to be given verbally to minimize the danger of it being intercepted and provide the sender the capability of easy denial. Booth was coming tonight, and it was necessary that the rifles stored there were available. After some conversation, she agreed. She told Lou Weichmann, a boarder at her house, that she found "... it necessary to go into the country to see about a debt owed me by John Nothey. Would you have any objections to driving me down?" Weichmann readily agreed and hired a horse and buggy for the trip.

Booth left for the Herndon House to talk with Powell and then down to the Kirkwood to see Atzerodt. Sloppy, disheveled, and reeking of alcohol, Atzerodt was as recognizable at the upscale Kirkwood as if he had a target painted on his back. He had not yet accomplished what Booth wanted; meet Vice-President Johnson and ask him for the passes. Atzerodt was at a stable trying to rent a horse and was not at the hotel when Booth called - but by asking for him at the desk, the actor established a crucial link between Atzerodt and himself. Taking a pencil from the lobby desk, Booth wrote the following note and handed it to the clerk on duty.

Don't wish to disturb you. Are you at home?
John Wilkes Booth.

He then took a seat in the foyer and composed a letter of justification for his actions, put it in an envelope and addressed it to the Editor of the *National Intelligencer*. He placed it in his pocket and casually strolled out of the hotel and into the sunshine.

The Plot Unfolds   121

Meanwhile, Davy Herold was negotiating with John Fletcher, the manager at Naylor's stables for a particular roan horse he wanted to rent for the evening. Fletcher tried to rent him a small mare, but Herold would have none of it. He wanted the roan, and Fletcher finally relented. After reviewing the saddles and bridles, he insisted on a pair of English steel stirrups rather than a leather pair and a double-rein bridle. As he mounted the horse, he asked how late he could stay out with him. Fletcher told him no later than eight o'clock or nine at the latest. Herold had the horse he was going to use to make his escape.

Booth walked up the street to Pumphrey's Livery Stable and rented a small mare. He trotted her around Ford's Theatre, carefully planning his escape route openly letting others see him on the horse, tipping his hat to the ladies and waving to passersby. He would later return to Pumphrey's Stables after dark and take a bay as his escape horse, but his promenade on the streets with the mare would misidentify his horse.

Booth then spotted stock actor John Matthews in front of Willard's Hotel. He rode over and asked him for a favor. Matthews and Booth had had a falling out not long before. During a volatile political argument, Booth had taken issue with Matthew's position. He held a grudge against him for both his pro-union statements and his Northern sympathies. He told fellow actor Samuel Chester "he would not care if he sacrificed him, Matthews was a coward and not fit to live". [64]

Eager to smooth things over with the volatile star, Matthews readily agreed to the favor. Booth told him that he may have to leave town that night but wanted a letter published in the *National Intelligencer*. If he did not leave town, he would pick it up from Matthews before 10:00 tomorrow. If Matthews didn't see him the next day, would he deliver the letter to the newspaper. Matthews agreed and put the letter in his pocket.

As Booth turned his horse, he noticed General Grant and his wife leaving Willard's Hotel in an open carriage. Booth galloped after it staring hard at the couple and their luggage making sure of what he was seeing. They were clearly heading towards the railroad station. Booth then returned to Willard's and asked where Grant was going. A porter told him "New Jersey."

Lincoln's cabinet meeting had ended, and Stanton thought Lincoln was more "cheerful and happy" than he had ever seen him. Grant had already made his excuses to Lincoln that he and his wife wanted to take the night train to New Jersey and visit their children. When he advised the president that he might want to reconsider going himself, Lincoln began to see the behind-the-scenes hand of his secretary of war and decided to have some fun at his expense.

The president went to the war department and told Stanton of Grant's cancellation. Seizing the opportunity, the Secretary at his stern and cautious best, urged the president to give up the theatre, but Lincoln remained reluctant. "Well," sputtered Stanton in frustration, "you ought to at least have a competent guard."

Lincoln smiled as his secretary had given him the opportunity he was looking for:

"Stanton, do you know that Eckert can break a poker over his arm?"

Surprised by the comment he said, "No, why do you ask such a question?"

"Well, I've seen him break five pokers, one after the other over his arm and I'm thinking he would be the kind of man to go with me this evening. May I take him?"

Stanton quickly recognized that Lincoln was manipulating his own words against him, and curtly replied that Eckert was busy that night.

But Lincoln decided to twist the tiger's tail a little more. "Well, I will ask the Major myself, and he can do your work tomorrow." He then went into the Cipher room and said, "Now Major, come along. You can do Stanton's work tomorrow."

Eckert realized that the president was needling his thin-skinned boss and wisely agreed with Stanton that he could not postpone the work.

Lincoln then jabbed his Secretary one last time with his punch line: "I'll take Major Rathbone because Stanton insists upon having someone to protect me, but I should much rather have you since I know you can break a poker over your arm."[65]

Gleeful at his one-upmanship Lincoln left the war department for a carriage ride toward the Navy Yard with his wife. "I never saw him so supremely cheerful – his manner even playful," Mary wrote a friend. "He was so gay that I said to him laughingly, dear husband, you almost startle me by your great cheerfulness."

Until now, all of Booth's bases were covered, but as one of his prey rode away, he had a decision to make. If Grant cancelled his appearance at the theatre, did that mean that Lincoln cancelled too? With Grant leaving town, he would have to adjust his plans if the General were to become one of his victims.

Quickly weighing the pros and cons he may have decided that Grant was too big a target to let escape. He, more than anyone, was responsible for the South's defeat and the deaths of thousands of his countrymen. Booth's solution was to reassign the assassin he had targeted for Johnson and send him on the 6:00 train after Grant. He would deal with the Johnson situation later.

Atzerodt later identified a man named James Donaldson as the possible hit man:

"James Donaldson, a low chunky man about 23 or 24 years of age, small-potted, dark complexion (not very) deep plain black suit; only saw him one time & this was Wednesday previous to the murder, he was having an interview with Booth and told him to meet him on Friday eve & he replied he would….. I was under the impression he came on with Booth."

Atzerodt believed that Donaldson was part of the group, but he never showed up on Friday evening at the Herndon House for final instructions with the rest of the conspirators. Did Booth send him on the train with Grant? Baltimore police records show an arrest for a James Donaldson on May 13, 1865, for "treasonable language". They released him on May 16 for unrecorded reasons. He was then lost to history.[66]

In 1880, Grant talked of the assassination with Ward Lamon. Grant turned down the offer of going to the theatre because his wife wanted to leave for Burlington to visit their daughter. While leaving for the station, "a horseman rode rapidly by us at a gallop, and wheeling his horse, rode back, peering into our carriage as he passed us. Mrs. Grant identified him as the man who sat near us at lunch that day with some others and tried to overhear our conversation. The horseman was later identified as Booth. A few days afterward, I received an anonymous letter stating that the writer had been detailed to assassinate me; that he rode in my train as far as Havre De Grace, and as my car was locked, he failed to get in. He now thanked God he had so failed."⁶⁷

If Booth sent Donaldson on the train with Grant, it would have left him one assassin short in Washington. Had he known that Grant was going to be in town and would be a vulnerable target two days earlier, he might have been able to bring Surratt back from Canada. There was no time, however, to bring in anyone now. To solve his problem, he decided to play a long shot. He would order, intimidate, and pressure Atzerodt to do the job. If Atzerodt refused, he would give the job to his reliable toady Herold.

The primary reason that Booth brought the heavy-drinking Atzerodt from Port Tobacco to Washington was to keep him secluded. Try as he may, George just could not keep quiet. With the kidnap plot now changed to assassination the boatman was expendable. Booth concluded that he could be beneficial to the escape plan if he could draw the manhunt away from the escape route and point the search parties in the wrong direction. Now, the goal of decapitating the government depended on Atzerodt, the alcoholic boatman, becoming a murderer and shooting Johnson.

Despite his newspaper characterization as a dim-witted, cold-hearted monster, Thomas Eckert's interviews with Lewis Powell after his arrest, showed him to be a soldier who had a sense of honor. Recruited to help burn New York in November 1864, he refused to take part because it would destroy private property and sacrifice innocent lives. ⁶⁸

While working with Booth to kidnap Lincoln, he turned down three opportunities to shoot the president. The last time occurred during Lincoln's Louisiana speech the night of April 11 when an enraged Booth ordered him to 'take out his revolver and fire'. Why then would Powell decide to take part in the assassination plot three nights later? His attorney William Doster asked the same question. Powell replied, "I believed it was my duty."[69] Powell also told the Reverend Gillette that he "thought he was doing right in attempting to kill Secretary Seward as he still claimed to be a Confederate Soldier. He thinks now it was all wrong and blames *Rebel Leaders* for his death". [70]

The reason that Powell felt that it was 'his duty' to become an assassin was due to his presence with Booth in New York, when the details of the Torpedo Plot was made known to the New York branch of the Confederate underground. It explains his later comment to Eckert regarding the number of conspirators in the plot when he told him that – "you have not got one-half of them."[71]

We don't know if Booth's action was the official Confederate backup plan to the Torpedo plot or if he was acting on his own accord but it's easy to imagine that on the night of the assassination, Booth appealed to Powell's sense of duty and honor. Informing him of Harney's capture and that they were now duty bound to complete the mission would have likely motivated the stoic soldier into action.

John Surratt certainly knew about the Harney plot. When he first read of the assassination, there was no mention of the assassin's name and Surratt immediately believed Harney and his group were successful.

> "It never occurred to me for an instant that it could have been Booth or any of the parties to our conspiracy, for the simple reason that I had never heard anything regarding assassination spoken of during my intercourse with them. I had good reason to believe that there was another conspiracy afloat in Washington: **in fact we all knew it**."[72]

The Torpedo Plot is evidence that the leaders of the Confederacy had arrived at a grim decision. The well-being of their society and nation, their 'Southern rights' would soon be gone with the wind. At this point, they felt compelled to deal with the dangers posed to their way of life. The restraints of their morality could no longer be limited due to the drastic situation they faced. The extreme measures they were willing to employ were no longer shocking to them and in their minds became justifiable. The delegation of the task to a lower-level operative eased any guilt allowing them to keep their hands clean.

To decapitate the government the Confederates were aware that the president, the vice-president, and the secretary of state would have to die simultaneously. With the office of the president vacant, the Presidential Succession Act of 1792 would be in force. Under this law, the secretary of state would call together the Electoral College and oversee the election of a new president. If there were no secretary of state to perform this duty, there would be constitutional chaos and political infighting on a grand scale. During this period of confusion and disorder the South would be given time to regroup, melt into the countryside and return as guerrilla units. As Jefferson Davis remarked upon hearing of the assassination,

> *" If it were to be done at all, it were better that it were well done; and if the same had been done to Andy Johnson, the beast, and to Secretary Stanton, the job would then be complete."*[73]

This was the goal of the Torpedo Plot.

Judah Benjamin

Judah Benjamin, Confederate Secretary of State, formed the Canadian Secret Service with the purpose of disrupting the elections of 1864, helping the Democrats oust Lincoln, sabotaging supply lines, stirring up riots in the cities, compelling Washington to place troops in Canada and forcing Britain to enter the war. Benjamin's association with Jacob Thompson and John Surratt lay at the center of the accusation of conspiracy against Jefferson Davis.

When Richmond fell, Benjamin escaped to Great Britain. Of all the officers of the Confederacy, he was the only one never to return to the United States. Secretary of State Seward firmly believed that Benjamin was the man behind the assassination.

The Night of the Assassins

At around 5:30 Booth entered the restaurant by the side of Ford's Theatre. Ed Spangler was sitting out front, and Booth invited him in for a drink and conversation. After dinner, Booth got together with Davy Herold and told him to find Atzerodt for a meeting at the Herndon House.

By 7:00, Booth was back in his hotel room readying himself for the night. He changed into black clothes, calf length boots, and new spurs. He made sure that his trunk contained the clues he wanted the authorities to find. He loaded a single shot derringer with a .44 caliber lead ball. In his pockets, he put a compass, his appointment book, and the derringer. Inside his pants, he carried a long bowie knife.

Around 7:30, Davy Herold met up with Atzerodt in his room at the Kirkwood. He told him that Booth had called a meeting and wanted to see him. Before leaving, Herold left his coat, knife, and pistol in the room. Inside the coat pocket were Booth's bankbook and a map of Virginia. Atzerodt locked the door and took the key with him. The pigeon's nest was set.

Authorities would believe that the weapons in the room and it's location near Johnson's proved that Atzerodt was the assigned triggerman for the vice-president. History would forever label him as the cowardly assassin. Atzerodt did not understand that his inability to kill was not a legal defense.

Booth held his last meeting with the conspirators at approximately 8:00 p.m. that night. Powell's assignment was to kill the secretary of state and he was ready to perform his duty. Booth then turned to Atzerodt and ordered him to shoot Johnson in his hotel room as close to 10:15 as possible.

A shocked Atzerodt immediately refused to comply and Booth began his rehearsed routine to goad him into action. Using all his acting vigor Booth flashed his angry eyes at the boatman threatening to shoot him on the spot, but Atzerodt held firm. A disgusted Booth then called him a coward telling him that young Davy Herold had "more pluck" than he did. The chastised Atzerodt conceded the point, but still refused to be provoked into murder.

Finally, Booth played his last card, inevitability. He told Atzerodt it was too late to back out; the government would know that he was involved in the plot and would hang him even if he quit now. Atzerodt finally spoke up and told Booth that he agreed to be part of a kidnapping not a murder and would not be a part of it. Booth realizing that Atzerodt did not have enough pride to be shamed into action finally relented giving the job of killing Johnson to Herold. He then asked Atzerodt if he would get his horse and meet them at the Eastern Branch (Navy Yard) Bridge to guide them to the proper roads in Maryland. A thoroughly intimidated Atzerodt finally agreed, and the conspirators parted company.[74]

Shaken by this frightening conversation, Atzerodt promptly went on a drinking spree, pub-crawling his way throughout the town. At 11:15, thoroughly inebriated, he found himself on a horse car heading for the Navy Yard Bridge. On the car, he recognized an old acquaintance named Washington Briscoe who was on his way home. When the car reached the end of the line, Atzerodt reeking of liquor and trembling, asked Briscoe if he could spend the night with him. Briscoe refused. He then asked if the car could take him back to the city and out to Georgetown. Briscoe said it could and gladly put the stumbling drunkard back on the car. At approximately 2:00 a.m., George finally got a room at the Kimmel House and poured himself into a bed.[75]

At 10:00 P.M. Lewis Powell pulled up to the Seward Home. Powell, for all his experience as a Mosby Ranger, seemed to be easily confused by the circle of streets that make up the layout

The Plot Unfolds

of Washington. The horse he was riding was the one-eyed bay owned by Booth, the horse that John Surratt said had a tendency to pull up and stop at unexpected times. Not the kind of horse one would use for a quick getaway. On a suggestion by Herold, Powell used a ruse of being a pharmacist assistant coming from Seward's physician Dr. Verdi with some medicine to give him. Perhaps the vial contained a fast-acting poison that Herold always bragged about being able to formulate, but this is speculation. After bullying his way past William Bell, the Seward family's black servant, Powell, was stopped at the top of the stairs by Frederick Seward, who refused to let him wake his sleeping father. His sister Fanny peeked out of her father's room.

"Is the Secretary asleep?" he asked.

"Almost," she replied.

Powell again impatiently demanded that Frederick let him give the Secretary his medicine. Frederick, in turn, demanded that Powell either give the medicine to him or return it to Dr. Verdi. Fanny closed the door as Powell glared hard at young Seward. He then turned his back and began to follow Bell back down the stairs. With the battle of wills seemingly over, Frederick turned to go to his room. Powell then whirled, bounded back up the stairs, pulled a navy revolver from his pocket, leveled it at the surprised Seward, and pulled the trigger.

The gun misfired. Rather than pulling back the hammer to re-cock the pistol, Powell smashed the barrel of the gun on Frederick's head breaking his skull and knocking him unconscious. The blow was so savage that it broke the steel ramrod on the pistol, jamming the cylinder and rendering it useless. Powell dropped the revolver and rushed for the bedroom pulling a bowie knife from his belt.

As Fanny opened the door to see what the ruckus in the hall was all about, Powell pushed aside the young girl and charged the sick bed of the Secretary. The old man saw the flash of the knife, and as he rolled to avoid the blow, the knife cut through the side of his face from his cheek to his jawbone but fortunately no fatal arteries were severed.

Seward's Nurse George Robinson pulled the assassin off Seward and was rewarded with two slash wounds and a powerful punch from Powell that knocked him to the floor. Before Robinson could get back into the fight, Powell delivered two more blows to Seward breaking the Secretary's jaw. But, Seward's rolling action exposed only his neck brace to his attacker, shielding him from a fatal blow. As Fanny screamed, Seward's other son Augustus arrived in time to help Robinson wrestle the muscular Powell off the Secretary and into the hallway. During this life or death, hand-to-hand struggle, Augustus lost half his scalp and Robinson was streaming blood from multiple knife wounds to his chest and shoulders.

William Bell recognized that more help was needed and hastily ran from the house and into the street screaming, "MURDER! MURDER!" Herold, upon hearing the uproar decided to abandon Powell and head for the Navy Yard Bridge.

Finally, the powerful Powell broke free from his bleeding and determined adversaries and bounded for the stairs screaming, "I'M MAD, I'M MAD!" On his way down, he ran into Emerick Hansell, a State Department messenger. As the unarmed Emerick tried to beat a hasty retreat, Powell made him his fifth victim by stabbing him in the back. He then composed himself, exited the house, mounted his horse, and coolly trotted down the street. Bell, the hysterical servant, pursued the hit man on foot pointing and screaming, "MURDERER! ….. MURDERER!" until Powell finally spurred his horse and made his escape.[76]

When Booth arrived at the back door of Ford's Theatre, he called for his drinking partner Ed Spangler. "Ned", he said, "hold this mare for about ten or fifteen minutes for me."

The Plot Unfolds

Spangler turned and called to Joseph "Johnny Peanuts" Burroughs to hold Booth's horse. Peanuts protested that his job was to guard the backstage door. Spangler told him that it was ok and that he would take the blame if anything went wrong. Thus, reassured Burroughs took the reins and agreed to hold the horse. This event was likely a pre-arranged charade to give Spangler a much-needed cover story for what was to occur that night. Booth's backstage door to escape was now open and unguarded.

Booth's horse must have anticipated her rider's intentions for she was extremely restless constantly stomping on the stones outside the door. Her agitated disposition forced Johnny Peanuts to walk her around the alley in an attempt to calm her.[77]

As Act III began, Orchestra leader William Withers was a frustrated man. He was supposed to present his new featured song *Honor to our Soldiers,* after the second act but the stage manager told him that Laura Keene was too nervous to perform it. He would now have to play the song at the conclusion of the play, while the audience was leaving the theatre. Keene's angst preserved the critical timing factor for the simultaneous attacks.

Meanwhile, Booth coolly walked up the stage to the dress circle and along the wall to the president's box. Captain Theodore McGowan was sitting in the aisle leaning by the wall toward the door of the president's box when Booth asked him to move so that he could pass. He stopped three feet away and casually surveyed the house. He took a small pack of visiting cards from his pocket, selected one and replaced the others, stood a second or two and then showed it to Charles Forbes, Lincoln's footman seated outside. With a nod and a smile, Booth entered the outer box passageway grasping his knife expecting to stab Lincoln's bodyguard.

To his surprise, the guard John F. Parker had abandoned his post leaving the passageway empty. Booth barred the door behind him and peeked into the president's box. With all the occupants seated as expected, Booth calmly reached for his gun and waited for his cue.

> "I am aware, Mr. Trenchard, "said the mother, "that you are not used to the manners of good society and that alone, will excuse the impertinence of which you are guilty!"

The two actresses exited the stage just under the president's box leaving actor Harry Hawk alone near the rear of the stage. The president leaned forward as Hawk delivered his line:

> "Don't know the manners of good society, eh!"..........

Lincoln's laughter blended with that of the rest of the theatre and masked the sound of the box door opening. Booth put the gun behind the president's ear and fired. He then dropped the one shot pistol, pulled out his knife and lunged at Major Rathbone who was sitting directly behind Lincoln. Rathbone parried the blow with his arm resulting in a gush of blood. Booth then turned toward the stage, planted one hand on the railing and dropped from the corner of the box. The decorative union flag bunting adorning the outside of the box caught the assassin's spur and came crashing down with him to the stage floor.

The laughter of the audience quickly turned to bewilderment as the matinee idol tumbled onto the stage and began to trample and stomp on the flag in an effort to disentangle his foot. Hawk, ran from the stage in fear. Some believe that at this point Spangler was supposed to cover Booth's escape by extinguishing the lights as Booth originally called for in the kidnapping plot.

If so, he was unable to do so because actress Jeannie Gourlay was discussing Withers' plight with him in front of the meter box blocking Spangler's access.[78] This miscue left the assassin exposed in front of the audience, but the actor was up to the challenge. With a theatrical flourish he raised his knife above his head, and dramatically shouted "*Sic Semper Tyrannis*!" he then rushed from the stage.

Mary Lincoln's piercing cry of anguish broke the spell and the theatre exploded with rage. As Booth dashed from the stage, Colonel Joseph B. Stewart, a lawyer (said to be the tallest man in Washington) climbed onto the stage and sprinted after him.[79] Withers and Gourlay found themselves in the backstage passageway directly in the path of the knife-wielding Booth. The hard-charging actor quickly pushed Gourlay away. Withers turned to elude him but the assassin's knife slashed through his coat as Booth knocked him aside. Booth threw open the unguarded door and raced into the alley grabbing at the reins that Johnny Peanuts held for him. The nervous horse panicked as the rider mounted her and pulled away leaving Booth with one foot in the stirrup and the other in midair. With brute strength, he quickly gained control of the animal. Stewart came barreling through the exit door just in time to see Booth gallop down the alley.

Actor John Matthews was in a saloon a block away from the theatre. With his work in the theatre done for the night, he was relaxing at the bar when the news of the assassination came. Word murmured through the crowd that some actor named Booth had shot the president.

Matthews stunned by the news, remembered the letter that Booth had given him for the *National Intelligencer* editor. He made his way back to his hotel and opened the envelope. What he read shook him to his core. He realized that his association with Booth would put him under strong suspicion. His mere possession of the assassin's note would implicate him in the crime as a fellow conspirator. Holding his death warrant in his hands, he immediately burned the letter in his fireplace, telling no one about it for years.[80]

Lewis Powell

Lewis Powell was a veteran of Mosby's Raiders when he was recruited to be a part of Booth's plot. A powerfully built man and mentally toughened by the death of two brothers in service to the South, he stayed silent about the conspiracy except to say that not even half of the conspirators had been caught. He claimed that on three occasions he refused Booth's orders to shoot Lincoln when he had the opportunity.

He later apologized to Fredrick Seward for the injuries he caused.

The Petersen House

That night Edwin Stanton had finished working on the Reconstruction Plan that Lincoln wanted ready by the next cabinet meeting. The Secretary was preparing for bed when around 10:30, an unknown man knocked on the door to tell him of the Lincoln shooting. As he got his coat, a war department attorney arrived with the news of the Seward attack. Somewhat confused over the conflicting reports, Stanton headed for Seward's home. As he arrived, he met Sergeant Koerth, who just came from Ford's Theatre and confirmed the first report of the Lincoln attack. Stanton immediately recognized that the entire government was under attack and ordered Koerth to find soldiers and guard the homes of cabinet members and the Vice-president.

Gideon Welles arrived on the scene, and the two secretaries surveyed the carnage on the third floor as the beleaguered Dr. Verdi tended to the stricken Seward and the other four victims. The rugs on the floor oozed blood with every step as they learned that the Secretary's condition was critical and Frederick's "hopeless". Quartermaster General Montgomery Meigs arrived and urged them not to attempt to go to Lincoln. Thousands of frenzied people were milling the streets as well as uniformed Confederate soldiers recently paroled from Lee's surrender. Stanton froze momentarily, but Welles urged that they go and try to control the situation. Meigs ordered some passing soldiers to join him and provide the two men a bodyguard detail.

Upon their arrival shortly after 11:00, the two men learned that soldiers moved the stricken Lincoln from the theatre to the Petersen house across the street. Establishing the house as his headquarters, Stanton began to take charge of the situation and make sense of the confusion surrounding the scene.

At this point Stanton knew that the president was dying as was Secretary Seward and his sons. He did not yet know how many terrorists were involved, where they were hiding, or who they were. Rumors were circulating that Stanton himself was a target along with the vice-president and the remaining members of the Cabinet. When word spread of the two terrorist attacks, there was panic in the streets of the capitol. Angry crowd leaders were urging the torching of Ford's Theatre with all the actors inside. Washington was on the verge of descending into anarchy.

"It was a terrible night, surcharged with tragedy, treason and murder. Everybody looked upon everybody else with distrust and suspicion, and many people both civic and military did not hesitate to say they believed that the vice-president was mixed up in the affair .... I will say right here that in none of my engagements, from the Wilderness to Petersburg, did I feel so nervous and shaky as I did on this eventful night." **George Ruehle   Company C, 27th Michigan Volunteer Infantry**

At Stanton's request, District of Columbia Chief Judge Cartter began taking testimony from witnesses. So many people had so much to say that it became obvious that recording their statements by longhand was too cumbersome.

General Augur commandant of Washington made a request for a shorthand expert and a man on the balcony next door told him that there was one in his house. Twenty-one year old Corporal James Tanner, a double amputee from the second Battle of Bull Run had just arrived home after hearing of the assassination at the Grover's Theatre. Answering the call, he made his way to the Petersen House and was shown to the back parlor headquarters.

Here he found the distraught Stanton writing dispatches to General Dix and others, and giving orders to General Thomas M. Vincent (Assistant Adjutant General) to be responsible for the people coming in and out of the Petersen House and to guard Ford's Theatre. Stanton listened and wrote as Judge Cartter questioned the witnesses. Shortly after Tanner's arrival at midnight, Stanton called cabinet members to a meeting and told Tanner not to take notes. Also in attendance was Judge Cartter, Major Richards of the Washington police, Assistant Secretary of War Charles Dana, General Augur and Major O'Beirne of the U.S. Marshals office.

At this meeting, he ordered General Augur, to secure the routes out of the city. He told Dana to telegraph General Grant at Philadelphia of Lincoln's impending death and to have him return at once to Washington. Not knowing the extent of the conspiracy, he advised Grant to watch every person approaching him and to have a detached locomotive precede his train on its way to Washington to clear the way in case the tracks were disabled. He then had Dana wire President Garret of the Baltimore and Ohio railroad to run a special train to transfer Grant to the Capital. Major O'Beirne was told to summon the vice-president at the Kirkwood House. He then wrote and dispatched a note to Chief Justice Chase to be ready to administer the oath of office to Vice-President Johnson.[81]

Later critics of Stanton would claim that he assumed dictatorial powers during this critical time. Implied in this criticism was that Stanton usurped powers that Vice-President Johnson should have been exercising. However, it should be noted that other than casting a deciding vote in the Senate, the vice-president has no constitutional authority to issue commands to anyone. Stanton issued instructions only to people who would normally report to his department in some capacity. If Stanton had wanted to use the military to take over the government, he had the perfect opportunity to do so that night. These critics were largely partisan supporters of Johnson in his later fight with the secretary of war.

As Tanner compiled the statements of the people who had been in Ford's Theatre that night, the horror of the crime held the witnesses back from positively identifying the assassin as Booth. According to Tanner, "No one said positively that the assassin was John Wilkes Booth but the sum total left no doubt as to the identity of the assassin." Harry Hawk, the only actor on the stage at the time said, 'To the best of my belief, it was Mr. John Wilkes Booth, but I will not be positive.' [82]

In the Ford Theatre audience, that night was former Wisconsin Governor Leonard Farwell. Farwell was a friend of Andrew Johnson who lived on the same floor at the Kirkwood House. Upon witnessing the shooting of the president, he immediately left the theatre and hurried to Andrew Johnson's hotel room. A few moments after calling loudly for him and rapping on the door, the vice-president rose from his bed and answered his call. Farwell told him of the assassination, locked and bolted the door, isolating him from the mob forming in the streets and insisted the hotel place a guard outside his room.[83]

Acting on his own authority, Major O'Beirne had also sent a man to guard the vice-president as soon as he heard the news of the attack. At the end of his meeting with Stanton, O'Beirne, secured a buggy and fought his way through the crowds to summon the vice-president at the Kirkwood House.

Upon arriving, he sent up his card as Provost Marshall of D.C. with a message from Stanton to come with him and be prepared to take the oath of office. After a while, Johnson sent word to O'Beirne to come to his room.

Asked by Johnson if the president was dead, O'Beirne replied that he was not when he left the Petersen House but death could come at any moment. He then told him, "It is the wish of Mr. Stanton that you come down to the Petersen House, in order to be sworn in when Mr. Lincoln dies. And I believe it is intended to hold a cabinet meeting in the parlor of the house."[84]

Johnson insisted upon walking the three-and-a-half blocks to the Petersen House, despite O'Beirne's warnings about the danger on the streets. Neatly attired with a high silk hat he refused to take the buggy that the Major had secured. Undoubtedly, he believed that a dignified entrance in this moment of crisis would ease the sting of the inaugural fiasco.

The Plot Unfolds

O'Beirne, a Medal of Honor winner argued strenuously against Johnson's decision. "Mr. Vice-President, I don't usually get stampeded when there is any trouble around, but I like to take every reasonable precaution for safety, especially when I have a responsibility". Johnson stubborn and unruffled stood his ground and O'Beirne finally relented.

Against his better judgment, O'Beirne took Johnson by his left arm and led the way edging through the mob on the street, worrying that someone in the large crowd would recognize the vice-president and attack him from the rear. As he got nearer the house, the mob was so dense that it was difficult for people to make way for them despite O'Beirne's commands to do so. Slowly the huddled mass parted a path and the Provost Marshall and the vice-president walked into the front parlor together.

The time of Johnson's arrival in the Petersen House is crucial since it seems to have served as a catalyst for succeeding events. Senator Charles Sumner was at Lincoln's bedside the entire night and said Johnson arrived 'about two o'clock in the morning'. According to the Senator, Johnson remained only two minutes in the Lincoln's room, because Mary wanted to visit her husband again.[85]

Best estimates put his stay in the Petersen house somewhere between 20 to 30 minutes. Since Johnson's visit to Lincoln's deathbed was so brief, we have to assume he spent the majority of his time conferring with Stanton. Johnson had been a virtual prisoner in his room after the attack and was anxious to learn as much as possible. He continually queried his guards over Lincoln and Seward's condition. He even asked Farwell to go in person to see the president and not be satisfied with second or third hand information.

After a briefing on the details of the attack and learning the identification of the assassin, Johnson finally made his way to Lincoln's room.

Senator Sumner knew that Mrs. Lincoln had a strong dislike for Andrew Johnson and thought it best that she not see him hovering over her husband. With his briefing with Stanton finished, Johnson excused himself and disappeared into the night. What happened next became a mystery and controversy.[86]

Putting together a timeline of events that occurred in the Petersen House from the statements of the people who were there is a difficult task. The intensity at which they worked skewed their time estimates. James Tanner admitted to this phenomenon two days later when he wrote:

> I was writing shorthand for about an hour and a half, when I commenced transcribing it. I thought I had been writing about two hours when I looked at the clock and it marked half past four A. M.. I commenced writing about 12 M. I could not believe that it was so late, but my watch corroborated it. The surrounding circumstances had so engrossed my attention that I had not noticed the flight of time.[87]

The only people that we know who were actually looking at their watches and recording the time of events were Stanton as he dispatched orders and Dr. Ezra Abbott who was recording Lincoln's pulse readings.

Upon hearing of the attack, Robert Lincoln called Mary Lincoln's friend Elizabeth Dixon to help comfort his distraught mother. Arriving at 11:00 P.M, she wrote that Mrs. Lincoln left her husband's side only *twice* the entire evening.[88] From Dr. Abbott's notes, we know that the first time she left was 2:10 a.m. returning to his side at 3:00 a.m.

> **1.30** o'clock. Pulse 95; appearing easier.
> **1.45** o'clock. Pulse 86; very quiet; respiration irregular; Mrs. Lincoln present
> **2.10** o'clock. Mrs. Lincoln, with Robert Lincoln, retired to an adjoining room.
> **2.30** o'clock. Pulse 54; President very quiet; respiration 28.
> **2.52** o'clock. Pulse 48; respiration 30.
> **3.00** o'clock. Visited again by Mrs. Lincoln.[89]

The second and last time was twenty minutes before his death confirmed by the accounts of Dr. Leale and Mrs. Dixon.

> ...She sprang up suddenly with a piercing cry, and fell fainting to the floor. Secretary Stanton, hearing her cry, came in from the adjoining room and with raised arms called out loudly, "Take that woman out and don't let her in again." Mrs. Lincoln was helped up kindly and assisted in a fainting condition from the room. Secretary Stanton's order was obeyed and Mrs. Lincoln did not see her husband again before he died.[90] – **Dr. Charles Leale**

> ...They then asked her to go into the adjoining room and in twenty minutes came in and said, "It's all over! The President is no more.[91] – **Elizabeth Dixon**.

If the Dixon and Sumner accounts are true, then Johnson's briefing with Stanton occurred sometime between 2:10 and 2:52 am when Mary Lincoln was absent from the room. Since Johnson left just before she reclaimed her position at Lincoln's bedside, we have to assume the vice-president left the building shortly before 3:00 am.

At 7:22 Lincoln died. Upon Lincoln's death, Stanton remarked, "Now he belongs to the ages." Throughout the following long days of securing the nation, Stanton wept bitterly at the mention of Lincoln's name. He impounded the chair Lincoln[92] sat in when he was shot and kept it in his office for over a year. Many of his associates who were accustomed to the harsh bureaucrat were shocked at the uncontrollability of his grief. He later eulogized Lincoln with the words, "There lies the most perfect ruler of men the world has ever seen."

Remarkably, President Andrew Johnson gave Lincoln no eulogy at all. Nor did he offer any condolences to his widow or his family. When Robert Lincoln offered to sell Johnson the former president's carriage, horses and other trappings of the office, he refused to consider it. He also refused to set foot on the boat Lincoln used to sail on the Potomac. Furthermore, his actions at the Petersen House seemed callously irresponsible. Stanton's purpose for calling him, according to O'Beirne, was to keep the government functioning by not leaving the position of president vacant. Johnson's abrupt departure left the impression that Lincoln was not dying fast enough for him.

Senator William Stewart, one of the last people to see Lincoln at the White House before leaving for the theatre, met Chief Justice Chase outside the Petersen House, just after Lincoln's death. Together they then left for the Kirkwood House along with the head of the Republican caucus Senator Solomon Foote of Vermont. The following is an excerpt from Stewart's book called *Reminiscences* published in 1908:

> After some delay, Johnson opened the door and we entered. The vice-president was in his bare feet and only partially dressed, as though he had hurriedly drawn on a pair of trousers and a shirt. He was occupying two little rooms about ten feet square and we entered one of them, a sitting room, while he finished his toilet in the other. In a few minutes Johnson came in, putting on a rumpled coat, and presenting the appearance of a drunken man. He was dirty, shabby, and his hair was matted, as though with mud from the gutter, while he blinked at us through squinting eyes, and lurched around unsteadily. He had been on a "bender" for a month. As he came in the room we were all staring. Johnson felt for a chair and sat down. Chief Justice Chase said very solemnly:
>
> "The president has been assassinated. He died this morning. I have come to administer the oath of office to you." Johnson seemed dazed at first. Then he jumped up, thrust his right arm up as far as he could reach and said in a gruff, hoarse voice: "I'm ready". The Chief Justice administrated the oath. President Johnson – went back to his bedroom and retired.
>
> There were only three persons present besides Johnson when he was sworn in – Chief Justice Chase, Senator Foote and myself. All statements to the contrary are completely false…So far as I am aware nobody knows where he spent the night although his appearance clearly indicates what he was doing… Stanton and I went back to the Kirkwood House and with the coachman dressed him and put him in the carriage. We took him to the White House and Stanton sent for a tailor, a barber and a doctor… the president was bathed and shaved, his hair was cut and a new set of clothes fitted to him.[93]

This first-hand account by a United States Senator has long been ignored by the school of revisionist Johnson biographers who denied that Johnson had a drinking problem or derided as a lie on the grounds that Stewart was a political opponent of

Johnson. Others point to the fact that Johnson never occupied the White House until Mrs. Lincoln moved out weeks later, conveniently ignoring the possibility that he was ever a brief visitor. Most biographers use the Chase account;

> "I went to see the vice-president and found him in his hotel, calm apparently but very grave. Soon after Secretary McCulloch and Attorney General Speed came in – they said they were on their way to my house to ask my attendance for administering the oath of office as President to the Vice-President – Some consultation followed as to time and place and it was agreed that it should be in the parlor where we then were and at 10 o'clock." [94]

Although the *New York Herald* records the swearing in to have occurred at eleven o'clock, careful readings of both accounts do not necessarily cancel out each other. It would make sense that Chase would give the oath as soon as possible and set the formal swearing in later, when Johnson was presentable. Secretary McCulloch and Attorney General Speed could have arrived after the first informal ceremony. We know that Stewart was in Johnson's room as he took the formal oath of office[95]. Why would he make up such a story out of whole cloth? It is true that Stewart and Johnson would later become rivals, but most politicians of the time were opponents of Johnson.

It is difficult to assess what is true when dealing with politicians since what they tell you is usually calculated to give themselves a political advantage. However, the real problem with Stewart's story is that Chase and Foote were both dead at the time of publication and could not verify the narrative. Stewart's account came out almost thirty-five years after Johnson's death, during a time when the historical legacy of Andrew Johnson was undergoing a successful rewrite, courtesy of a former politician turned author, David Miller DeWitt. It seems odd that Stewart would make up a false story just before his own death. A deathbed type of statement such as this is usually respected not reviled. But, Tennessee historian George F. Milton a major defender of Johnson, derided it as 'an outrageous lie' and it's been discredited by Johnson's biographers ever since.

It is far more likely that Stewart kept this episode secret as a 'political favor' to Johnson. In 1897, he gave a similar account in a *New York Times* interview[96]. Although he described Johnson's slovenly appearance in much the same manner, he avoided mentioning that Johnson had been drinking and there was no repudiation made. Eleven years later, he told the whole story.

Stewart had a proud list of accomplishments in his life and a random story about Andrew Johnson's drunkenness in his memoirs certainly would not have increased book sales in 1908. It is treated as a minor incident in his book and it seems unlikely that at that late a date Stewart had a political axe to grind.

Johnson knew his inebriated performance and public humiliation at his Vice presidential inauguration would be hard to overcome if his political career was to continue. He was a strong-willed individual, however, who, if he were not an alcoholic, should have been smart enough to avoid the temptation. Yet something happened to him in the Petersen house that seems to have triggered a drinking binge.

The Plot Unfolds

Senator William M. Stewart

William Stewart was lured to Nevada by the silver discoveries of the Comstock Lode and became wealthy litigating the claims of miners. It was estimated that Stewart received some $500,000 for his efforts. Stewart became a strong proponent of Nevada statehood and was elected to the Senate in 1865 serving for twenty –eight years.

Stewart supported the re-entry of southern states on moderate principles, but due to Andrew Johnson's actions he soon advocated more radical policies. He was one of the principal authors of the Fifteenth Amendment.

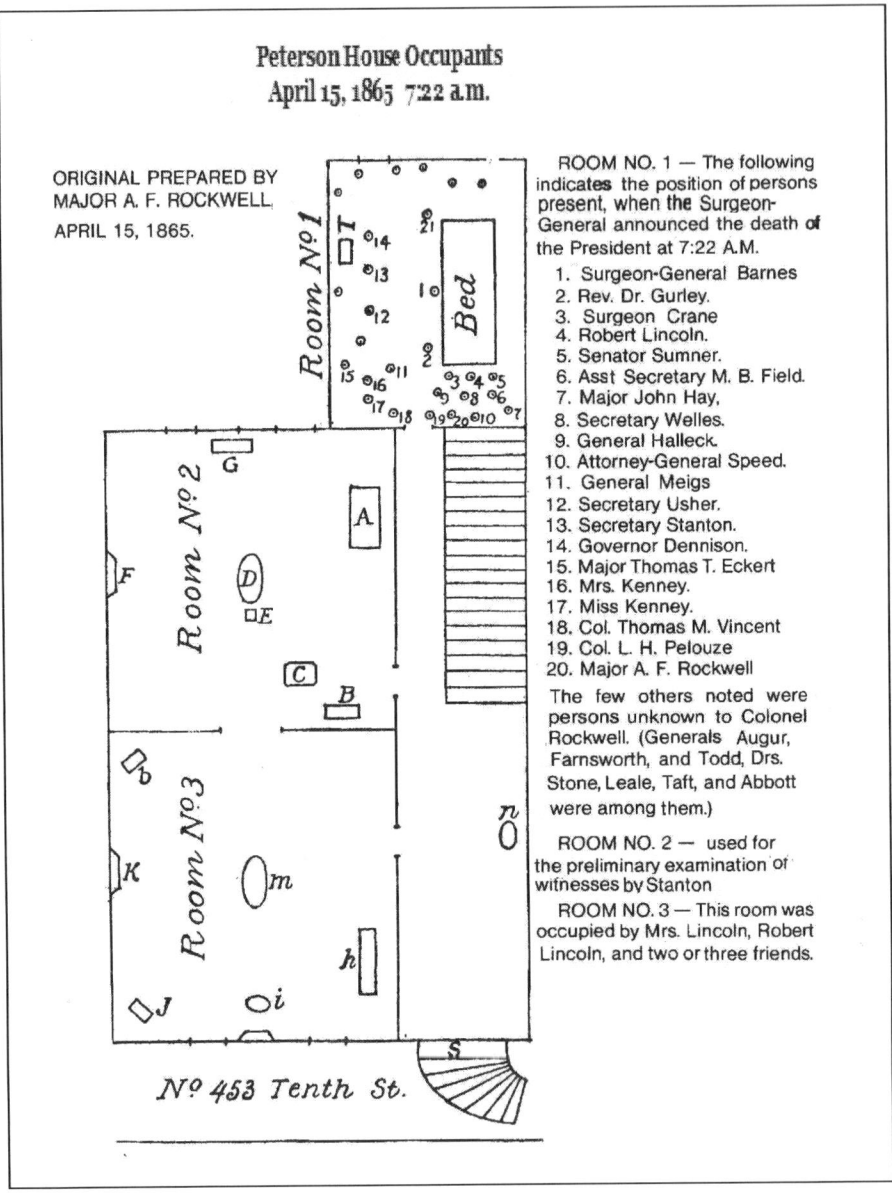

As part of the official investigation a sketch was ordered to document the occupants of the Peterson House present at Lincoln's death.

Chapter 5

The Great Manhunt

Eight Roads out of Washington

Major General Christopher C. Augur was a veteran of two wars. He served with Grant in Mexico and was wounded at Cedar Mountain in July 1862. He recovered to serve in the Louisiana campaign where he was brevetted as a Brigadier General. In March 1865, he received the brevet of Major General largely for his work in repulsing Jubal Early's attempt to take Washington the previous year. He had been the commandant of Department of Washington since October 1863 and served the position admirably. "Augur and myself have always worked together as one man," wrote General Sheridan. In short, he was a veteran of the war who knew the city and how to react in a crisis.

On the night of the assassination, Augur reviewed all avenues of escape from Washington and issued his orders. Although the civil telegraphs were down for two hours, the military telegraph was running all night, and Augur and Stanton put it to good use. The police in the railroad terminals would inspect each person on every car. Secretary Welles sent out messages to his naval commanders already stationed along the Potomac and Chesapeake to intercept any travel by water. Since the spring thaws turned most of the back roads into mud, the most likely route of escape would be the eight main turnpikes out of town, and Augur moved to have them rapidly covered.

Just the year before, Confederate General Jubal Early had moved his army to the gates of Washington before being driven back. Much of the army that repulsed him was still garrisoned in a ring around the city. Augur moved quickly to block the routes and tighten the noose.

- Route #1 was the eastern road over the Benning's Bridge. This pike led to Upper Marlboro, Maryland. Army camps were already present on the road and quickly notified by Augur to block the route.
- Route #2 was the northern Montgomery County Pike, which turned eastward and intersected with the northeastern Bladensburg Pike leading to either Baltimore or Annapolis Maryland. Early alarms to Baltimore and Annapolis blocked these roads.
- Route #3 was the northern Montgomery County Turnpike leading to central Maryland. Again, the early dispatches to Baltimore blocked these roads.
- Route #4 was the northwestern Rockville road through Georgetown leading to Frederick Maryland. Augur notified the cavalry at Darnestown to block this road.
- Route #5 was the western route through Arlington, leading to Falls Church Virginia. Augur's warnings to the army at Fairfax blocked this route.
- Route #6 was the southern route using the Long Bridge out of Alexandria Virginia. The route led to Occoquan, Fredericksburg and Richmond. Augur had the road blocked at Alexandria and Occoquan.
- Routes #7 and #8 had one thing in common. In order to get to them one had to cross the Navy Yard Bridge. Once across one could go from Piscataway to Port Tobacco or to Surrattsville and Bryantown.

For some reason Augur did not issue orders to the cavalry stationed just south of Port Tobacco. Either this was an error of omission on his part or he felt that the order not to let anyone cross after 9:00 p.m. was being rigidly enforced.

The latter seems to be the better reason considering that the bridge was the strategic choke point for the two roads south. The bridge led to the most pro-Confederate area in the Union, and Southern agents operated freely in the area.

It was not until early in the morning of the 15th that a cavalry detail headed by Lieutenant David Dana (brother of Assistant Secretary of War, Charles Dana) crossed the bridge to cut the route at Piscataway by 7:00 a.m. By that time, Booth and Herold were beyond the roadblock and waking to breakfast in the home of Samuel Mudd. [97]

Why the route was so late in being blocked is another mystery that has no explanation in documented form. Lincoln scholar Osborn Oldroyd offered one possible reason. Davy Herold had rented a horse at Naylor's livery stable from foreman John Fletcher to perform his part of the Seward operation with Lewis Powell. His escape route led him past Naylor's stable. When Fletcher called to him that he was out past the time the horse was due back, Herold galloped past and raced to the Navy Yard Bridge. Fletcher mounted up and gave chase. When Fletcher arrived at the bridge, he asked the sentry:

"Did a man on a roan horse cross a few minutes ago? He had an English saddle and metal stirrups."

The guard nodded and said, "Yes, he had gone across."[98]

When he informed the sentry that that man had stolen a horse and asked if he could give pursuit, the guard granted permission but warned him he could not return until morning. The disgusted Fletcher then decided to let the police handle the matter rather than spend the night searching in the dark. He returned to town and went to police headquarters to register his complaint.

A Threat to the Republic

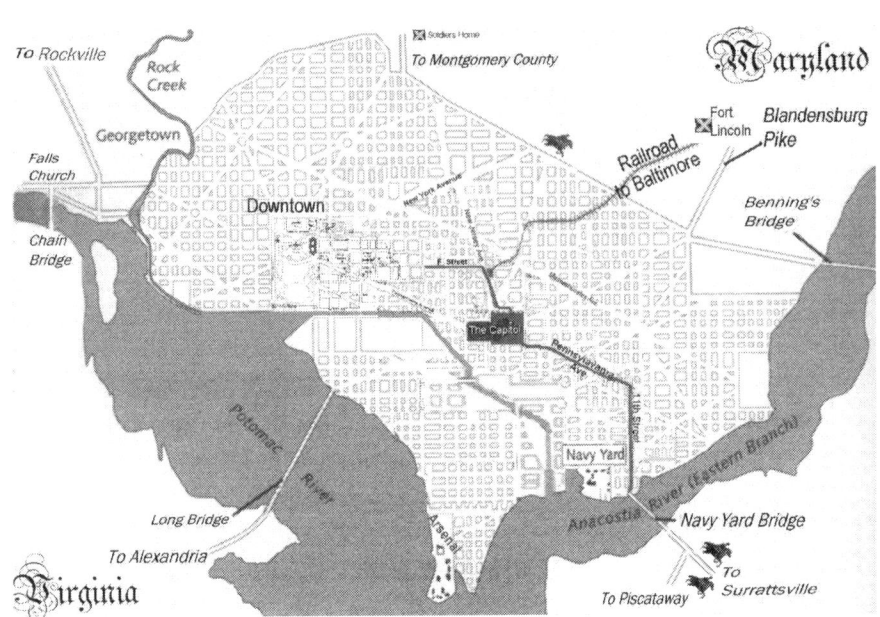

Primary Routes out of Washington – April 1865

Major Richards, superintendent of Washington police, supposedly deduced from Fletcher's story that Booth had taken flight across the Navy Yard Bridge. He later said that he offered to pursue the assassin if the government would provide him the horses; but due to the red tape involved, Auger refused Richard's request. Richards himself thought the military was jealous of his police.[99] This "government red tape" excuse combined with the sentry's faulty discretionary judgment have been the bedrock belief ever since of how Booth escaped the dragnet.

It is doubtful, however, that this scenario played out as presented. It sounds more like grandstanding after the fact since Richards judgment had come into question following the assassination. He had no explanation as to why he assigned a man like John F. Parker, who had one of the worst records on the Washington Force, to guard Lincoln. Among the blights on his record included; insubordination, unbecoming conduct, foul language, sleeping on the job, drunk on duty, and arresting streetwalkers who refused him free access to their favors. Nor did he present any reason why Parker had deserted his post on the night of the assassination. Parker was charged with neglect of duty on May 1 and the complaint was dismissed on June 2nd. The facts concerning the investigation of his disappearance that night were mysteriously *lost*. One has to take his charge that Augur would be jealous of his record with a huge grain of salt.

Fletcher's name was on the police ledger as one of the witnesses interviewed that night. After a traumatic event police are usually flooded with conflicting eyewitness accounts, Fletcher was one of *seventeen* on the blotter before midnight. If Richards had believed Fletcher's story, what would make him immediately link Davy Herold with the assassin? Rather than asking the government for a string of horses to give pursuit, why didn't he send someone to the bridge to confirm the story? Lastly, if he sincerely needed horses the anxious Fletcher could have easily provided them since he had a stable full. Fletcher had a legitimate complaint about the stolen horse, but no one was going to waste resources chasing after a thief when they were looking for the president's assassin.

Furthermore, Lafayette Baker, head of the Secret Service, in his book *History of the Secret Service* states that the Fletcher clue was wasted: "Fletcher learned that two suspicious characters had just crossed the Navy Yard Bridge on horseback. He returned to General Augur's headquarters about one o'clock on Saturday morning, and reported the fact. Here begins the first series of blunders in this attempted search for the assassins. Fletcher's statement was entirely disregarded. No steps were taken by those in possession of this information to follow up on the clue thus given until sixteen hours afterward. This delay enabled the assassins to get entirely beyond the reach of those sent in pursuit."

In Jim Bishop's *The Day Lincoln Was Shot*, the author twisted the facts by speeding up the timetable to back up Oldroyd's theory. In Bishop's scenario, Augur learned from Fletcher that Davy Herold and Atzerodt were friends and that he suspected Atzerodt as the first rider across the bridge.

Meanwhile, Major O'Beirne sent detective John Lee to the Kirkwood House. While there, the clerk told him of a suspicious looking fellow in room 126 named George Atzerodt. Finding the room locked, Lee forced open the door and began inspecting the room. Besides finding a revolver and knife, he came upon the bankbook of John Wilkes Booth in a coat hanging by the door. Lee's discovery of the Atzerodt - Booth link connected the dots for Augur to assume that Booth had crossed the Navy Bridge ahead of Herold.

> The Secretary of War now had an unmistakable cross reference between John Wilkes Booth and George Atzerodt. And, from Fletcher through General Augur, he had a cross-reference between Atzerodt and David Herold...Two hours and thirty five minutes after the attacks, Mister Stanton knew who was wanted.[100]

To make this scenario work Bishop made a big assumption. During his sworn testimony at the Conspirators Trial, Lee testified that his actions occurred on the night of April 15th, the night *after* Booth shot Lincoln. With an asterisk, Bishop tells his readers that Lee probably meant *'after midnight of the fourteenth'*.

Unfortunately, Lee meant exactly what he said. At the trial Robert R. Jones, a clerk at the Kirkwood confirmed Lee's testimony under oath.

> I went to the room occupied by Mr. Atzerodt after it had been opened on the night of the 15th of April, and I saw all the article that were found there...The bed had not been occupied on the night of the 14th, nor had the chambermaid been able to get into the room the next day.[101]

Bishop's claim that Stanton knew all in a mere 'two hours and thirty five minutes after the attacks' fit well within the confines of his book, which is an hour by hour description of Lincoln's last day. However, in the 1860's without telephones, radios or computers cross-referencing detective work was slow.
With Jones confirming that, Lee made his discoveries at the Kirkwood House almost 24 hours after the shooting, the Oldroyd theory that Bishop supported falls apart and Baker's assertion that police disregarded Fletcher's information seems validated. The question then remains, how did Augur know that Booth used the Navy Yard Bridge as his escape route that night?[102]

Various authors have vilified Stanton for keeping Booth's name secret after witnesses identified him as the 'probable' assassin. Although Tanner was convinced of Booth's guilt after fifteen minutes, Stanton was trying to get his arms around the entire conspiracy. Logistically, it was unlikely for Booth to be Seward's attacker so he was convinced this was a widespread plot. How many were involved, he had no idea. There were uniformed Confederate soldiers in the streets and the city was teeming with Southern sympathizers. Was this a final attempt to destroy the government? Until he knew the extent of the threat, he could not commit to a pursuit.[103]

Stanton's first objective was to secure the functionality of the executive branch by protecting the cabinet members. He made certain that the routes in and out of the city were 'locked down' to contain the assassins in a small geographical area. With these actions, he could afford the time to assess the situation.

Shortly before 3:00 a.m., Stanton came into possession of information leading him to believe that that he did not have the assassins isolated in the city. He began writing messages to New York and Baltimore identifying Booth as the assassin for the first time and instructing General Morris to lock down Baltimore.

War Department
Washington, April 15—3 A.M.

Major-General Dix, New York—

The president still breathes, but is quite insensible, as he has been ever since he was shot. He evidently did not see the person who shot him, but was looking on the stage as he was approached from behind.

Mr. Seward has rallied, and it is hoped he may live. Frederick Seward's condition is very critical. The attendant who was present was shot through the lungs, and is not expected to live.

The wounds of Major Seward are not serious. Investigation strongly indicates J. Wilkes Booth as the assassin of the president. Whether it was the same or a different person that attempted to murder Mr. Seward remains in doubt.

The Chief Justice is engaged in taking evidence. Every exertion has been made to prevent the escape of the murderer. His horse has been found on the road near Washington.

EDWIN M. STANTION, Secretary of War

War Department
Washington, April 15—3 A.M.

Brigadier-General Morris, Baltimore—

Make immediate arrangements for guarding thoroughly every avenue into Baltimore, and if possible arrest J.Wilkes Booth, the murderer of President Lincoln. You will acknowledge the receipt of this telegram, giving time, &cc.

EDWIN M. STANTION, Secretary of War

Despite these warnings to his Lieutenants, Stanton did not send a cavalry in pursuit across the Bennings Bridge towards Baltimore. Instead, he chose to send it southward across the Navy Yard Bridge implying that he was acting upon information that Booth was heading south not east. The sentry at the bridge went off duty at midnight and did not learn of events until the next morning, so there was no communication between the two of them until after Augur sent the cavalry. Who then could have tipped off Stanton about the route of the assassins?

In Atzerodt's statement to Col. H. H. Wells, Booth wanted Atzerodt to obtain a travel pass from Andrew Johnson. He also states that Booth and Herold had already seen Johnson. If true, it suggests that the vice-president was the most probable source of the tip, telling Stanton of the passes he issued to Booth and his friend shortly after learning of the assassin's identity at the Petersen House. Informed that the assassin carried a travel pass would have invalidated Stanton's previously held assumption that sentries would keep the Navy Bridge closed to traffic. The evidence suggests that whatever information Stanton received was trustworthy enough for him to order Augur to "search and patrol the roads leading from Washington, particularly in the direction of the Occoquan (Virginia)"[104].

Augur ordered a detachment of the 13th New York Cavalry to saddle-up for Piscataway sometime after 3 a.m. The commander of this group reported his arrival in Piscataway at 7 a.m. so the estimated time of his departure from Washington was approximately 4 a.m.

The timing of these orders came immediately after Johnson left the Petersen House. If this 'tip' came from Johnson, it would serve to explain his odd decision to retreat to the isolation of his hotel room rather than help manage the situation with Stanton. It would also help to explain why he disappeared from written documentation after visiting the president at that time until Stewart's account that began at approximately 7:30 a.m.

This was the most important night and event in Johnson's life. Where did he go? What did he do? The silence on his whereabouts is deafening. Illustrators of the day placed Johnson in the death room with Lincoln dying in his arms, which we know was not true, but it gave the correct political spin that the country needed to see. By having no written account on the matter, Johnson's biographers leave us with the impression that he simply returned alone to his room at the Kirkwood and went back to sleep waiting for Lincoln to die. If true, Johnson was the only man in Washington who slept that night. With every self-serving politician in D.C. trying to get into the Petersen House and anarchy running rampant in the streets, the accounts of the vice-president's actions have been completely expunged. He simply disappears from history.

We know that somehow he made it back to his room at the Kirkwood House. Uncertain that by the next morning he would be President of the United States or under arrest for treason, it seems very likely that he used the remainder of the night to drink himself into a stupor.

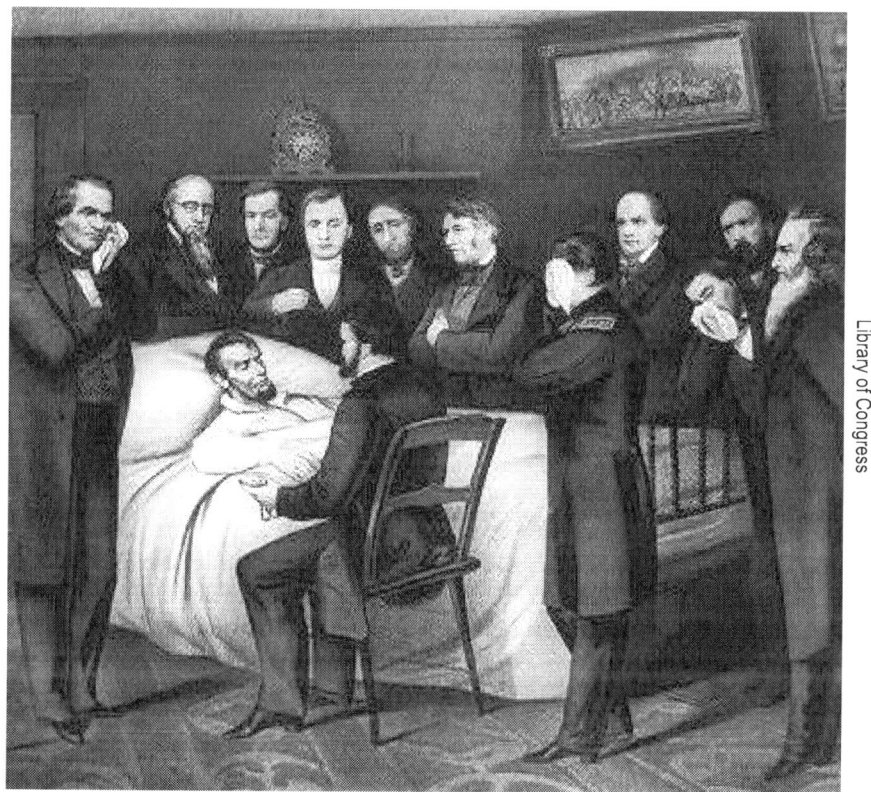

This Currier & Ives lithograph is similar to others in showing the Vice-President as being at Lincoln's side when he died. In fact, he was alone drinking in his hotel room.

The Flight of Booth and Herold

The full moon of Easter was playing hide and seek among the clouds as John Wilkes Booth approached the Navy Yard Bridge. Sergeant Silas Cobb and his two fellow sentries heard the coming hoof beats as he approached, and they readied to challenge the rider. As the horse stopped, one of the sentries grabbed the reins and held the horse as Cobb began his interrogation.

"Who are you, sir?"
"My name is Booth."
"Where are you from?"
"The city"
"Where are you going?"
"I'm going home"
"And where would that be?"
"Charles."
"What town?"
"No town."
"You must live in some town"
"I live close to Beantown, but I don't live in the town."[105]

After three or four more minutes of conversation and inspection, Cobb nodded to his fellow sentries who swung the barrier open allowing Booth to pass.

Once he was over the bridge, the first stop in Booth's escape plan was to be Mary Surratt's tavern at Surrattsville. There he would meet up with the rest of the group, load up with rifles, and continue their journey. However, somewhere between the Navy Bridge and the tavern, Booth had an accident. The bay that he was riding hard on the potholed road missed a step in the night and threw him from the saddle, breaking his left leg. That accident gave Herold enough time to catch up with him and help him back on the horse.

The Great Manhunt 161

The myth that he broke his leg in his leap from the stage got its start by Booth himself, in the first melodramatic entry in his notebook. Angry at being vilified for his action, Booth decided to write his own account, twisting events to his own advantage. This was not Booth's first attempt to portray himself as a living legend. It was similar to his twisting the witnessing of John Brown's execution to actually being involved in his capture. It made for good press, as the dramatist would have known, but the evidence brought forth in the trial and eyewitness accounts soundly contradicts this fairy tale.[106]

> J.W. Booth - Diary
> ....I walked with a firm step through a thousand of his friends, was stopped, but pushed on. A colonel was at his side. I shouted Sic semper before I fired. In jumping broke my leg. I passed all his pickets, rode sixty miles that night with the bone of my leg tearing the flesh at every jump ......

The eyewitness accounts recorded in 1865 by members of the audience, give no hint that Booth fractured his leg while he was in Ford's Theatre. They described him as running across the stage with no mention of a limp, much less a broken leg. All witnesses from the orchestra seats, described the assassin's movement as "rushed" or indicate that he "ran" across the stage.[107] The testimony of the young man who held Booth's horse further dispels the myth:

> **Joseph "Peanuts" Borroughs**
> Q. What did he say when he came out?
> A. He told me to give me his horse.
> Q. Did he do anything besides that?
> A. He knocked me down.
> Q. With his hand or not?
> A. He struck me with the butt of a knife.
> Q. Did he do that as he mounted his horse?
> A. Yes, sir, he had one foot in the stirrup.
> Q. Did he also strike or kick you?
> A. He kicked me.
> Q. As he got on the horse?
> A. Yes, sir.[108]

Unquestionably, Booth was filled with alcohol and adrenaline as he ran off stage and onto his horse. However, putting a broken left leg into a stirrup and expecting it to support one's full weight while getting into a saddle AND kicking with the right at the same time is a physical impossibility. Booth's mounting of his horse, as witnessed by Johnny Peanuts, was the last time he would ever get on a horse again without assistance

Lastly, Booth rode only thirty miles that night, not sixty as claimed. The broken leg he suffered was a simple fracture, not compound, so no bone could have been tearing at his leg with every jump. The entire passage was a complete falsification.*

Dr. Samuel Mudd who set the leg confirmed this fact. In his opinion, he did "not regard it as a particularly painful or dangerous wound". It took no more than 45 minutes from examination to the setting of the leg. Both Herold and Mudd also testified that Booth told them he had broken his leg when his horse fell on him. Thomas Davis, a farmhand at Dr. Mudd's, took care of Booth's horse when he was at Mudd's farm. He told detectives that the horse had a badly swollen left front shoulder and a fresh cut on his leg. Injuries that would have been obvious to Johnny Peanuts and the sentry at the Navy Yard Bridge if the fall had occurred before crossing the bridge. It was not until the Butler commission discovered Booth's suppressed diary two years later that the myth of "the broken leg from the leap to the stage" was born.[109]

Davy Herold woke tavern keeper John Lloyd from his liquor-induced sleep around midnight. "For God's sake, make haste and get those things," Herold demanded.

---

* Despite the overwhelming evidence that Booth did not break his leg on his leap to the stage, the myth has become so strong that it will continue to be repeated whenever American history is taught. It has become an accepted truth similar to the 'shots from the grassy knoll' contention regarding the Kennedy assassination almost 100 years later.

Lloyd staggered downstairs. The "things" Herold was talking about were the two Spencer carbines, ammunition, and field glasses that his landlady, Mary Surratt, had told him to get ready earlier in the day. Herold brought them to the tavern a month earlier after the aborted kidnapping attempt where John Surratt stored them. Herold went into the bar and grabbed a bottle of whiskey for Booth. Booth was in pain and did not bother to dismount. His broken leg was swelling in his boot forcing him to abandon any plans to dismount, re-saddle fresh horses and ride hard that night. He sat and scanned the roads as Herold gave him the bottle.

When Lloyd came out with the equipment, Herold took one rifle, but Booth turned down the other one. He was in too much pain to carry it. Booth then told Lloyd some news he was dying to share: "I'm pretty certain that we have assassinated the president and Secretary Seward."

Lloyd stood dumbfounded wondering if he was sure of what he had heard. Booth and Herold took the road south to the village of T.B.

By the time Lieutenant Dana of the 13th Cavalry arrived in Piscataway at 7:00 a.m., he realized that Booth had probably taken the Surrattsville road rather than the Piscataway road. He then decided that Bryantown would be the assassins' next destination and arrived there by noon on April 15.

An Alternate Route?

T.B. was a small crossroads community with a tavern. It got its name from a stone that marked the property of Thomas Brooke. Booth's injury caused a major revision to his escape plan and timetable. The kidnapping plan called for the abductors to get fresh horses at T.B. and ride non-stop to Port Tobacco, then cross the Potomac River into Virginia. Port Tobacco was 36 miles or an approximate six-hour ride from Surrattsville.

However, now that the plot was changed from kidnapping to murder there was a faster route to freedom that was available. Less than 40 miles to the north was the railroad station in Baltimore, Maryland. If Booth could have gotten fresh horses at Surrattsville and ridden hard that night, he would have had time to make the 9:00 train to New York City arriving at 5:37 in the afternoon. From there he could have caught the 12:15 "Midnight Special" which would have completed its run in Montreal, Canada.[110]

The train route was one with which Booth was familiar having recently made the trip to New York with Powell on March 25. The fact that Davy Herold spent the night before the assassination with his distant cousin Joseph Huntt at T.B. suggests Booth may have been setting up his new escape plan.

Furthermore, we know from Louis Weichmann that during a conversation with Mary Surratt on the day of the assassination she told him "Booth is done acting and is going to New York very soon, never to return".[111] Did Booth in a moment of candor tell her of his ultimate destination?

The Great Manhunt

According to Huntt family folklore, Joseph Huntt's wife Laura was feeding her newborn child when she heard the village dogs barking and horses approaching the house. The horsemen did not stop but rode past their house and out of the village.[112] Booth's broken leg needed treatment and Dr. Samuel Mudd, a trusted Confederate would have to be his next stop.

When B.F. Stringfellow, the Confederate master spy, managed to escape from his captors on April 3, he realized that with Richmond in Union hands there would be no safe haven for him in Virginia or anywhere in the United States. Instead, he used the Confederate secret courier lines and safe houses to work his way north and found refuge in Canada. With Jefferson Davis already fleeing for his life, it's probable that Booth also recognized that going south was not to be the preferred route of escape.

Although Booth scouted the Southern Maryland area six months before the assassination, there is no evidence of any more recent advanced planning by him for the route he took southward down the Maryland peninsula. John Surratt, in his one public discussion of his role in the kidnapping conspiracy in 1870, said this in regards to using the Navy Bridge during their March meeting at Gautiers:

> We had called a meeting in Washington for the purpose of discussing matters in general, as we had understood that the government had received information that there was a plot of some kind on hand. They had even commenced to build a stockade and gates on the Navy yard bridge; gates opening towards the south as though they expected danger from within, and not from without. At this meeting I explained the construction of the gates, etc., and stated I was confident the government had wind of our movement, and the best thing we could do would be to throw up the whole project."[113]

It would be difficult to believe that Booth would be racing for a bridge with a stockade ready for him unless he was certain that he could cross it. There is no evidence that Booth ever tried to cross the Navy Yard Bridge at night, so why with his life on the line, would he believe he could talk his way past a sentry?

Booth was a bold man and a careful schemer. Few people would have been daring enough to put a gun to the president's head in a crowded theatre and still believe he could escape, except a man who was prepared to the nth degree with the location, timing, and escape route.

It is doubtful that he would have thought that charm and bluff would have gotten him by the sentry on the bridge. It also seems illogical that when crossing the Navy Yard Bridge that Booth would tell the guard that his destination was Beantown (in southern Maryland) unless that was where he intended to lead his pursuers. This is further evidence that his broken leg occurred after he crossed the bridge forcing him to alter his intended route.

There is little doubt that Booth planned to lure his pursuers southward. Planting the map of Virginia in Atzerodt's room left enough clues to link the boatman to the conspiracy and the Port Tobacco route to Virginia. Booth was smart enough to realize that other than knowing the roads and rivers in Southern Maryland, the talkative Atzerodt was more of a liability than an asset. He hoped his sacrificial lamb would point the posse in the wrong direction.

The Great Manhunt

Bennings Bridge may well have been the destination of Lewis Powell. If he had taken a right turn onto H Street at the top of Lafayette Park, it would have taken him to the Benning Road and then to the bridge. On the other side of the bridge, a fork in the road offered two options: turn right and follow Booth's escape route; turn left and head for Baltimore. Mary Surratt's attorney, John Clampitt, quoted Powell as saying he intended to escape to Baltimore, likely with the intention of reuniting with Booth. [114]

After releasing his horse, Powell spent three days hiding in a cedar tree while skirmishers passed below him.[115] Cold and hungry Powell fashioned a skullcap by cutting off a sleeve of his undershirt and disguised himself as a normal laborer. To complete the costume he took a pickaxe from a gravedigger's shed in a nearby cemetery. With no friends close by and believing, Mrs. Surratt was completely ignorant of the plot; he decided to head for the only safe house he knew of in the area. His timing could not have been worse. He arrived at the boarding house just as police were arresting Mary Surratt.

Thinking quickly, Powell told the police that he was there to dig a gutter for Mrs. Surratt. However, the frightened woman vehemently denied that she had ever seen him before. The police decided to take both into custody. William Bell identified him at the police station.

Sleeping under the stars was definitely not part of the John Wilkes Booth lifestyle. He took no supplies for living outdoors making him completely dependent upon the kindness of strangers. Again, this fact illustrates the probable change in escape plans caused by his broken leg. He knew that his only chance of true escape was to get out of the country as quickly as possible. His broken leg thwarted any plans he may have had of using the train system north to Canada.

Booth arrived at the door of Dr. Samuel Mudd at 4:00 am. In a great deal of pain, Herold helped him dismount from his horse and enter the house. After setting the leg, Mudd offered the fugitives a place to sleep. Booth had met Mudd twice before when he was scouting the area for Southern sympathizers who could aid him in the kidnapping plot. At that time, Mudd entertained Booth in his home and introduced him to John Surratt as well as George Gardiner, the man who had sold him the one-eyed bay used by Powell.

The next morning Herold related the story of Booth's riding accident and told them that they wanted to reach the Potomac that day. He then inquired about the roads in the area and 'shortcuts' through the Zekiah Swamp about 150 yards from Mudd's house.

Booth did not eat the breakfast that the Doctor's wife prepared for him. He complained that he injured his back in the fall from his horse and was in too much pain. Instead, he asked for some brandy.

Early the next afternoon Mudd and Herold went to Bryantown four miles away to run errands and find a carriage for Booth. There they ran into Dana's 13th New York Cavalry detachment sent from Washington. Rather than risking capture, Herold decided to return to Mudd's home. When Mudd heard the news of the assassination, he galloped back to his farm and ordered the fugitives to leave his property immediately. Booth and Herold told him that they wanted to "go to Mosby" whom they believed was still operating in the Northern Neck of Virginia. They then set out for the farm of Samuel Cox at 5:00 in the afternoon.

The Great Manhunt

At 9:00 that night, they met Oswald Swann, who for twelve dollars agreed to take them to the home of Colonel Cox. Cox guided Booth and Herold through a dense undergrowth of pines to a spot two miles south of his house. The hiding spot to which Captain Cox led the assassins was an old tobacco-bed covered with broom-sedge in a dense thicket of young pines, which was not near any roadway. He then arranged for his stepbrother, Thomas A. Jones, to care for them for the next six days until they could make their way across the Potomac River.

Cox and Jones were longtime members of the Confederate underground. Jones spent six months in prison for his activities from September 1861 until he signed an oath of allegiance in March 1862. After Booth's departure, prosecutors tried to build a case against both men confining them in the old Capitol prison at Washington for nearly two months. Henry Woodland their former slave lied to authorities in order to gain their release. Woodland's perjury probably saved the lives of both men.

The story of their actual involvement would have most likely remained unknown had not Frederick Stone, the legal counsel to both Herold and Dr. Mudd in the Lincoln assassination trial, hinted at Jones' participation to journalist George Alfred Townsend in 1883. After nearly twenty years, Jones acknowledged his role to Townsend and told him his story.

A Threat to the Republic

Major James O'Beirne

Born in Ireland, O'Beirne received the Medal of Honor for heroism during the battle at Fair Oaks, Virginia. As Provost Marshal of the District of Columbia, he accompanied Andrew Johnson to the Peterson House the night of the assassination and was then assigned to track down the assassins.

He arrested both John Lloyd and Samuel Mudd and telegraphed Booth's presumed whereabouts to the war department. While investigating another possible lead, Booth was cornered by Detective Everton Conger and Lt. Edward Doherty. Stanton awarded O'Beirne $3,000 in reward money affirming that it was his information which led to Booth's capture.

The Great Manhunt

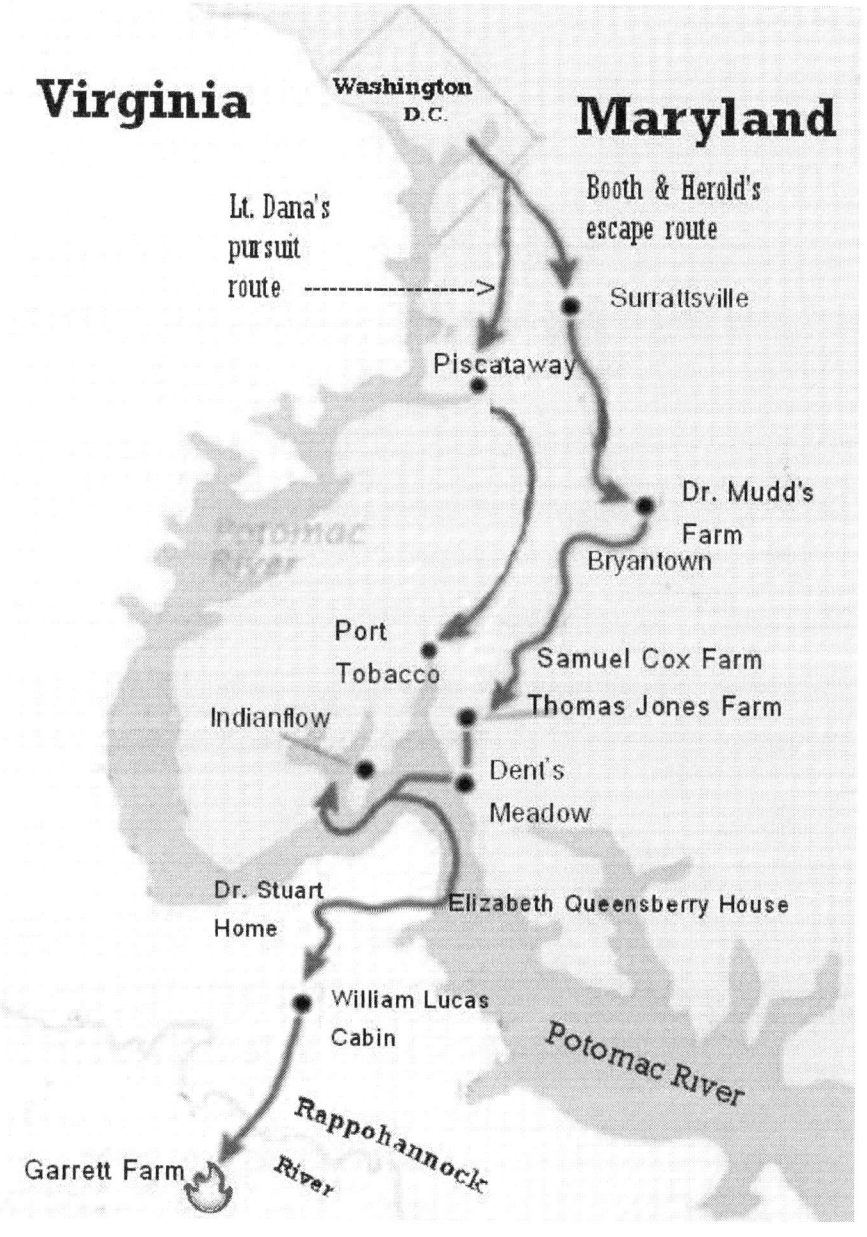

**Routes used by John Wilkes Booth and his pursuers
April 14 – April 26, 1865**

Life in the Zekiah Swamp

The Zekiah swamp was a combination of bogs and the overflows of various tributaries and small river branches in an area south of Bryantown. To traverse this area in the early spring was a particularly wet and miserable time unless one knew the way around via the small paths. The area was a favorite for trappers who fed on possum, muskrat, and raccoons. In a small patch of a nearby thicket, Jones hid the hunted pair.

The historical record is quiet on what Booth did during his six days in the Zekiah swamp. All we have on the topic is the little that the taciturn Jones decided to reveal. According to Jones all Booth wanted was food, newspapers and help crossing the river. He expressed no regret for the act, and knew all the consequences involved. [116]

The only other source we have are the notes left in Booth's diary. The word diary is a misnomer in this case. The book was actually a small appointment book that Booth purchased in St. Louis the previous year. Each page of the book had three days printed on them in consecutive order for the year 1864. When discovered, the pages from January 1 through June 10 were missing. On the page beginning June 11, he had a hand-drawn calendar and an entry. He skipped the pages beginning June 17 and June 20 and began writing again on page June 23 finishing on page June 29. The rest of the book was blank except for four missing pages, one in July, one in August, and two between August and September. [117]

The Great Manhunt

What happened to the missing pages is lost to history. Booth did use two of the missing pages in notes to a Dr. Richard Stuart, sarcastically thanking him for his lack of hospitality after he crossed the Potomac. The first note he wrote to Stuart did not seem strong enough to strike home Booth's point. He decided to rewrite the note and put the first note in the flap of his book. This note was in the book when the diary was found on April 26, 1865, along with the pictures of five women. In Booth's first diary entry, he wrote:

> I can never repent it, though we hated to kill. Our country owed all her troubles to him, and God simply made me the instrument of his punishment. The country is not what it was. This forced Union is not what I have loved. I care not what becomes of me. I have no desire to outlive my country. The night before the deed I wrote a long article and left it for one of the editors of the *National Intelligencer*, in which I fully set forth our reasons for our proceedings. He or the gov'r-...

At this point, Booth stopped and never returned to this thought in the diary. Perhaps Herold or Jones interrupted him, or perhaps he had gotten an epiphany. Obviously, he was about to go into a rant about how the government would not allow him to be heard through the newspapers, when he probably realized that he still could be heard through his friends in the Confederate underground. Richmond had fallen, and all contacts there were gone. However, the Confederate agents in Canada were still operating, and Jones could still get messages to them in short order. The historian Osborne Oldroyd uncovered this fact in 1901 when he walked the route of Booth and Herold talking to people who were still alive at the time.

> "I am the only living white person living who knew the whereabouts of Booth and Herold after they left Colonel Cox's on Sunday morning, April 16, 1865, and were launched upon the Potomac by Thomas A. Jones and Henry Woodland, Friday night, April 21, 1865...." Mr. Cox pointed out a piece of ground to the right of the road.surrounded by a dense forest. Mr. Cox saw a historic stump dug up near this spot. The cavity in the stump was used as a deposit for the Confederate mail. The mail that was going to Richmond and Southern points during the war, and from the South to the North, was deposited in this stump, and called for by the properly assigned agents. The letters from the South were then dropped into

the United States post offices after placing the proper stamps upon them; then they were delivered to their destination. "Samuel Cox jr. son of Col. Samuel Cox (1901) [118]

Booth was hiding in the middle of the Confederacy's information superhighway for six days. He had the means and the time to communicate with his spymasters in Canada. It seems inconceivable that he would not do so. This, of course, is speculation since no written records exist. However, we do know that he was well enough to write in his "diary" at this time, so it is possible that Jones delivered some of those torn pages to friends of the cause.

The Navy Yard Bridge used by Booth and Herold to escape into Maryland

Escape to Virginia

Thomas Jones kept his guests well hidden from the man hunters who were canvassing the area. He understood that keeping the horses that brought them from Washington was now an unneeded risk. They were as recognizable as their riders, and any sounds they made could bring the cavalry to their hideout. It was decided that Herold take them to a nearby swamp, execute them with a shot to the head, and let their bodies sink beneath the quicksand to avoid vultures that would circle the horses' bodies and give away their location.

Jones had a small boat that he would use to move the assassins across the Potomac. He had his former slave Henry Woodland hide the skiff in an isolated inlet called Dent's Meadow and constantly monitored the area for the right moment to move Booth and Herold to the river.

The cavalry already knew Booth's connection with Atzerodt, and the town teemed with detectives looking for clues. Jones went to the local bar to pick up the latest gossip as to where the army believed Booth was hiding. At this bar, army detective Captain William Williams recognized Jones and approached him. As Jones sipped his drink, Williams told him that he would "give one hundred thousand dollars to anyone who will give me the information that will lead to Booth's capture".

Jones nodded and replied, "That is a large sum of money and ought to get him – if money can do it." The war had been hard for Jones, but he had been loyal to the Confederate side and was not about to sell out his loyalty now. His personal honor was not for sale.

On Thursday, April 20, while scouting the village of Allens Fresh, Jones heard a rumor of a Booth sighting in St. Mary's County. Upon hearing the news, the cavalry quickly abandoned the town, and headed for the new hunting ground. Jones realized that the opportunity he was waiting for had come. If Booth was going to cross the Potomac, this was the night to accomplish the task.

The night was dark and misty, a beautiful night to cross the river undetected. Jones fed Herold and Booth one last time and gave them a compass and candle by which to read it. Before they left, Booth offered Jones a fistful of dollars. Jones refused the gesture, taking only $18, the price he had paid for the boat. He then shoved them off "to the mercies of the dark water". Their destination was Machodoc Creek on the Virginia side where a Mrs. Quesenberry would probably house them.

Unfortunately, Davy Herold was not a sailor. After five hours of fighting the current in total darkness and rowing to avoid gunships anchored in the river, the tiny boat ended up in Nanjemoy Creek still on the Maryland side of the river. Luckily, they found people in the area that fed them and gave them refuge until they could try again the next day.

When the refugees finally arrived at Mrs. Quesenberry's, she called for help in the person of Thomas Harbin, the chief Confederate agent in the area. Harbin was the brother-in-law of Thomas Jones, who along with John Surratt had helped Booth recruit George Atzerodt and purchase Richard Smoot's escape boat. For this mission he enlisted a William Bryant and two horses.

The Great Manhunt

The condition of Booth's leg had worsened, so Harbin told Bryant to take him to Dr. Richard Stuart. Stuart took one look at the party, quickly surmised who the men were, and refused to take them in or even look at Booth's swollen and blackened leg. When asked where they could find a wagon to transport Booth, he pointed them down the road to a neighbor named William Lucas who occasionally rented out his wagon.

Stunned by the lack of hospitality on Stuart's part, Booth wrote him a stinging rebuke and took out his frustration on the hapless Lucas. Threatening him at knifepoint, the fugitives took over his cabin forcing Lucas and his family to spend the night on their porch. The next day they "rented" his wagon and Lucas' twenty-one-year-old son to drive them to Port Conway. Crossing the Rappahannock River was their next goal.

Davy Herold

Trained as a pharmacist, Davy Herold was a sharp shooting bird hunter and outdoorsman. He was assigned to shoot the Vice-President after Atzerodt refused. Atzerodt claimed that Booth thought, Herold had "more pluck" than he did. Atzerodt said that Booth's chosen role for him was to "back up" Herold and "give him more courage".

Herold failed because his weapons were locked in Atzerodt's hotel room and Atzerodt refused to give him the key. Herold then accompanied Lewis Powell when he attacked Secretary of State Seward. Trapped in the tobacco barn with Booth, he surrendered to U.S. Troops and was sentenced to hang.

Garrett's Farm

Colonel John Mosby was in a quandary. On April 16, he had received word of Lincoln's assassination. On the same day, he received a recommendation from General Lee that he disband his rangers. As he negotiated surrender terms with General Winfield Hancock, he realized that with Booth still on the loose there was a good chance the fugitive may reveal Mosby's role in the kidnapping and torpedo plots, which would implicate him in the assassination. Stanton was cognizant of Mosby's contacts and told Hancock that; *"if Mosby is sincere he might do much toward detecting and apprehending the murderers of the president"*.

As the negotiations dragged on Stanton retracted his previous request for Mosby's help as he began to receive reports of Mosby's probable involvement. He wrote to Hancock;

"There is evidence that Mosby knew of Booth's plan, and was here in the city with him; also that some of the gang are endeavoring to escape by crossing the upper Potomac to get with Mosby or the secesh (secessionists) there." [119]

After pondering the situation for a few days Mosby decided to disband his organization and allow his men to petition for their pardons, but he did not personally surrender. Instead, he and a group of his raiders headed toward Richmond. He needed to be able to either intercept Booth and bring him to safety or get himself out of the country if the army captured Booth alive.

On April 24, Colonel Lafayette Baker, head of the Union Secret Service, received a telegram from Major O'Beirne informing him that reliable witnesses informed him that two men had crossed the river into Virginia, and that Booth and Herold were somewhere between the Potomac and Rappahannock rivers. It is believed that these witnesses were the people who fed the pair when they landed at Nanjemoy Creek.

The Great Manhunt

From his office across the street from the Willard's Hotel, Baker requested a cavalry force of twenty-five men. General Hancock responded by sending him the Sixteenth New York Cavalry under the command of Lieutenant Edward Doherty. Baker gave Doherty his orders and sent with him military detectives Lieutenant Colonel Everton Conger, and Lieutenant Luther Baker, Lafayette's cousin, both dressed in civilian clothes. Conger, the ranking officer, assumed "courtesy command" while Doherty remained in charge of the uniformed soldiers.

At the ferry landing in Port Conway, Va., Booth and Herold had finally met some returning Confederate soldiers who befriended them. Two of the men, Major M.B. Ruggles and Lt. A.R. Bainbridge, were part of the recently disbanded Mosby's raiders. The other, Capt. William Jett was a veteran of the 9th Virginia Cavalry. At that time, Booth was hopeful to make contact with Mosby and with his help be able to flee the country. Upon learning that they had finally made the contact for which they were hoping, they identified themselves as the assassins of the president.

Colonel John Mosby

Colonel John Mosby was responsible for infiltrating Thomas Harney through the lines and into Washington. Although he surrendered his command on April 16th he did not personally surrender until June 17th.

By then the government's case in trial of the conspirators was completed and his participation in the Conrad abduction and Harney Torpedo plots remained unrevealed. With Booth dead his only connection to the kidnapping and assassination plot was Lewis Powell, a 'deserter' from his ranks.

Jett was awestruck by the revelation but found Booth reluctant to talk about the deed saying it was "nothing to brag about". After almost ten days of living like a hunted animal, Booth was feeling pangs of regret and depression. He told Jett of his intentions if captured. "If they don't kill me, he told Jett, I'll kill myself."

Major Ruggles, in a conversation with Booth that he related in 1890, said that "Booth seemed to feel that he had been spurred on to the deed through a duty he owed the country to bring the war to an end, and that he would never be taken alive".[120]

Once they crossed over the Rappahannock to Port Royal, the soldiers escorted the fugitives to the farm of Richard Garrett. Jett was the son of an old friend of Garrett's. He introduced Booth as John W. Boyd, a soldier wounded at Petersburg who needed to rest before he could travel to his home in Maryland. Garrett agreed to take him in for a day or two. Once Booth settled down at the farm, the rest of the group headed towards Bowling Green.

Bainbridge, Ruggles, Jett and Herold rode five miles down the road and spent the night at Mrs. Clarke's, tavern called the Trappe. The tavern was a favorite stop for men along the road to see cockfights, dogfights, or spend some time and money on Mrs. Clarke's very friendly daughters. Jett left the group saying he was anxious to see his sweetheart and get his parole. He proceeded on alone to Bowling Green, spending the night at the Goldman Hotel.

Booth spent the night at the house in the room of Garrett's two sons, Jack and Robert. News of the assassination had not yet reached this section of the country since there was no telegraph or mail service available. The next day Booth asked one of the boys to take down a map from the wall. He then traced a water route from Norfolk to Charleston and from Charleston to Galveston Texas. When asked where he wanted to go, Booth replied, "Mexico". Herold returned the next day and made the remark that "when we get our fortune in Spain, we'll be alright."[121]

Spain was the future home of Booth's fiancée Lucy Hale and had no extradition treaty with the United States at that time. Apparently Booth was dreaming of "a happily ever after" reunion.

A few hours later, Ruggles and Bainbridge galloped up and told Booth that the Federal cavalry was coming up the road. Booth and Herold ran into the woods while their friends raced off in another direction. Doherty's unit passed by the farm but did not enter. Nevertheless, the reactions of his houseguest made the owner of the farm very suspicious. He ordered them to leave his property but after much pleading allowed them to spend one last night in his tobacco barn. A Negro neighbor was supposed to call for them early the next morning. [122]

The cavalry bypassed Garrett's farm, because they were following up on the most recent sighting of Booth at the ferry landing along with three soldiers. One of whom was identified as Willie Jett, who had a girlfriend in Bowling Green.

The cavalry arrived at nightfall in Bowling Green. At the Goldman Hotel, Everton Conger and his soldiers stormed the room of the sleeping Jett rousting him from his bed with guns in his face. Knowing what they wanted, he agreed to show them where Booth was located as long as Conger would not arrest him for aiding in Booth's escape. Conger agreed to the deal and doubled back to Garrett's farm early in the morning of April 26. The soldiers involved were in their saddles for almost eighteen hours, and the accounts of exactly what happened are not necessarily consistent with one another.

About 2 a.m. the soldiers knocked on the door demanding that Garrett tell them where Booth was hiding. Garrett had no idea that the man he knew as Boyd was actually Booth. He pleaded ignorance and the soldiers threatened to hang him for assisting the assassin. As they were about to make good their threat Garrett's son told them that two men were sleeping in the barn. The soldiers quickly surrounded the barn as Booth called to them trying to determine if they were Federals or Confederates.[123]

Among the soldiers, surrounding the barn was Sergeant Thomas Corbett. Corbett was a bible thumping, voice thundering man of God. An immigrant to Troy, New York, he learned the trade of a hatter. Just like the Mad Hatter in *Alice Through The Looking Glass*, the fumes of the chemicals he used (probably mercury poisoning) drove him to madness and drink. One night in Boston, he saw the light and became spiritually reborn, renaming himself Boston Corbett. He became a Salvationist, hearing voices from God, preaching on street corners, and wearing his hair down to his waist. One night, two attractive streetwalkers enticed him seductively. To prevent himself from engaging in future temptation he decided to castrate himself.

When Lincoln called for volunteers in April 1861, Corbett announced in his church that he was going to enlist. In a religious fervor, he told his fellow churchgoers that when he met the enemy "I will say to them, God have mercy on your souls- then pop them off." Corbett's God was the Old Testament version, filled with vengeance and always ready to punish evildoers. The war provided Corbett the perfect opportunity to be God's avenging angel.

As the soldiers surrounded the barn, Conger and Baker demanded that the pair surrender. Booth defiantly refused. After a series of threats and counter-threats, Herold saw their situation as hopeless and begged Booth to let him surrender. Booth relented and Herold left Booth to his fate.

Conger and Baker were both physically tired and knew they were in 'secesh country'. If the issue was not soon resolved, they risked a local uprising if word got out that they had the assassin trapped. Corbett filled with the spirit, volunteered to rush the door and drag him out. Conger told him to take his position on the side, because he was going to force Booth out by firing the barn. Booth was obviously playing for time and it was time to end the negotiating.

The fire illuminated the crippled man as he raged his defiance. Booth pleaded for a 'sporting 'chance to fight his way out. As he raised his carbine, a gunshot dropped him to the ground. Soldiers rushed the barn and dragged Booth taken to a safe distance.

As they laid him on the ground Booth told them, "This man's property is being destroyed and he doesn't know who I am." These words probably saved Garrett from immediate execution.[124]

At this point, an argument developed between Conger and Baker. Baker insisted somebody shot Booth while Conger insisted Booth shot himself. Conger then interrogated the troopers, asking if any of them saw anybody shoot Booth. Corbett volunteered that he fired the fatal shot.

"God Almighty directed me," Corbett said.

"I guess He did," said the incredulous Conger, "or you could never have hit him through that crack in the barn."

As Booth lay in mortal agony Conger and Baker began to rifle his body as if he were already dead. Conger removed the appointment book from the dying man's pocket and examined its contents. When he finished he closed it with a snap and thrust it into his own pocket.

Although he was physically drained the sleep deprived Conger then turned to Baker and told him that he was leaving for Washington immediately. Baker was told to care for the prisoner and to follow him as soon as possible. Whatever Booth had in that booklet, Conger determined it to be important enough to relinquish his command, leave his men and head for the capitol without delay.

Doctor Charles Urquhart was called from Port Royal to examine the dying man. He determined that the bullet had pierced his spinal cord and the paralysis was shutting down his vital organs. The wound was mortal.

As dawn began to break Booth's last thoughts were of the women in his life. He whispered to Baker, "Tell my mother I died for my country." He then asked to see his paralyzed hands. Baker lifted them up to his face. Booth stared at them, unable to bring them to his lips for one last kiss of Lucy's ring, he gasped and wheezed and faintly whispered "Useless. Useless". Then he died.

The Great Manhunt

When the soldiers returned to Washington with Booth's body, the story of Corbett's action turned him into a desperately needed hero. Lafayette Baker, in an attempt to discredit Corbett and gain a larger share of the reward money, spread the rumor that Corbett fired the fatal shot against orders. The partisan Copperheads spread the rumor that Booth actually committed suicide to vilify the Union forces.[125]

A war department investigation into the shooting credited Corbett's claim. Conger testified under oath that no one had given orders to the soldiers to shoot or not to shoot. Corbett explained that he took the shot because Booth raised his gun putting fellow soldiers in danger. Booth died because he knowingly forced the hand of the soldiers.

When Corbett returned to civilian life, he took his popularity on the lecture circuit where he was a disaster. His wild religious sermons quickly showed the congregation that he was not a man in possession of all his faculties.

He went west drifting from town to town and job to job preaching incoherently. At a soldiers' reunion in 1875, Corbett pointed his revolver at several of his fellow veterans who had alleged that Booth committed suicide.

In 1887, while serving as the assistant doorkeeper at the Kansas House of Representatives in Topeka he overheard two pages mocking a longwinded preacher during the legislature's opening prayer. Corbett pulled out his revolver, and opened fire at the "heretics".

Fortunately, no one was hurt but the lawmakers fearing for their lives, sent Corbett to the Topeka Asylum for the Insane. On May 26, 1888, disgusted by the shameful treatment his nation had given him, "God's Avenging Angel" jumped on a horse and escaped to a friend's ranch in Neodesha, Kansas.

His friend, Irwin Deford gave him some food, money and a blanket for the next part of his journey advising him never to return. Corbett readily accepted Deford's suggestion. On June 1, 1888, Boston Corbett rode off into the sunset never to be seen again, his final resting place known only to God.

Thomas Boston Corbett

Thomas Corbett was born in London, England, in 1832. After he allegedly shot Booth he was placed under arrest, but with the public's thirst for vengeance quenched, his sudden hero status caused the charges to be dropped. Stanton said, "The rebel is dead. The patriot lives." Corbett received his share of the reward money which amounted to $1,653.85. In his official statement of May 1, 1865, Corbett claimed he shot Booth because he thought Lincoln's assassin was getting ready to use his weapons

The Great Manhunt 187

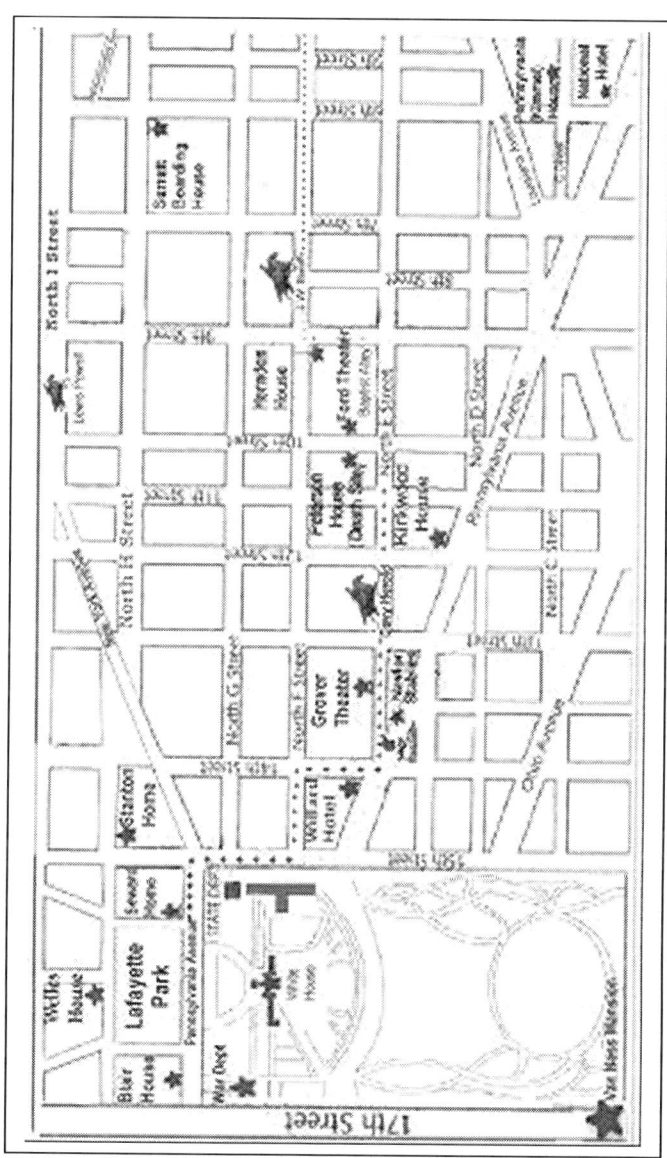

This downtown map of Washington 1865 shows the distance between the buildings involved in the attack and the routes taken by the assassins.

A Threat to the Republic

The White House in the 1860s had deteriorated by the heavy traffic from citizens, soldiers and office seekers interested in visiting the Lincolns or just taking home souvenirs. The lack of nominal security to prevent such abuses in public areas made the home a target for destruction by use of a mine. A greenhouse (on the left) built by James Buchanan near the west entrance was unguarded and planned to possibly be used by Harney's group to enter the basement and plant their bomb. In 1902, the greenhouse was removed by Teddy Roosevelt to build the West Wing.

Mary Surratt (left), David Herold (center) and George Atzerodt (right) are prepared for their execution.

Chapter 6

The Secrets of Mars

Lonesome George

"I am in trouble," moaned the prisoner, "and I shall never be shut of it." George Atzerodt was indeed in big trouble. Before the war George and his brother John, two German immigrants, owned a carriage painting business in Port Tobacco, Maryland. When the war began, the business dried up and John decided to take a job as a detective in Baltimore. George, his happy-go-lucky brother, found an opportunity to make some easy money by smuggling Confederate operatives across the Potomac River from Port Tobacco, Maryland, to Virginia. With this side business, he was able to supplement his income as a carriage painter for merely a few hours work. He had little interest in politics other than agreeing with whoever was buying the drinks. Then came the day when his friend and best customer, John Surratt, introduced him to the famous actor John Wilkes Booth, who promised him riches and glory for only a few hours of his time. Now he sat alone in a cell awaiting his fate.

How he managed to elude the dragnet put out for him by Federal authorities was an amazing piece of blind luck. After leaving the Kimmel House the day after the assassination, he sold his revolver for ten dollars and took the Rockville stage heading for his relatives in Germantown. Caught in a traffic jam of wagons at an army checkpoint, he decided to leave the stage and stroll up to the roadblock to see if he could help. Always good-natured, he jabbered with police, drank hard cider with them, and helped them inspect wagon upon wagon coming up the road. After a while, he hitched another ride on a just-released wagon of a farmer named Gaither, said goodbye to his new friends, and rode off. The army report was brutally frank:

> During that time he treated the guard to several drinks, and finally induced them to allow him to proceed in a wagon of one John Garther, who took him as far as Rockville, when he left and proceeded to his own house. [126]

He might have gotten away permanently if only he could have kept quiet at Easter dinner, but being reserved or taciturn just was not part of George's easygoing nature. Residing with his cousin, Hartman Richter, in Germantown, their neighbors, the Metz family invited him to supper. The house was full of people for Easter dinner, and the topic was naturally the assassination. Somebody at the table mentioned that he heard that General Grant was a target, but the assassins missed him.

"Ja", said Atzerodt knowingly, "if the man had followed General Grant that was to have followed him, he would have been killed."

James Leaman, another guest, then asked George if the assassins murdered Grant. "No, I don't suppose he was," George replied. "If it was so, someone must have gotten on the same cars that he did." [127] Silence overtook the table but George kept right on eating, smiling, and flirting with the host's daughter, oblivious to what he had said and enjoying the fact that he suddenly became the center of attention.

With troops scouring the countryside, questioning anyone who looked out of place, it was only a matter of time before troopers learned about the know-it-all living at his cousin's house.

At this point in the investigation, the police were specifically looking for him. They had no doubt that Atzerodt was involved. The search of his room at the Kirkwood House confirmed that he was part of the conspiracy. Booth had securely tied Atzerodt's fate to his with a hangman's knot. However, George firmly believed that he had done nothing wrong. He asserted that he had saved Andrew Johnson's life, and in fact, the evidence shows that to be true. Co-conspirator Lewis Powell backed Atzerodt's claim of innocence, stating that he heard Atzerodt tell Booth he would not participate in the scheme.[128]

Reverend Butler was a minister who came to Atzerodt's cell to offer him comfort. According to Butler, Atzerodt said he first learned of Booth's plan to assassinate the president less than two hours before the shooting. Atzerodt claimed that Booth wanted David Herold to assassinate Vice President Johnson because, Booth thought, Herold had "more pluck" than he did. Atzerodt said Booth's chosen role for him was to "back up" Herold and "give him more courage."

In a statement to Col. H.H. Wells, while aboard the prison ship *Montauk* Atzerodt said;

"He (Booth) and Herold had been ***and seen*** Andrew Johnson and found out where he was. He then asked if I was willing myself to assist them. I said that I did not come for that and was not willing to murder a person. They said they did not want me to do any act but only to show them the road into the lower part of Maryland and if I did not I would suffer for it. I said I would do all I could on the road. They said will you get a horse and stop near the Eastern Branch Bridge? We then came out. Herold wanted me to go to the Kirkwood House and asked me if I had the key to the room. **I told him no.** I did not go to the hotel and we parted then and I have never seen them since."[129]

The Eastern Branch Bridge was another name for the Navy Yard Bridge. It seems from this statement that Booth was hoping to have Herold as his guide in the dark Maryland countryside, but if he had to use Herold as an assassin, there was no guarantee that he would make it to the bridge. Atzerodt, now free from his assassination duties, would be the logical replacement.

Each member of Booth's team was equipped with a knife and gun. However, Herold had left his colt revolver and bowie knife in Atzerodt's room when he planted the coat with the incriminating evidence. By Atzerodt's refusal to give him the key, Herold had no access to the weaponry needed to perform his new assignment. This accounts for why the bird hunter did not take a more active role in the assassinations. With no weaponry, he became a mere tagalong for Powell, keeping the directionally challenged hit man on the proper course.

The police were now looking for names and information, and George promised to tell them all he knew in an attempt to save his neck. Not only was his brother, John, on the police force but his brother-in-law, John Smith, was as well. He felt sure that they would understand and help him out of this predicament.

Interred in the Old Penitentiary on the grounds of the Washington Arsenal, George requested that his brother-in-law and his boss Provincial Marshal James McPhail visit him. He wanted to make a statement. The following is a transcript of Atzerodt's remarks to questions asked by police. In parenthesis are the real names of the people to whom Atzerodt was referring. Unfortunately, transcripts of the questions are lost. The numbers were added to provide a logical break in the statement.

Statements of George A. Atzerodt

To: Provincial Marshal James McPhail
Witnessed by: John L. Smith
May 1 – 1865 bet 8 & 10 P.M

1. James Wood (*POWELL*) sometimes called Mosby boarded with Mrs. Murray an Irish woman on the corner of 9 & F St. in a three story house, front on the upper end of the P.O. and South End of Patent Office - with basement entrance on the left side going up 9th St. from Avenue. He was a little over six feet, black hair, smooth round face, gray coat black pants, & spring coat mixed with white & gray. Saw him last time on Friday evening about 5 o'clock with Booth. He sent for letters to the post office with James Hall. He was brought from New York. Surratt told me so. He said he had been a prisoner in Balte, near the depot. He was arrested for whipping a Negro woman. Mosby was Wood (*POWELL*)'s nick name - did not know him by any other name than mentioned.

2. Gus. Howell now arrested in Old Capitol was one of the party. He went also by name of Gustavus Spencer, Surratt and Spencer came from Richmond, together just after it had fallen.

3. James Donaldson, a low chunky man about 23 or 24 years of age, small-potted, dark complexion (not very) deep plain black suit; only saw him one time & this was Wednesday previous to the murder, he was having an interview with Booth and told him to meet him on Friday eve & he replied he would and left and went up Penn. Avenue towards the Treasury building. I was under the impression he came on with Booth.

4. Arnold, O'Laughlin, Surratt, Herold, Booth and myself met once at a saloon or restaurant on the Avenue between 13 & 14 St.

5. The Samuel Thomas registered on the morning of the 15th April at Penn Hotel, I met on my way to hotel, he was an entire stranger to me. I left the Hotel alone on the morning of 15th of April. A Lieut. in room No. 51 will prove this.

6. Surratt bought a boat from Dick Smoot & James Brawner living about Port Tobacco, for which they paid $300.00 and was to give one hundred Dolls. extra for taking care of it till wanted.

7. Booth told me that Mrs. Surratt went to Surrattsville to get out the guns (Two Carbines) which had been taken to that place by Herold. This was Friday. The carriage was hired at Howard's. I saw a man named Weightman *(Lewis Weichmann)* who boarded at Surratt's at Post Office. He told me he had to go down the Country with Mrs. Surratt. This was on Friday,

8. Also, I am certain Dr. Mudd knew all about it, as Booth sent (as he told me) liquors & provisions for the trip with the president to Richmond, about two weeks before the murder to Dr. Mudd's.

9. Booth never said until the last night (Friday) that he intended to kill the president. Herold came to the Kirkwood House, same evening for me to go to see Booth. I went with Herold & saw Booth. He then said he was going to kill the president and Wood *(POWELL)*, the Secy. of State. I did not believe him. This occurred in the evening about 7 1/2 o'clock. It was dark. I took a room at Kirkwood. Both Herold & I went to the room left Herold's coat, knife, & pistol in room and never again returned to it.

10. Booth said during the day that the thing had failed and proposed to go to Richmond & open the theatre. I am not certain but I think I stayed one night at Kirkwood (Thursday) we were to try and get papers to Richmond from

Mr. Johnson. Booth spoke of getting the papers. He would get them out of the theatre.

11. Wood (*POWELL*) & Booth were apparently confidential with each other. Plenty of parties in Charles County knew of the kidnapping affair. One of the men named Charles Yates knew all about it, he went to Richmond during the winter he was to row the president & party over. Thos. Holborn was to meet us on the road and help in the kidnapping. Bailey & Barnes knew nothing of the affair unless Booth told Bailey & he told Barnes. Booth had met Bailey on "C" St. with me. I did not meet Booth or any other of the party in Baltimore on or about the 31 of March. Boyle also killed Capt. Watkins near Annapolis last month, was one of the party, in the conspiracy.

12. I repeat I never knew anything about the murder. I was intended to give assistance to the kidnapping. They come to Port Tobacco (Surratt & Booth) several times and brought me to Washington. The pistol given me I sold or received a loan on it Saturday morning after the murder from John Caldwick at Matthews & Wells, Store, High St. Georgetown. The knife I threw away just above Mrs. Canby's boarding house the night of the murder about 11 o'clock when I took my horse to stable. I had the horse out to help to take the president. I did not believe he was going to be killed, although Booth had said so. After I heard of the murder I run about the city like a crazy man.

13. I have not seen Arnold for some time, but saw O'Laughlin on Thursday evening, on the Avenue at Saloon near U.S. Hotel. He told me he was going to see Booth.

14. Wood (*POWELL*) did not go on the street in daytime for fear of arrest. When he first came to Washington, he boarded at Surratt's. This was in February. He (Wood (*POWELL*)) went with Booth last of February to N. York. Booth we

understood paid the way. I know nothing about Canada. Wood (*POWELL*) told me he had horses in Virginia. Sam. Arnold and Mike O'Laughlin ought to know where the horses and pistols were bought. Sam and Mike have a buggy and horse kept at stable in rear of Theatre. Booth had several horses at same place. I think the horse's property was in Surratt's name. I sold one of the horses & paid part of the money to Booth and part to Herold, who said he would see Booth about it. The saddle and bridle belonging to Booth is at Penn House, where I left it.

15. I overheard Booth when in conversation with Wood (*POWELL*) say, that he visited a chambermaid at Seward's House & that she was pretty. He said he had a great mind to give her his diamond pin. Herold talked about powders & medicines on Friday night at Mrs. Condby's. Wood (*POWELL*), Herold, Booth, and myself were present. This was a meeting place because Wood (*POWELL*) could not go out for fear of arrest.

16. Kate Thompson or Kate Brown, as she was known by both names, put up at National & was well known at Penn House. She knew all about the affair. Surratt went to Richmond with her last March and Gust. Powell made a trip with her to same place. This woman is about twenty yrs of age, good looking and well dressed. Black hair and eyes, round face from South Carolina & a widow. I did not see Surratt for seven or eight days before the murder nor have I seen him since. Miss Thompson or Brown had two large light trunks, one much larger than the other. Young Weightman (*Weichmann*) at Surratt's ought to know about this woman.

17. This remark made by me in Baltimore on the 31 of March alluded to blockade running & privateering altogether & Booth said he had money to buy a steamer & wanted me to go in it. I was to be one of them. In this way I was going to make a pile of money.

18. Booth said he had met a party in N. York who would get the president for certain. They were going to mine the end of the pres. House, near the War Dept. They knew an entrance to accomplish it. Spoke about getting friends of the president. to get up an entertainment & they would mix it in, have a serenade & thus get at the president & party. These were understood to be projects. Booth said if he did not get him quick the N. York crowd would. Booth knew the New York party apparently by a sign. He saw Booth give some kind of sign to two parties on the Avenue who he said were from New York.

19. My Uncle, Mr. Richter and family in Monty. Co. Md. knew nothing about the affair either before or after the occurrence & never suspected me of any thing wrong as I was in the habit of visiting and working in the neighborhood & staying with him. My father formerly owned part of the property now owned by Richter.   Finis. [130]

George Atzerodt made this statement before his brother secured the legal services of General William. E. Doster. Most probably his brother-in-law, John L. Smith (the witness to the statement), secured a copy for his attorney. Upon reading the account, Doster realized that this document would get his client hanged. The conspiracy charge leveled against Atzerodt meant that if he were a part of a group doing something illegal and never told authorities of the activity, the law would deem him guilty of the charge even if he did not participate in the illegal act. This is exactly what Booth told him would happen if he backed out. Doster, at the trial, immediately moved to have this confession stricken from the official record on the grounds that the statement was given under duress.

The court overruled Doster on his motion but for some reason never put Atzerodt's confession into the official record. The complete statement would have left no doubt that Atzerodt was indeed a member of the conspiracy as well as Mary Surratt.

Statement #7 confirmed the later and crucial testimony of tavern keeper John Lloyd that Mary Surratt asked him to have the carbines ready for Booth. Lloyd's testimony was critical to her conviction, and many thought it unreliable because Lloyd admitted to being inebriated at the time she made the request. Had Atzerodt's confession been included in the official record, many years of controversy could have been avoided.

William E. Doster

William E. Doster was a Brigadier General who led his regiment during the Chancellorsville and Gettysburg campaigns. He practiced law in Washington and was appointed, by Judge-Advocate-Generals Holt and Bingham, to defend Lewis Payne and George Atzerodt.

Given no time to prepare a proper defense, Doster gave an impassioned and powerful argument that the Commission should spare his clients but his plea fell on deaf ears.

Passes to Freedom

What Booth was doing the two days before the assassination is largely a mystery to us. Atzerodt reveals in statement #10 that they were trying to get papers to go to Richmond from Andrew Johnson.

> Booth said during the day that the thing had failed and proposed to go to Richmond & open the theatre. I am not certain but I think I stayed one night at Kirkwood (Thursday) we were to try and get papers to Richmond from Mr. Johnson. <u>Booth spoke of getting the papers</u>. He would get them out of the Theatre.

"The thing" Booth was referring to was the kidnapping plot. He told Atzerodt the same story he gave to O'Laughlin, Arnold, and Sam Chester, that the kidnapping scheme was finished and he was going to open a new business in Richmond. This helps to confirm the previous statement in which Atzerodt was stunned when Booth suddenly announced he was going to kill the president. The "<u>papers to Richmond</u>" could only mean travel passes. Anyone who wanted to cross over the bridges after 9:00 needed a pass. Lincoln confirmed this fact himself by a pass he issued the day before the assassination to General James Singleton.

> Allow General Singleton to pass to Richmond & return
> April 13, 1865   A. Lincoln

[131]

Singleton was a noncombatant general from Illinois who Lincoln was sending to help Mrs. Lincoln's half-sister B.H. Helm from losing her property to Union troops. [132] If a general needed a pass from the president, it gives an indication of how strictly the army was still controlling travel.

Ironically, just before Lincoln left for the theatre, two Southerners asked him for a pass so they could travel safely to Richmond and Petersburg. He hastily scrawled a note and had it delivered to them:

> "No pass is necessary now to authorize anyone to go and return from Petersburg & Richmond. People go and return just as they did before the war.
>
> A. Lincoln" [133]

This last note by Lincoln was the result of his approval that day of Stanton's orders to halt the draft, stop recruiting, curtail purchases, reduce the number of officers and remove all traffic restrictions. On April 14, Stanton issued brigade commanders orders to stop asking citizens for passes. [134] Unfortunately, this development came too late to alter Booth's plans.

Lincoln knew it would take time to process this change order down the line, so in order to facilitate the process he wrote a "note" rather than a "pass" and used the word *now*, because he knew it would be the first time that sentries would be aware of the change. It was a well-known fact that if one wanted to cross one of the bridges out of Washington at night, a pass was required.[135] The two Southerners who asked for the pass were aware of the restriction as was Booth, who had been actively trying to obtain them from the vice-president.

General Order No.5, issued on 24 January 1863, by Major General Samuel P. Heintzelman, was still in effect the night of the assassination and posted at the Navy Bridge. The basic order remained unchanged for over two years.

> None other [passes] will be recognized unless issued from these Head Quarters or by superior authority. No person excepting General Officers will be passed over any of the several crossings [of the Potomac] between the hours of 9 p.m. and daylight without the countersign and a pass.[136]

A pass signed by the vice president would surely qualify as a "superior authority". If Booth asked Johnson for such a pass, it would explain another mystery that has puzzled researchers. Why would a man who is fleeing from a murder committed in front of a large audience that can readily identify him use his real name at a bridge checkpoint? Some have speculated that Booth was being egotistical when he revealed his identity to the sentry. The more logical reason is that the name he gave had to match the name on the pass that he received from Johnson .

When Col. Roger E. Cook of the 13th Maryland Infantry received the news from Washington early on April 15th he immediately passed along the following order: "Maj. You will immediately cause all your pickets along line of Railroad to be instructed to arrest all persons attempting to pass the lines **with or without passes** who are not known to be trustworthy...". This order to disregard passes is an indication that authorities were aware that Booth had a pass. [137]

In Atzerodt's *Montauk* account, he stated, "He (Booth) and Herold had been *and seen* Andrew Johnson" it is likely that at this meeting Herold obtained a pass using Booth's connection under the alias 'Smith'. If Johnson knew the actor personally or if someone was representing Booth to Johnson, it would have been impossible for Booth to use an alias. Johnson would have issued one of the passes directly to the famous actor

The prosecution in the trial of the conspirators released most of the evidence to the public through the press before presenting it in court. Neither this portion of the confession nor the torpedo plot was ever "leaked" to the press by government sources. In fact, after McPhail's testimony, the entire statement and the information it contained disappeared from war department files.

Johnson, being an ambitious Southern politician, was not a very well-liked man by people in the North or South. By virtue of his sudden promotion, he came under immediate suspicion in some quarters. Rumors that Booth escaped due to the assistance of someone 'higher-up' swirled through Washington with Johnson being the prime suspect. Any mentions of his name with that of Booth or any of the conspirators were quickly denied.

Government apologists quickly denounced such rumors calling them political attacks and smears upon Johnson. They defended the sentries saying that since the war was almost over, the rule was relaxed. Booth and Herold's stories were reasonable enough to allow the sentries to let them pass. These plausible denials were enough to quell the criticism.

Senator Jacob Merritt Howard from Michigan, co-sponsor of the Fourteenth Amendment, was one who was suspicious of the highly ambitious Johnson. In a conversation with his good friend Stanton, he told him that in his opinion "Johnson was an accessory *before* the crime". Knowing that Howard was looking for confirmation on his statement, Stanton did not answer but merely shrugged his shoulders. Howard said that he interpreted the gesture to mean "I could disclose a great deal of very interesting information on that subject, but it will not do to tell even you".[138]

Every politician who ever did a favor for a friend knows that sometimes it could come back to haunt him. Booth duped Johnson into helping him, and he was by no means the only one. Booth was extremely charming and persuasive as he ruthlessly used people to achieve his objectives.

It is obvious that Booth purposely left behind many of the items found in his room at the National Hotel to implicate both friends and enemies. He kept outdated letters of Arnold and Ella Starr Turner to implicate them in his plot as well as one that incriminated his own brother Edwin. It's not known what was contained in the letter burned by Matthews, but it's safe to assume that he too was an intended victim. Many other people did innocent favors for him not realizing that he was compromising them to achieve his ultimate goal. Andrew Johnson was one such victim.

George Atzerodt

Two hours before the assassination, Booth told Atzerodt that he was now to shoot Vice-President Andrew Johnson. Atzerodt refused claiming that he joined for a kidnapping not a murder and proceeded to drink himself into a stupor.

After his capture, Atzerodt told all he knew about the conspiracy to the authorities hoping for mercy. His statement made shortly after his capture disappeared for 112 years.

The Elephant in the Room

Andrew Johnson has always been an enigma to his supporters, detractors, and biographers. Growing up as poor white trash in Raleigh N.C., he apprenticed to a tailor's trade. Raised in the poor underclass of Raleigh he had a poor white feeling of inferiority. He took comfort, however, in the fact that he was not on the bottom rung of the social ladder. That place belonged permanently to the Negro.

Young Andrew, who had never attended school for even a single day, was bound as an apprentice tailor when he was 14. In 1826, when he had just turned 17, he broke his indentured service determined to seek his fortune in Tennessee. He was eighteen when he married sixteen-year-old Eliza McCardle the daughter of a local shoemaker. By all accounts, the marriage was a happy one despite the fact that Johnson was frequently away from home for long spells.

Eliza taught her husband reading, writing and arithmetic. As the tailor business flourished, she would read to her husband while he worked. Johnson's shop soon became a gathering place for political discussion. To improve his debating skills he joined a debate club at a small college four miles from his home. With Eliza's encouragement, he entered politics.

Andrew Johnson's political career advanced rapidly. He became a council member of Greeneville, Tennessee, in 1828, and two years later, won election to become mayor of the town. In 1835 and 1839, Johnson won election to the Tennessee House of Representatives. In 1843, he won election to the U.S. House of Representatives and won the four following elections to retain his seat until 1853.

Returning to state politics, Johnson won the 1853 Tennessee gubernatorial election and re-election in 1855. During his term as Governor of Tennessee, he provided as benefits to the state a public school system and a state library. On the eve of the Civil War in 1857, Johnson became a U.S. senator from Tennessee.

Washington D.C. was the farthest north he had ever been before he became president. In an attempt to save the Union from war, he proposed a constitutional amendment guaranteeing that the office of either president or vice president always be held by a slave-state man and providing for an even division of the Supreme Court into justices from free and slave states. For this, secessionists in Tennessee burned him in effigy.

As a politician Johnson's style was confrontational and incendiary. He had neither diplomacy nor tact and was blindly stubborn, frequently mistaking his sternness for consistency. He neither trusted nor confided completely in one person. He detested the planter aristocrats who looked down on him and blamed them for the war. Throughout the war, he simultaneously raged against both secessionists and abolitionists as dangerous to the existence of the Union and the Constitution.

His Secretary of the Treasury, Hugh McCulloch, described him as a man who was never happy "unless he had someone to strike or denounce". All these traits were reminiscent of his hero Andrew Jackson. In fact he often called himself a "Jacksonian Democrat" while his opponents derided him as Andrew the second.

As a president, Jackson was successful in several confrontations with Congress, although many of these shortsighted victories were not always in the best long term interests of the country. Due to his alienating attitude and actions, Andrew Jackson was the only president officially censured by an Act of Congress. Johnson would exceed his hero's dishonor through impeachment.

Throughout the war, Johnson strongly supported the Constitution and the Union, soundly rejecting the Confederacy. He was the only Southern senator to remain in the U.S. Senate after his State seceded, and he seemed to revel in the rejection of his aristocratic associates. His support of the Union won him great acclaim in the North and infamy in the South. His one-man stand against the Confederacy brought him the notoriety he craved.

Union victories in Tennessee placed a large portion of the State under federal control. In 1862, President Lincoln appointed Johnson to the post of Military Governor to administer the Union held territory. Johnson ruled with a firm hand silencing sources of anti-Union sentiment and using the State as a laboratory for reconstruction.

Though Johnson was deeply committed to saving the Union, he did not believe in the emancipation of slaves. During his term as Military Governor, Johnson convinced the president to exempt Tennessee from the Emancipation Proclamation. By the summer of 1863, however, he began to favor emancipation strictly as a war measure.

Early in 1864, Lincoln was deeply concerned about his chances for reelection. Congressman George Julian of Indiana believed that probably not one in ten members of his party in Congress favored Lincoln's re-nomination. Often mentioned to replace Lincoln at the top of the ticket was General John C. Fremont and Secretary of the Treasury Salmon P. Chase. Bolstering the ticket with a sound War Democrat for the vice-presidency would help balance and broaden the appeal of the ticket. Lincoln's first choice for the position was General Benjamin Butler, who, like Johnson, was a War Democrat.

Although Lincoln greatly distrusted Butler with power, the move would have had a twofold effect. It would balance the ticket and remove Butler from his military position to which he was terribly incompetent. However, "Old Cockeye", who was in charge of the garrison at Fortress Monroe, Virginia, turned him down.

The ambitious Butler was planning an ill-fated military offensive that would take Richmond and give him the opportunity to replace Lincoln on the top spot of the ticket. Thus, the rebuff by Butler opened the way for Johnson, a Southerner, to replace Hannibal Hamlin an abolitionist from Maine as vice-president.

After the assassination Butler declared, "If I had been in Mr. Johnson's place this tragedy would never have occurred." Southern sympathizers hated Butler so much more than they hated Lincoln that they "would not have wanted me in the White House." [139]

Johnson's inclusion defused the Democrats criticism that Lincoln was merely a tool of the abolitionists. It showed the electorate that the Republicans represented all loyal men throughout the country. Secondly, it sent a message to those countries abroad debating about intervening by increasing Union sentiment to have a Southern man on the ticket.

Whether or not Johnson actually helped Lincoln to secure the presidency is matter of mixed opinion. Union victories in the field doomed the 'peace at any price' Democrats in the election of 1864. The Lincoln-Johnson ticket was the political equivalent of a shotgun marriage. Neither man liked the other very much but both used the other for political gain. Neither exchanged congratulatory telegrams on their nominations and there was very little communication between them afterwards. Before the second inaugural, Johnson wrote the president saying that he didn't think it was necessary for him to be in Washington for the inauguration. Lincoln showed the letter to a reporter and commented; "This Johnson is a queer man."[140]

Reversing the momentum of the war not only retained the White House for Lincoln, but also finally gave an overdue amount of credit to the beleaguered secretary of war, and Johnson reciprocated quickly. After Johnson took the oath as president, the members of the cabinet were ready to tender their resignations allowing Johnson to choose his own advisors. Stanton was the first to make the offer when Johnson immediately replied, "No, you must keep the machinery moving. We must retain the chief engineer by all means; I hope you are not thinking of resigning!"

According to Charles A. Dana, "Vice President Johnson took the oath of office as president and his first act, most becomingly performed, was to thank the secretary of war for all that he had accomplished and ask him, while they still held each other by the hand, to stand by him as he had stood by Mr. Lincoln."[141] Stanton would stay and protect the republic against any threats.

Johnson needed all the help he could get from his cabinet. His inebriated performance on inauguration day was still in the minds of the nation. The official story became that a recent bout of typhoid weakened the exhausted Johnson on his long trip from Tennessee. This exhaustion coupled with a glass of whiskey caused the embarrassment.

However, his former colleagues in the Senate knew better. A few days afterward, a senatorial caucus seriously considered the propriety of asking him to resign as their presiding officer. Although he was able to edit the official record of his speech, opposition newspapers had a field day with the story.

According to the accounts, Johnson took to bed in illness and mortification. A week later, a newspaper reported that he had called in several physicians for consultation with a view for making a case of temporary insanity.

Johnson went into seclusion after the speech and did not preside over the Senate. This absence gave rise to more rumors that he was still on a drinking binge. He did not reappear until he met with Lincoln on the afternoon of the assassination to complain about the terms Grant gave Lee at Appomattox.

Two days after the inauguration, a worried Secretary McCulloch informed the president of concern in certain quarters of the government based upon Johnson's inauguration debacle. What would be the fate of the country should Johnson need to replace him? Lincoln hesitated and then replied with a curious graveness, "I have known Andy for many years. He made a bad slip the other day but you need not be scared. Andy ain't a drunkard."[142]

Johnson biographers have used this quote by Lincoln as a self-evident truth of Johnson's sobriety and that his alcoholism was merely a smear tactic used by his enemies. Many of his biographers dismiss the drinking issue with barely a mention while some quote contemporaries as never seeing him drunk in their presence.

Hans Trefousse in his excellent biography of Johnson stated, "Some days he would consume two to four glasses of whiskey and some days none at all. Former Assistant Secretary of War Charles Dana saw him imbibe heavily throughout his governorship, but never saw him drunk."[143] Claude Bowers in his book *The Tragic Era* used Johnson's success as proof of his sobriety. "A penniless and obscure youth, without family prestige or influential friends, who, within a few years, accumulated a modest fortune, and through sheer ability rose to a position of authority, could not have been a drunkard."[144]

When it comes to alcoholics, one must always be aware of the "elephant in the room" syndrome. This frequently occurs within the families of alcoholics where friends and family are reluctant to discuss the person's problem, thus aiding in the denial. In politics, the denial of the obvious is a tactic often used to avoid discussing an issue and putting the onus of slander upon the accuser.

Johnson's ability to 'imbibe heavily but not be drunk' is an indication of chronic alcohol consumption. A man with this condition is a drinker who has developed a tolerance for at least some of alcohol's effects. This means that after continuous drinking, consumption of a constant amount of alcohol produces a lesser effect. Increasing amounts of alcohol are necessary to produce an intoxicated effect.

If this is the case, Johnson probably drank secretly throughout the day, never enough to show the effects of alcohol abuse in the forms of slurred speech or loss of motor skills, but enough to affect his personality. The tendency to erupt with frequent and intense episodes of anger, which was part of Johnson's personality makeup, may well have been alcohol induced.

His inauguration day fiasco could have been the result of an alcoholic phenomenon called *acute tolerance*. This occasionally occurs in people who have developed a tolerance for alcohol. This experience produces alcohol-induced impairment soon after the beginning of consumption rather than later in the drinking session. A person with this condition could actually appear to be sobering up as he continues to drink.

In the 1970s, scientific studies documented that alcoholism does run in families.[145] However, it has not yet proven if it runs in families because a child learns to become an alcoholic from parents and the home environment, or because a child inherits genes that create a predisposition for alcoholism. Johnson's sons Charles and Robert both suffered from alcoholism.

Charles Johnson died in April 1863 after falling from his horse in an inebriated state. Robert Johnson, made a Colonel in the Union Army by his father, was frequently drunk on duty. Eventually, he was sent home to avoid further embarrassment to the Military Governor. Robert's drunken escapades in the White House were a source of constant humiliation for his father ending with Robert's suicide in 1869.

If Senator Stewart's account of Johnson's inebriation the morning after the assassination is true, one can imagine the scene at the White House that morning. Mary Lincoln, grief stricken, somberly taken to her room while Stanton goes about feverishly trying to sober up her husband's successor. Perhaps it contributed to her negative view of Johnson when she wrote:

"...that, that miserable inebriate Johnson, had cognizance of my husband's death - Why, was that card of Booth's, found in his box, some acquaintance certainly existed - I have been deeply impressed, with the harrowing thought, that he, had an understanding with the conspirators & they knew their man... As sure, as you & I live, Johnson, had some hand, in all this...."[146]

The sanitation of political reputations was (and still is) a common practice for biographers. A politician's record never included personal vices and trysts. Washington brothels made their living off Congressmen and Senators who would leave their families in their respective districts while Congress was in session. It left one Reverend to lament how good a town Washington could become if only the representatives would bring their families. Johnson's wife never accompanied him to the Capitol.

One person who recognized the elephant in the Johnson White House was Norman Judd, a former envoy to Berlin. He vigorously complained to Senator Lyman Trumbull, "There is too much whiskey in the White House, and harlots go into the Private Secretary's office unannounced in broad daylight!"

Gideon Welles diary recorded a statement made in 1866 by Senator Samuel Pomeroy that he called at the White House and found the president, his son, and son-in-law all drunk and unfit for business and that the president kept a mistress.[147] When pressed on the statement, Pomeroy later denied that he saw the president drunk, only the members of his family.[148] There was no known denial of the mistress. In fact, Johnson had received letters from a pardon broker named Jennie A. Perry, who attempted to blackmail him with a story of an illegitimate son.

Johnson's personal bodyguard William Crook, in his memoirs, pushed the accusations of adultery a little further when he wrote, "Johnson had an amiable weakness for women, particularly for pretty women. Those of us who were on duty in corridors and in anterooms saw many evidences of this fact [149]

Chapter 7

Trial and Cover-up

Reducing the Confederacy's Exposure

The trial of the conspirators would focus the attention of the nation and divert it from the primary task of reconstruction. Stanton argued in the cabinet that the trial should begin at once in front of a military commission, where the rules of evidence would be less constricting and the outcome would be decided much faster. President Johnson agreed if Attorney General Speed concurred that, the proceeding was legal. Speed issued a one-sentence opinion, the shortest ever by an Attorney General, and the government's case began.

Much of the press, who previously sided with the Copperhead Democrats at the time disagreed with Speed's decision and insisted that the proceedings were unconstitutional. Speed elaborated on his decision, giving his reasoning and analysis to justify his position. However, it was too late. The press had already deemed the trial illegal and were not about to change their position. An adversarial relationship developed upon which critics to the administration built a bias.

The responsibility of the trial was entirely in the hands of Judge Advocate General of the Army, Joseph Holt. Like Stanton and Johnson, Holt was a War Democrat and a cabinet member for former President James Buchanan. None had supported Lincoln in 1860 but became strong Unionists when the war began. The detail of the Court consisted of: Major-General David Hunter, Major-General Lewis Wallace, Brevet Major-General Augustus V. Kautz, Brigadier-General Albion P. Howe, Brigadier-General Albert S. Foster, Brigadier-General Thomas M. Harris, Brevet Brigadier-General James A. Ekin, Colonel C.H. Tompkins, and Lieutenant-Colonel David T. Clendenin. John A. Bingham and General Henry Burnett were assistants or special Judge advocates.

The ten conspirators were John Wilkes Booth, John Surratt, Lewis Powell, David Herold, George Atzerodt, Edman Spangler, Sam Arnold, Michael O'Laughlin, Samuel Mudd, and Mary Surratt. All charged with conspiring with each other, with Booth and with persons unknown through Jefferson Davis to murder Abraham Lincoln.

Additional charges included; Powell with the attempted murder of Secretary Seward, Herold and Spangler with aiding and abetting Booth's escape. Atzerodt and O'Laughlin with laying in wait to assassinate Andrew Johnson and General Grant; Sam Arnold with aiding and abetting before the crime; Samuel Mudd with aiding and assisting in the concealment of the conspirators and Mary Surratt for aiding Booth and others with knowledge of their conspiracy. Charges against John Surratt would wait until his capture.

The backbone of the government's case against the ten conspirators came from two primary sources. The first was the testimony of Lewis Weichmann, a boarder and good friend of John Surratt, who described the times and events that occurred between the conspirators at the Surratt boarding house. The second were the statements of George Atzerodt, which gave an inside, look at the group and fit well within the framework of Weichmann's testimony. Once the framework was complete, other witnesses filled in additional details.

Unfortunately, there were no primary sources to establish their grand conspiracy case linking Jefferson Davis to the Canadian Confederate leaders, Jacob Thompson and Clement Clay, and subsequently to Booth. The case against these men was piecemealed together from testimony of witnesses willing to come forth.

Among these was Richard Montgomery, the primary Union spy working in Canada. Montgomery was a Confederate courier who gave copies of his dispatches to the Union before delivery to their final destination. He quoted Thompson, in January 1865 as saying that it would be a "blessing" to "rid the world" of Lincoln, Johnson, and Grant. Montgomery also stated that Thompson revealed that a "proposition" was made by a group of "bold, daring men" to do just that.

Spymaster George Sanders was still a free man in Canada and was determined to undermine the government's case against the leaders of the Confederacy. To do this he launched a disinformation campaign with the help of New York newspapers sympathetic to the Southern cause. He charged that Andrew Johnson was the leader of the conspiracy against Lincoln since he had the most to gain from Lincoln's death. To disrupt the trial he called upon a master con artist named Charles Dunham. Using the alias of Sanford Conover, Dunham recruited James B. Merritt, another con man, and gave him a story that would match the tale that he would give to chief prosecutor Joseph Holt. Once these lies became part of the official testimony, Sanders would expose them publicly and implicate the government.

Sanford Conover, (a.k.a. Charles A. Dunham), (a.k.a. James Watson Wallace) was formerly employed as a reporter for the *New York Tribune* in 1864. He was an outstanding liar who could tell you what you wanted to hear and concoct it in a way that made it seem plausible.

What we truly know about him is shrouded in mystery since like all good con men what he says is difficult to confirm. We do know that before the war he was involved in a number of swindles and that he was in Niagara in 1864, reporting on the peace conference staged by George Sanders. He may well have been a double agent working for both sides. His testimony showed an intimate knowledge of Confederate personnel and operations in Canada. After his testimony, he returned to Canada and conferred with Sanders.

Unlike the James Bond secret agent of fiction, most spies come from the lower parts of the societal ethics chain and sell their information not for patriotic reasons but for simple greed. They eventually become trusted informers when confirmations of their reports are received by other sources. However, in an open court where their dubious character can be exposed, their information can be easily made to look highly suspect.

For security reasons the testimony of the witnesses in the Grand Conspiracy was taken in secret session. This secrecy precaution worked in Sanders's favor implying a government cover-up. He then leaked the essential part of Conover's testimony to the Canadian press on June 5 and pointed out the inconsistencies and falsehoods. The press, of course, denounced Conover for his fabrications. In an effort to keep feeding the circus of criticism, Conover then denied he ever presented the testimony. In a stunning show of audacity, he claimed that "someone" had used his good name and lied under oath!

Conover and Merritt's testimony was decidedly false and designed to destroy the government's case, which it did. Moreover, they essentially tainted everyone who gave proof of Booth's Canadian ties and damaged anyone's testimony that came forward implicating the Confederacy to the assassination.[150]

Sanders' propaganda and counter intelligence operation successfully changed American history to the view that the Confederacy was totally innocent in the assassination of Lincoln.

Judge Joseph Holt

President Buchanan appointed Judge Holt commissioner of patents in 1857, postmaster-general, in 1859, and secretary of war in 1860.

A southern conservative who stayed loyal to the Union, he was appointed the first Judge Advocate General of the U.S. Army in 1862.

After prosecuting the conspirators in the Lincoln assassination, he was beleaguered by the smear campaign of Andrew Johnson.

Reducing the President's Exposure

With Judge Holt taking the responsibility for the trial, Secretary Stanton took it upon himself to gather evidence of the plot and review testimony with critical witnesses. In order to minimize Johnson's exposure, certain witnesses had to be careful what they said when giving their testimony. The president's first exposure was Booth's calling card:

Robert R. Jones – May 13

Q. Are you a clerk at the Kirkwood House in this city?
A. I am.
Q. Do you know anything about J. Wilkes Booth having called that day and inquired the number of Vice-President Johnson's room?
A. I do not know that he inquired about the room. I gave the card of J. Wilkes Booth to Colonel Browning, Mr. Johnson's secretary. It was put in the box. I gave him that card as it was left for Colonel Browning.
Q. Did you receive it yourself from Booth
A. I have no positive recollection of having received it, although I may have done so. [151]

The prosecution tried to get Jones to corroborate that Booth was seeking the vice-president on the day of the assassination but the clerk refuses to confirm that point. Jones testifies that Booth's card was in the box of Colonel Browning. How it got there is a mystery since Jones has no recollection of receiving it, yet he claims that it was left for Colonel Browning. Did Booth actually leave the card for Browning? At this point, it is not apparent, so the following testimony of Browning will need to address this issue.

WILLIAM A. BROWNING – May 16

Q. Will you state if you are the private secretary of the president?
A. Yes sir: I am.
Q. Were you with him on the 14th of April last?
A. I was

[Exhibiting a card to the witness]

Q. What knowledge, if any, have you of that card having been sent to him by John Wilkes Booth?

A. Between the hours of 4 and 5 o'clock in the afternoon, I left Vice President Johnson's room in the Capitol, and went to the Kirkwood House, where I was boarding with him. Upon entering, I went up to the office as was my custom, and I noticed a card in my box. Vice-President Johnson's box and mine were adjoining: mine was 67, his was 68. In 67 I noticed a card. The clerk of the hotel, Mr. Jones, handed it to me. This I recognize as the card.

Q. Will you read what is on it?

A. *Don't wish to disturb you; are you at home?*
   J. WILKES BOOTH.

[The card was offered in evidence without objection]

Q. You do not know anything about the handwriting of Booth?
A. No, Sir.
Q. You had no acquaintance whatever with J. Wilkes Booth had you?
A. Yes, sir: I had known J. Wilkes Booth when he was playing in Nashville, Tenn.; I met him there **several** times; that was the only acquaintance I had with him.
Q. Did you understand the card as sent to the president, or to yourself?
A. At the time, I attached no importance to it. I had known him in Nashville; and seeing the card I remarked to the clerk, "It is from Booth; is he playing here?" I had some idea of going to see him. I thought perhaps he might have called upon me, having known me; but when his name was connected with this affair, I looked upon it differently. It was a very common mistake in the office to put cards intended for me into the vice-president's box, and his would find their way into mine; they being together. [152]

Booth played in Nashville in February 1864 at the opening of the Woods Theatre.[153] Browning's testimony implies that he knew Booth more than casually since he saw him "several" times in that week and after reading the card, he assumed that Booth came to call on him.

Johnson rarely attended the theatre but one can assume that Browning would have introduced him to Booth one of the evenings after his performance. If Booth were smuggling for the Confederacy at this time as he claimed, it would have been in his best interests to make Johnson's acquaintance and gain a pass for his cargo. Browning would seem to have been the perfect conduit.

It is hard to believe that it was a "common mistake" for the hotel office to place correspondence for the vice-president in another person's box. The Kirkwood was a premium hotel, and Washington is a city where information is the gold standard, especially during war. It is doubtful that a mistake like this would be "common" and all we have is Browning's opinion that Booth meant the card for Johnson. However, since this exchange did not affect any of the conspirators on trial, there was no cross-examination.

The more dangerous exposures were the military passes that Booth and Herold obtained to cross the Navy Bridge that night. If Johnson was to remain above reproach, the testimony of the sentry on duty was critically important:

SERGEANT SILAS T. COBB. 3rd Massachusetts Heavy Artillery – May 16

Q. Will you state whether or not, on the night of the assassination of the President, you were on duty at what is called, I believe, The Navy–Yard Bridge?
A. I was
Q. Do you remember two men passing rapidly on horseback that night? And if you did so, at what hour was it?
A. There were three men approached me rapidly on horseback and two of them passed.
Q. At what hour?
A. Between half-past ten and eleven o'clock in the evening.
Q. Did you challenge them?
A. The sentry challenged them; and I advanced then to recognize them.
Q. Did you recognize them?

Trial and Cover-up

A. I satisfied myself that they were proper persons to pass and passed them.
Q. Do you recognize either of those persons among the prisoners here?
A. No Sir.
Q. Could you describe either of those me or both of them?
A. Yes sir, I could describe them.
Q. Do you think you would recognize them, or either of them by a photograph?
A. I think I would.

[A photograph of J. Wilkes Booth, Exhibit No. 1, was shown to the witness.]

A. That man passed first
Q. Alone?
A. Yes sir.
Q. I thought you said the three were together?
A. No sir, I did not. I said that two of them passed me; but they were not together.
Q. Did you have any conversation with him as he passed?
A. I had, for about three or four minutes.
Q. What name did he give?
A. He gave me his name as Booth
Q. What did he say? Anything special besides the desire to pass?
A. I asked him, "Who are you, sir?" He said, "My name is Booth." I asked him where he was from. He made answer, "From the city." "Where are you going?" I said; and he replied, "I am going home."

I asked him where his home was. He said it was in Charles. I understood by that he meant Charles County.

I asked him what town. He said he did not live in any town. I said, "You must live in some town." Said he, "I live close to Beantown; but do not live in the town." I asked him why he was out so late; **if he did not know the rule that persons were not allowed to pass after 9 o'clock.**

He said it was new to him; that he had had somewhere to go in the city, and it was a dark night, and he thought he would have the moon to ride home by. The moon rose that night about that time. I thought he was a proper person to pass, and I passed him.
Q. How long after him was it that the other two men came?
A. The next one came, I should think, in from five to seven or perhaps 10 minutes at the outside, not later.
Q. Did they seem to be riding rapidly or leisurely?
A. The second one did not seem to be riding so rapidly as the first, or his horse did not show signs of it as much as the first
Q. What did he say to you?

A. I asked who he was, and he said that his name was Smith, and that he was going home; that he lived at the White Plains.

I asked him how it was that he was out so late. He made use of a rather indelicate expression, and said that he had been in bad company.

Q. Was that a large or small man?

A. He was a small sized man, not a large man.

Q. Did you have a good look at his face? Was there a light?

A. I did I brought him up before the guard-house door, so that the light shone full in his face and on his horse

Q. How would he compare in size with the last man on the row in the prisoner's dock?

[The accused, David E. Herold, was directed to stand for identification.]

A. He is very near the size of the second horseman; but, I should think, taller, although I can not be sure, as he was on horseback. He had a lighter complexion than this man

Q. Did you allow him to pass after that explanation?

A. Yes, sir.

Q. What became of the other man?

A. The other man I turned back. He did not seem to have any business on the other side of the bridge that I considered of sufficient importance to pass him.

Q. Was he on horseback also?

A. Yes sir.

Q. Did he seem to be the companion of these other men?

A. No sir.

Q. Did they come up together?

A. No sir, they were some distance apart.[154]

Trial and Cover-up

The tone of Sergeant Cobb's testimony gives one the impression that he is a man who is quite sure of himself as well as one who handles his responsibilities seriously and appropriately. There was no hesitation in his story and one can assume that he practiced his testimony with Secretary Stanton before he took the stand. The Judge Advocate was careful not to ask him what criteria he used to determine that Booth and Herold were "proper" to pass. He leaves the impression that it was entirely his decision, which is the notion that Stanton wanted to leave. To a court made up of Generals and Colonels, that implication must have raised red flags. However, this impression was only for public consumption. It did not alter the fact that Booth did indeed cross the bridge.

Cobb's standing orders for the night of April 14 were not part of his testimony, so the requirement for the pass is never mentioned. However, Cobb let slip a little when he described the third horseman (Fletcher's) business as not "of sufficient importance to pass him". Fletcher was in hot pursuit of Herold, who had stolen his horse. Fletcher's reason for requesting passage certainly sounds better than Herold's excuse that he was in "bad company". Apparently, Cobb thought so as well. According to Fletcher's later testimony, Cobb offered to permit Fletcher to pass but not to allow him to return until the next morning when normal traffic would be re-established. Fletcher then decided to return to town.

Stanton's intelligence in preparing Cobb for the witness stand was apparent when Cobb, who had such a keen eye for detail, could not positively identify Herold as the second rider. As later testimony would prove, Herold was undoubtedly guilty of aiding and abetting after the commission of a felony. Cobb's testimony of how Herold crossed the bridge was insignificant to this fact. By not being able to positively identify Herold, as the second horseman there was no need for Herold's attorney to cross-examine Cobb since his testimony did not affect the case against Herold. Thus, Cobb's testimony remained unchallenged and the secret of the passes preserved.

Further evidence that Sgt. Cobb was holding back something in his testimony comes from the interrogatory conducted before the trial about his actions that night found in the war department files:

..."Said I, what is your object to be in town after nine o'clock when you have such a long road to travel?
Said he, It is a dark road and I thought if I waited a spell I would have the moon.
The moon rose about that time that night.

I said, I will pass you but I don't know as I ought to.
Said he, "Hell! I guess there'll be no trouble about that. "
He then turned and crossed the bridge...."[155]

The easiest thing for Cobb to do that night would have been to execute the orders that had been in effect for the past 30 months. Why would he suddenly take it upon himself to disobey a long standing order? If he was reluctant to pass Booth why did he?

Booth's reply holds the key. He implied there would be trouble if the sentry did not honor a pass from the vice-president. Thus, it is not surprising that this passage is not in the testimony Cobb gave in the courtroom. He replaced it with the true but limited statement:

Trial and Cover-up

"I thought he was a proper person to pass, and I passed him".

Did the sentry perhaps act within Stanton's new orders issued that day that passes were not required? His later statements refute that possibility. As he continued with his interrogatory, Cobb implied that there had been no change in orders for the bridge crossing in some time. In his recollection of his discussion with Herold, he said:

"I asked him to advance and be recognized and asked him where he was going.
He said 'Home to White Plains'.
I said 'you can't pass it is after nine o'clock, it is against the rules'.
Said he 'how long have these rules been out?'
I said 'Some time ever since I have been here.'
He said 'I didn't know that before'."[156]

It was not unusual that there was a lag between Stanton's rescinding of the passes and getting that order out to the field. That particular Friday was Good Friday, and Stanton had already given the war department the day off for religious observations. Most probably, Lincoln approved the order at the cabinet meeting, which ended sometime after 12:00 noon. With this red tape delay and the implications given in Cobb's interrogatory, it is obvious that Cobb was operating under the old orders. He said as much to Booth when he asked him:

"If he did not know the rule that persons were not allowed to pass after 9 o'clock".

If Cobb had been operating under the new orders, there would have been no need to continue securing the bridges. Sentries received Stanton's order the following day and immediately discontinued guarding the bridges.

During this same interrogatory of Cobb, we get a glimpse of how his testimony was prepared for trial. We do not know who Cobb's questioner was in this interrogatory, but it could well have been the "Iron Secretary" himself:

COBB: Between ten and fifteen minutes after this man had passed another horseman came up. He asked me if a light roan had gone along and I told him yes. He asked what kind of looking man? and I described him to him. He asked if he was going fast and I told him not very. He said "God! I'm after him." I said "How are you going to get back?" He asked "Why?" I said because_____

QUESTIONER: You are mistaken Sergeant! I will tell you, the fact is, the first man passed as you have said on a light bay horse. The next that passed was an iron-gray or roan horse with a long tail, single footed pacer as they were called. After the roan horse had passed a short time, a third horseman came up and asked you if the roan horse had passed, and you said yes. He then asked you if you could go after him, you said yes, He asked if he could come back and you said no.

COBB: That is true in relation to the three men.[157]

It is very curious that the questioner seems to have cut off Cobb just as he was about to reveal the reason the third horseman (Fletcher) could not come back over the bridge. The reason is clear that although Cobb would bend the rules for a man in hot pursuit of a thief, he could not vouch for his fellow sentries on the other end of the bridge nor the man who would relieve him at midnight. They would follow the rules that after nine o'clock one needed a pass. Stanton obviously wanted no mention of a pass to be brought up anywhere in any testimony.

If Cobb let Booth and Herold cross the bridge without a pass, he was clearly derelict in his duty and subject to severe disciplinary action. Yet the war department did not bother to order an investigation of his conduct. In the Civil War, soldiers could and were in fact, executed for such gross neglect; Cobb did not even merit a reprimand. In fact, the only reason we know of Cobb's name was to give testimony in the trial.

Trial and Cover-up 227

The names of his fellow sentries on duty that night, which could have corroborated Cobb's testimony, were never recorded. The orders for his company, 3rd Mass. Heavy Artillery, from March 4 through July 8, 1865, are missing from the war department records. General Augur's non-action in this case could only mean that Cobb did indeed follow orders and both riders had the required passes, confirming Atzerodt's statement. Since there was no formal investigation of Cobb's actions, no written record exists for Augur's reasoning on this matter.[158]

After passing the two main dangers the only man who could damage the president was Atzerodt. His defense attorney Doster saw an opportunity to prove that Atzerodt never intended to kill the vice-president, but he needed Johnson's testimony to corraborate his client's story. Johnson was not about to give the man who held the key to his political career an opportunity to use it. Therefore, Johnson gave no testimony in the trial and ignored the subpoena given to him.

William A. Browning

Courtesy of James O -Iall Research Center

William A. Browning had been Andrew Johnson's private secretary since 1861. The son of a tailor, his testimony in the trial suggested that Booth's calling card was actually a mailbox mix-up and diffused its political impact.

Nine months after testifying, Browning died suddenly at the age of thirty in Washington D.C.. Johnson's son Robert then filled his position as secretary.

In his memoirs about the trial Doster said:

> "Atzerodt from the time I first saw him until he was executed told the same story which he afterwards told in his confession – that he knew nothing of the assassination plot, until 2 hours before it was carried out and that he refused to have anything to do with it. Being in as far as he was he had to keep up appearances. His part was to kill Mr. Johnson, he said. He had ample opportunity but did not intend to do it. His defense lay mainly in showing this: that he had abundant occasion to carry out such an intention had it existed, that the President (Johnson) was in his room all night with his *door open*. The only witness who could have shown this was the President himself. I subpoenaed him to appear and testify, but he did not come. I issued another subpoena. He then sent me word through his private secretary (General Mussey) that he did not intend to come.
>
> I pressed Mr. Johnson no further, for I did not care to irritate the very man who could pardon the prisoner, and also must have known that to Atzerodt's unwillingness he was indebted for his life. The sequel showed, however, that he did not consider this."[159]

The practice of presidents ignoring subpoenas began with Thomas Jefferson when he insisted that the president could not maintain independence of the judiciary if "he were subject to the *commands* of the latter". This of course presents a problem. Who would put the president in jail for contempt? For this reason, scholars argue that the president can only be viewed a constitutional officer rather than as a private individual. Thus, when Johnson sought to claim "the same rights as every other citizen" during his impeachment trial, Benjamin Butler opposed his claim. Butler argued that the constitutional rights of a president are secondary to the presidential responsibilities of the officeholder

Doster tried to confirm Atzerodt's story of the unlocked door through the cross-examination of Leonard Farwell, but Farwell's testimony was inconclusive.

I believe the door was locked, but am not certain. I can not say whether I took hold of the handle or not. I did not see any one apparently lying in wait near Mr. Johnson's door.[160]

Trial and Cover-up

Although Doster could have embarrassed the president by pointing out to the press that he refused to testify, he clearly thought it was in the best interests of his client not to do so. He may have even thought he had an understanding with Johnson that the president would be magnanimous with the fate of his client because he refused to perform the murderous act.

> "There was nothing about this prisoner's appearance to win favor with a court of military men. He looked demoralized and low. During the period that elapsed between his sentence and execution, he oscillated between a condition of moaning stupor, kneeling and crying, "Oh! Oh! Oh!" and again begging in piteous accents to know whether there was no hope at all. It was heart rending to see. He appeared to think that his confession to Marshal McPhail and to Captain Monroe had secured his pardon". [161]

In Doster's closing arguments, he maintained that Atzerodt was not an accessory to the crime; neither before nor after the fact. He argued that to be guilty before the fact he would have had to procure, counsel, or command another to commit the crime. Since he had only agreed to help kidnap the president, the government needed to prosecute him under a new indictment. He could not be found guilty of being an accessory after the fact because he did not "receive, relieve, comfort or assist the felon" after the crime was committed.

Doster made a good legal argument, but the prosecution believed the kidnapping and assassination plot were one in the same, and since Atzerodt was aware of the plot to kill Lincoln and got drunk rather than tell the police, they found him guilty.

The end of the seven-week trial came on June 29, 1865, and the Military Commission began to review the evidence and make their decision. Death sentences required a vote of six members. A guilty verdict needed only a majority vote of the nine-member commission. The next day, the Commission reached its verdicts finding each of the prisoners guilty of at least one of the conspiracy charges. Four of the prisoners (Mary Surratt, Lewis Powell, George Atzerodt, and David Herold) were sentenced "to be hanged by the neck until he [or she] be dead." Samuel Arnold, Dr. Samuel Mudd and Michael O'Laughlin received a sentence of "hard labor for life, at such place at the president shall direct." Edman Spangler received a six-year sentence.

The decision to condemn Atzerodt while giving prison sentences to Arnold and O'Laughlin was somewhat puzzling. All three agreed to a kidnapping conspiracy, none agreed to a murder plot yet Atzerodt received the death sentence, taking his knowledge of the plot with him.

The decision to condemn Mary Surratt was the result of a compromise within the commission deciding her fate. When the first option to acquit her failed, they decided to render the same verdict on her as they did the other conspirators with a recommendation to the president of mercy for the woman. Judge Bingham wrote the petition for clemency and had it signed by the majority of the commission. The petition recommended to the president—that because of "her sex and age"-- he reduce Mary Surratt's punishment to life in prison.

Judge Advocate Holt forwarded the trial record along with the findings, the petition and the sentences of the Commission to President Johnson for his review. The petition was to become a controversial issue for many years. After reviewing the records for some two hours with Holt, Johnson approved the sentences of the Commission, including the death sentence for Mary Surratt. Johnson set the date of the executions for the *next day*.

Trial and Cover-up 231

The verdict to hang Mary Surratt was a surprise to most Americans. She would be the first woman ever executed under U.S. law. Many expected clemency in her case since the primary testimony against her was by a man who was habitually drunk. Surratt's lawyers hurriedly prepared a petition for habeas corpus that evening claiming that Mrs. Surratt was a citizen and not subject to a sentence by a military court. At 2:00 a.m., the next morning Judge Andrew Wylie of the Supreme Court of the District of Columbia issued the requested writ. When he received the court order, President Johnson quashed any effort to save Surratt from an afternoon hanging by issuing an order suspending the writ of habeas corpus "in cases such as this". General Hancock and Attorney General Speed went before Judge Wylie and explained that they could not bring Mary Surratt to him because their orders from the president to execute the prisoners superseded his order. Wiley, upset by Johnson's actions, realized that he could not compel the production of the prisoners held by a division of infantry.

The president twice refused to see Mary's priest, Father Walter. Walter bore with him a statement by Powell that Mrs. Surratt was completely ignorant of the assassination plot. Anna Surratt was prostrate with grief on the stairs of the White House begging for an audience but was refused admittance by Senators Preston King, James Lane, and soldiers with rifles and fixed bayonets.

Finally, Adele Cutts Douglas, widow of Senator Stephen Douglas arrived on the scene to plead Mary's case. Mrs. Douglas, the grandniece of Dolly Madison, was the premier Washington hostess and socialite at that time. She brushed aside the bayonets of the soldiers who backed off and let her pass to the president. Twice she came through the line to see the president, and twice Johnson refused to commute the sentence.

General R.D. Mussey, Johnson's private secretary, remembered that, Johnson told him he had approved the sentences and ordered the execution for Friday. Mussey asked him if that wasn't a short time to give the condemned for preparation. "He admitted that it was, but said that they had ever since the trial began for' preparation'. His design in making the time short was to give less opportunity for criticism, remonstrance, etc." Mussey was sure that Johnson told him of the recommendation for mercy, but said that sex was no proper plea saying, "*there had not been women enough hanged in this war.*" [162]

Andrew Johnson had the misfortune of always seeming to be in a state of ill health whenever a stressful or defining moment of his presidency occurred. Reportedly, Johnson had been "sick" during the last week of the trial and was not receiving visitors. Rumors continued to swirl that he had returned to the bottle and had been in an intoxicated state during that time.

Coincidently, this was the same time that the defense in the trial was presenting their case and calling their own witnesses. If the stress of the trial was contributing to Johnson's illness, he certainly knew the cure by sanctioning the executions to take place on the next day. Atzerodt's defense attorney William Doster had no doubts about the motive behind Johnson's swift and merciless decision.

> "The character of Mr. Johnson, as afterwards revealed, shows more clearly why these people were summarily hanged. His obstinacy and self-will when opposed by appeals for mercy or magnanimity of sentiment carried him to the opposite extreme of rigor. The suspicion that he might be one of them made him hasten to show by severity that his hands were clean". [163]

The Two Notes Theory

Three weeks after the assassination, Johnson reviewed the evidence compiled by Joseph Holt and the war department. The investigation showed that both Booth and John Surratt were agents of the Confederacy and reported to superiors in Canada. John Surratt was still at large and hiding underground somewhere near Montreal.

The primary links between Jefferson Davis and the assassination were Secretary of State Judah Benjamin's appointment of Jacob Thompson; the former Buchanan Secretary of the Interior, as head of the Canadian confederates; and John Surratt, as Benjamin's most trusted courier. The war activities of the Canadian confederates were well documented, and Holt was continuing to gather testimony to prove the grand conspiracy.

Benjamin had escaped to England, and Union intelligence officer General George Sharpe was sent overseas to trace his activities and determine who George Sanders' contacts were in London. The president had seen enough to convince him of their involvement. On May 2, 1865, Johnson issued a proclamation offering a reward of $100,000 and lesser sums for the Canadian cabinet of Jacob Thompson, William Cleary, George N. Sanders, Clement C. Clay, Beverly Tucker, and others for complicity in the assassination of Abraham Lincoln.

In an effort to blunt Johnson's allegation, Sanders and Tucker decided to make their case in the court of public opinion using the New York newspapers as their main outlet. Taking advantage of the safety provided by Canada to launch their attacks, the Confederates had a haven for their propaganda campaign that the government could not respond to without jeopardizing the trial in progress.

In an open letter to the *New York Times* on May 7, before the beginning of the conspiracy trial, George Sanders and Beverly Tucker responded to Johnson's accusation:

"Your proclamation is a living, burning lie known to be such by yourself and your surroundings," wrote Sanders. They then proceeded to defend themselves by implicating Johnson himself in the plot. Tucker wrote:

> "... is it impossible that Booth may have met Mr. Johnson in that lower circle they were both known to frequent, and thus formed an intimacy which a common vice begets? Andrew Johnson, let it be borne in mind, has been noted for many years past as an almost frenzied aspirant for the Presidency. All the arts and appliances which the fruitful brain of the unscrupulous demagogue could invent have been exhausted to attain this goal of his audacious ambition.... Andrew Johnson is the only solitary individual of the thirty five million souls in the land, who could possibly realize any interest or benefit from the perpetration of this deed, and that Booth was not captured alive, as he unquestionably could have been...leaves behind this bloody tragedy a fearful mystery."

This was powerful prose, which effectively mixed truth with innuendo. Johnson was very vulnerable to these types of attacks. He became vice-president by a brokered convention, and as a Southern man became president through the crime of a Southerner. Johnson ignored Tucker's implications, but his political enemies would soon echo these arguments.

The denials of Sanders and Tucker had an effect on the future trials of Confederates. Johnson, who was quick to approve the military trials of the conspirators, as well as Henry Wirz of Andersonville prison infamy, suddenly was no longer willing to approve the military trial of Jefferson Davis. Tucker's criticism of the "concealed manner in which the whole of judicial examination is conducted" ended the secret testimony recorded in the conspiracy trial and opened the trial to the public.

In defining Booth's relationship with Johnson, Tucker also questioned the reason Booth visited him on the day of the assassination:

"...What, then was the motive of his call and how came Booth to address the Vice-President of the United States in words of such familiarity...

'I do not wish to disturb you, but would be glad to have an interview.

(Signed,) John Wilkes Booth'

These are words of strange and mysterious import and are not to be lightly set aside in so great a matter as unmeaning and insignificant."

The note that Tucker quotes does not match the note presented in the trial. However, it does match an article published in the *New York Tribune* on April 16, 1865, which ignited a firestorm of speculation about the new president.

> **Attempt on the Vice - President**
> Special Dispatch to the N.Y. Tribune
> Washington April 16, 1865
>
> We have been shown the card sent to Vice-President Johnson's room at the Kirkwood House the afternoon of the day Mr. Lincoln was assassinated. It bears in legible pencil writing the following:
>
> "I do not wish to disturb you, but would be glad to have an interview. J. Wilkes Booth."
>
> Mr. Johnson, happening to be out at the time, did not discover till this morning that so suggestive a card had been lying on his table for these two memorable days...

This card, written in pencil and shown to the reporter of the story, never surfaced again. In the trial the card, that Johnson's secretary Browning swore that he found in his box said:

"I do not wish to disturb you, are you at home".

In addition, Browning gave no testimony that Johnson ever saw the card that was in Browning's box. Browning said that he assumed Booth intended the message for him. How then did this different card end up on Johnson's table for "two memorable days"?

The easiest explanation was that the report was a complete falsehood. The reporter never saw such a card, and it never found its way into Johnson's room. However, considering the controversy raised by the article, it is hard to believe that Stanton would not insist upon an immediate retraction of the report. Since Stanton did not deny the dispatch, we have to presume that he could not do so. One of the investigators must have shown the card to the reporter. However, Stanton could seize the card as evidence and present another card at the trial. Stanton's suppression of Booth's "diary" from the trial is ample proof that this card could just as easily been concealed.

In that case, the apparent explanation would be that Booth wrote two notes. His first note to Johnson would have been to ask him for an interview in order to discuss obtaining travel passes a day or two before the assassination as correlated by Atzerodt. This would explain how the note ended up in Johnson's possession on his table.

The revelation that Johnson actually met with Booth prior to the assassination would have been political dynamite and a death knell for his presidency. Combined with Johnson's Southern heritage and the disfavor he created by his inebriated inauguration speech, the country may well have been torn asunder. Tucker's use of the quote confirmed in Johnson's mind that Sanders and Tucker knew of the plot. Although Tucker may have been only quoting the newspaper report, Johnson was convinced that Tucker knew more. Johnson would later issue a pardon to all the rebels including Jefferson Davis. The one rebel Johnson never pardoned was Beverly Tucker.

The second card presented at the trial has both confounded and tantalized authors and historians for generations. The consensus through the years has been that the card was a red herring left by Booth in a poor attempt to implicate Johnson. However, for a man like Booth who was such a cunning planner, that opinion seems very weak. Especially, since at the time Booth left the note the evidence shows that he believed he had an assassin lined up for Johnson.

The public revelation that Booth had left the first calling card for Johnson presented a clear and present danger to the government that needed explanation. The government was already in denial that Johnson ever knew the assassin. The presence of this card would refute that assertion. The answer to the dilemma was a classic misdirection ploy.

Stanton confiscated the card to present later into evidence at Booth's trial, telling the press that the card supported the case for a larger conspiracy.[164] However, with Booth dead, there was no longer a legal need to present the card in court. Yet, the public knowledge of the card's existence forced Stanton to provide a plausible explanation. Substitution of the second card into the trial allowed Browning to defuse the situation by giving his explanation of a mere mailbox mix-up.

With Stanton in control of all the evidence, who could dispute that the card presented at the trial was the only card found? Had the *New York Tribune* not broken the story of the original card it is likely that the card presented in the trial would also have disappeared since it had no bearing on the outcome of the trial.

In 1959, Lincoln assassination writer Theodore Roscoe speculated (shockingly for the time) that perhaps the vice-president was entertaining a woman that evening which would account for his retiring early to his room.[165] The "cherchez la femme" theory of this calling card fits nicely with the "two notes" theory and ties together other loose ends.

We know that Booth ordered Atzerodt, at approximately 7:30 p.m. to assassinate Johnson at roughly 10:00 that night. What we do not know is how Booth was certain that Johnson would be in his room at that time. The carriage accident put Seward into a bedridden condition so Booth knew where the secretary of war state would be. Atzerodt also tells us that Booth charmed information from Seward's chambermaid (statement #15). Likewise, from testimony of the owners of the two theatres, Booth had suggested sending an invitation for Lincoln to be at one of the playhouses. For Booth to ascertain that Johnson would be waiting in his room at his hotel he most certainly would have had to make a previous contact with the vice-president.

Despite the benefit of inheriting Lincoln's office, there is no evidence that links Johnson to the plot. The fact that Booth planned to kill him is ample proof that he did not plan to have the vice-president accede to the presidency. However as Tucker alluded to in his rebuttal letter, Johnson was a man with a sexual appetite. There is far too much innuendo in the record to believe that he was strictly monogamous. The father of five children, his wife was an invalid, suffering from consumption throughout the war and was still in Tennessee at the time of the assassination. Hamilton Howard, son of Senator Jacob Howard, claimed in his book Civil War Echoes (1907) that detectives learned that when Johnson was Military Governor of Tennessee, he and Booth kept a couple of sisters as mistresses and were seen in each other's company.[166]

Among the letters found in Booth's trunk was a cache from actor and friend, William Donaldson. This man could quite possibly be the same Donaldson referred to by Atzerodt in statement # 3. Donaldson wanted to collaborate with Booth in setting up a brothel in the rebel capital. Apparently, he was confident that he and Booth, between them, knew enough 'talent' to make the place a high-class establishment.

Trial and Cover-up 239

With Richmond occupied by Union soldiers for the near future, it looked like the sort of get rich quick scheme that would appeal to the financially strapped Booth. In statement #10, Atzerodt states that Booth "proposed to go to Richmond and open the theatre" This may have been Booth's original reason for requesting the passes before impulsively deciding to become a "patriot" rather than a "businessman".

Although Atzerodt does not say when Booth and Herold received their passes from Johnson, it is probable that it occurred on Wednesday April 12, before Booth heard Lincoln's speech that evening. Atzerodt told Col. Wells that on Thursday at 10:30 am, he met with Booth at his room in the National Hotel where he "told me to go to the Kirkwood and get a pass from Vice-President Johnson. He said he would be there with a man to recommend me." [167] The man who would recommend him was most probably Booth's friend and Johnson's secretary William Browning.

Booth carefully set the stage for his tragedy leaving clues to implicate both friends and foes. Looking at the drama from the author's viewpoint it seems clear that Booth deliberately put his calling card in Browning's box not to incriminate the vice-president in Lincoln's assassination but to implicate Browning in the expected murder of Andrew Johnson. Browning's testimony at the trial was a smokescreen to obscure the obvious and offer a plausible alternative to the card found on Johnson's desk.

It is easy to imagine that in order to thank Johnson for the passes he received; Booth would offer to provide some company for him on Friday night. Paying for political string pulling with sexual favors has long been a second currency in Washington. Johnson's companion for the evening would have most likely been Ella Starr Turner.

Ella was a "hooker" (in the original sense of the term). Her mother was an established Baltimore madam who arrived in Washington in 1858. Her sister Mollie moved from Norfolk Virginia when her mother purchased a house on Ohio Avenue to run the family business. Ella was Booth's mistress and seen many times at the National Hotel[168]. The house was in the area known in Washington as Hooker's Division after the women who plied their trade on the soldiers in General Fighting Joe Hooker's army.

With Ella working on the inside, Booth would not only be assured of Johnson's whereabouts but could have also made sure the door was unlocked, making it easier for the assassin as Atzerodt claimed to his attorney.

Later that evening after learning of the assassination, Turner realized that Booth had duped her. Rather than face a government persecution and the rage of the crowd in the street, she went to her bedroom and placed a photo of John Wilkes Booth under her pillow, soaked a rag in chloroform and pressed her head against it trying to commit suicide. A doctor was able to revive her. Scared and depressed she did not bother to thank her rescuers for saving her life.[169]

She need not have worried. No one in the government would have dared to disclose that on the night of the assassination Andrew Johnson was entertaining John Booth's mistress. Leonard Farwell, wrote that he heard Johnson rise from his bed when he informed him of the attack on Lincoln. He never stated that Johnson was alone, nor would he confirm or deny that Johnson's door was unlocked as Atzerodt claimed.

Trial and Cover-up

On May 2, *The New York Times* reported the arrest of nearly 300 people on the suspicion of conspiracy. People who had no more than a casual acquaintance with Booth found themselves imprisoned and interrogated for days. However, Ella Starr Turner merits a scarce mention in the immense dossier assembled by the war department on the Lincoln murder case.[170] Although authorities found a letter from her in Booth's room along with the letter from Sam Arnold, Arnold was the one put on trial for conspiracy.

When officers arrived at the Starr boarding house at 5:30 a.m. Saturday morning April 15, officers took the freshly revived Ella and all the inhabitants to the Justice of the Peace for formal depositions. Police were very interested in questioning her since they had found the following letter in Booth's room.

My darling Baby,   Washington Feb 7th 1865

Please call this evening or as soon as you receive this note.
I will not detain you for five minutes – for gods sake come.

                                                                                      Yours Truly,   E.T.
If you will not come write a note the reason why   [171]

The war department never identified the woman in this photograph found among Booth's possessions. Speculation was that she was just another unidentified actress friend of Booth's.

She may also have been his Washington consort, the mysterious redhead, Ella Starr Turner.

The following is her statement to police.

> My name is Nellie Starr. My native place is Baltimore, State of Maryland. I have been in Washington D.C. since a week before Christmas. I am about nineteen or twenty years of age. I am not married. I have known John Wilkes Booth for about three years; he was in the habit of visiting the house where I live kept by Miss Eliza Thomas, number 62 Ohio Avenue in the city of Washington. The house is one of prostitution. I have never heard him speak unfavorably of the president. I heard him speak of the president as being a good man just as other people did. I do not distinctly remember how he was dressed, when I last saw him; I think he had on dark clothes. I think he wore a slough hat. I do not think it is the one shown me by the District Attorney. I know nothing about the case. I know nothing about whom he associated with, as I have not been on good terms with him for over a year. The last time I seen Mr. Booth was, two weeks ago at the said house. [Signed] Nellie Starr, Ella Starr, Fannie Harrison [172]

Ella's letter to her 'darling Baby' does not sound like an address that one would use for someone with whom one 'was not on good terms with for over a year. If she heard Booth speak of the president as 'a good man', she was probably the only one. Booth made a point of denouncing Lincoln in almost every city he played. Her entire deposition is an obvious whitewash to keep whatever she knew quiet. She signed the letter with three aliases, none of which used the surname Turner to disassociate her from the E.T. letter found in Booth's room. Government investigators recorded nothing else.

The trial began the day after the defendant's attorneys received the charges against their clients. With no time given to prepare a proper case, all that the defense attorneys knew of Ella was that she was a one-time girlfriend of Booth's and her one page denial of knowing anything. It is not surprising then that Atzerodt's attorney did not subpoena Turner to take the stand in the trial. Doster admits that he was ignorant of what she could offer as testimony as the reason he did not call her to testify:

> "The actor Booth (Edwin) had been subpoenaed on behalf of the prisoners to show the influence his brother exerted over weaker minds. He came but said he knew less of his brother, probably, than any one- that he had nothing to do with him for years. Booth's mistress, Ella Turner, a rather pretty, light haired, little woman was also on hand. But that sort of evidence was not very much to the point and they were dismissed without examination."[173]

The "cherchez la femme" and "two notes" theories are of course speculation. No one can be certain after almost one-hundred and fifty years after the event. However, they account for how Booth knew that Johnson was in his room that evening, while the rest of Washington was celebrating the end of the war throughout the wee hours of the morning.

They also offer a better explanation for Turner's attempted suicide that night rather than assuming the Victorian premise that she was merely a brokenhearted harlot atoning for her sins. Two known historical events ignored in the official narrative.

The notion that Booth merely assumed that Johnson would be alone in his room is simply not conceivable and suppressing any evidence of a connection between Booth and Johnson became imperative to preserve the function of government.

Johnson's usual excuse that he was sick was not plausible to explain why he was in his room. He seemed to be in good health when meeting with Lincoln that afternoon. Neither was he a man who would rather sit alone than drink with friends. To some of Johnson's early defenders, reading a book by gaslight seemed the only scenario that justified his being alone in his room that evening. So, even though the action is completely out of character for Andrew Johnson, to some of his early biographers that is what they speculated that he was probably doing during those critical hours.

It is far more likely that Johnson was alone in his ten-foot square room because he was expecting a visitor, most probably a female visitor. Booth had smartly directed each assassin and victim. If he was going to decapitate the government, he could leave nothing to chance. His late attempt to intimidate George Atzerodt into being an executioner was his only mistake.

Turner was not the only woman in Booth's life whom Stanton helped keep secret. Officially, there were pictures of at least five women found on Booth's body, but Stanton did not release their names to the public for fear of a backlash.

The pictures were reported to be all actress friends of Booth. It wasn't until many years later that one of the pictures was identified as his fiancée, Lucy Hale. When the clerk of the Aquidneck Hotel reported Booth's visit with Lucy there on April 3, investigators covered the trail by cutting out the "J.W. Booth & Lady" from the hotel register.

Early on the morning of April 27, Booth's body returned to Washington aboard the ship *Montauk* and met at the dock by two naval officers, a heavily veiled woman, and the former head of the Senate Committee on Naval affairs, John P. Hale. When shown the body, the woman reportedly shrieked and threw herself across Booth. An officer cut off a lock of Booth's hair and gave it to the woman. Since there was no official record of the ring that Chester identified either being in Booth's room or taken from his body, she probably received that as well.

Stanton was furious that the story of the mysterious veiled woman was making the rounds in Washington. People were bound to assume that she came aboard with Hale, and presume that the woman was his daughter. He immediately ordered that no one could board the ship without a pass signed by him and Secretary of the Navy Welles. To counter the story later reports said that the woman was an assistant to Surgeon General Barnes who was performing the autopsy. However, since her actions were hardly those of a nurse, the story became that the woman was a mistress of the assassin brought aboard to identify him. That was too close to the truth, so the final story was an admission that there was a woman on board but it had nothing to do with the assassin. She was merely a visitor on the ship.[174]

The truth of the Booth-Hale love affair stayed under the cloak of secrecy until 1878, when a Chicago newspaper finally broke the story that official Washington hushed up.

Jacob Thompson

There was little love lost between Stanton and Jacob Thompson head of Confederate clandestine operations in Canada. In Buchanan's cabinet, Stanton watched him play a double game advising Buchanan as Secretary of Interior and then passing information to the secessionists.

The day of the assassination Lincoln was told of his whereabouts but prevented Stanton from arresting him. Stanton reversed the order hours after Lincoln's death. Thompson escaped to England with over $600,000.

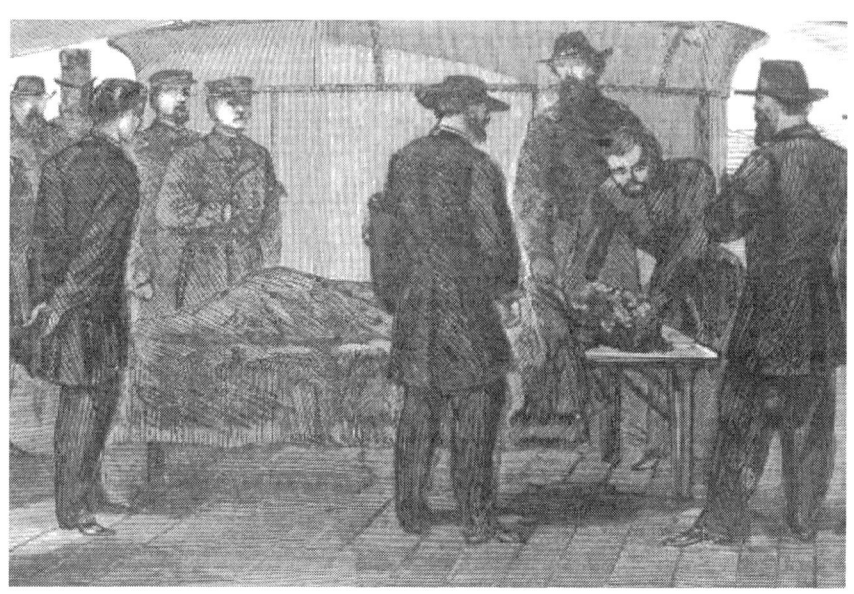

Harper's Weekly sketch of Booth's post-mortem examination aboard the monitor *Montauk*

Chapter 8

A Critical Rupture -1865

Presidential Reconstruction

As Andrew Johnson took over as president, he quickly sized up his assets and reviewed his primary tasks. His first decision was to retain Lincoln's cabinet in order to reassure the nation that Lincoln's policies would continue. This was a collection of various factions of the Republican Party, but all were very capable men. Among them were Hugh McCulloch, the newly appointed Secretary of Treasury; Gideon Welles, the Secretary of the Navy; and two of the greatest to ever hold their positions--William Seward, Secretary of State; and Edwin Stanton, Secretary of War.

The new president asked for an appraisal of the reconstruction progress in the South. Lincoln's first attempt at this project began in December 1863, as large portions of states gradually came under the control of the Union army. Working closely with Stanton, who was in the process of setting up rules and regulations for an Occupation Army, Lincoln announced his first attempt at a Reconstruction plan in a supplement of his annual message to Congress.

In it he offered a full pardon with restoration of most property rights to all persons implicated in the rebellion who would swear to thereafter uphold the Constitution, the Emancipation Proclamation, the Union, and all laws pertaining to slaves. This excluded only a few of the major rebellion offenders from this plan.

He also announced that when any State's number of voters equal to one tenth of those who participated in the 1860 election had taken the oath of allegiance, a state government, republican in form, could be re-established. Once done, he would recognize it and grant it Federal protection. He included an olive branch to Southern whites allowing them to solve their own race problem, provided their state governments were fair in relation to Negroes.

This was the plan that was currently in effect for Louisiana, Tennessee, and Arkansas. It proved to be a powerful war weapon helping sap the Southern will to fight throughout the military campaign of 1864. It enticed many captured rebel prisoners to become "galvanized Yankees". As propaganda, it was a very effective tool and worked hand in hand with the military victories in that year. However, it had not brought the political results in the affected States that Lincoln had hoped, and with the war now at an end, it was time to transfer the military power he had into political results.

In his last cabinet meeting, he had asked Stanton to present a plan for Virginia and North Carolina. In an effort to minimize the problems that beset the current plan, Stanton proposed dividing the South into military districts under the control of military governors. This would assure protection of the freedmen and hasten the reshaping of the South into political entities that would be acceptable to Congress. Lincoln asked his advisors to consider to the plan. At that meeting, Welles objected to the linking of Virginia and North Carolina since it would be an affront to the newly reunited state of Virginia's Unionist government of Francis Pierpont. Lincoln granted Welles the point and asked Stanton to change the plan separating the two States and they would review it again at their next meeting.

At Johnson's first cabinet meeting on Sunday, April 16, Stanton did not have copies of the revised plan but explained it to Johnson and members of the cabinet. That evening at the war department Stanton showed newly made copies of the plan to Sumner, Schuyler Colfax, Henry Dawes, and other members of Congress to gauge their reactions. At this meeting, Sumner declared that there could be no freedom for the Negro without the right to vote. He could not support the Reconstruction effort without this guarantee. At the time, Stanton did not feel that was necessary, knowing that including the provision would cause a split in the Republican Party. However, Sumner and Speaker of the House Colfax continued to lobby hard until Stanton inserted a clause in his North Carolina plan stating that all "loyal citizens" could vote.

On May 9, Stanton's North Carolina plan came up before the cabinet. Realizing that this proposal would likely be the pattern for reconstruction in the remaining States, the members carefully scrutinized it and decided that the main points of Lincoln's December '63 proposal should continue. The president would appoint a provisional governor. This official would see to it that a convention with elected delegates would draw up a new or revised State constitution that provides for a republican form of government. The State would then be able to resume its relationship in the Union. The clause that would allow "loyal citizens" to vote caused a split in the cabinet. Welles, Seward, Usher, and McCulloch opposed it while Stanton, Speed, and Harlan favored the clause. Johnson took no part in the discussion but reserved his decision for later.

On May 29, Johnson issued the proclamation without the "loyal citizens" clause. He had decided that he would not force Negro suffrage upon the South. He purported it to be a minor issue that would delay the reconstruction. Since the freedmen were economically bound to the big plantation owners, he felt that wealthy landowners would be able to control them politically.

He also decided that the terms of Lincoln's amnesty and pardons were too generous, and he would issue fourteen new exceptions to them. These included all civil and military officers of the Confederacy, disloyal Northerners, violators of Lincoln's 1863 Amnesty Proclamation, and Southerners who owned more than $20,000 worth of property and aided in the rebellion. The plantation aristocrats were a particular source of Johnson's ire. He believed they were the backbone of the rebellion and were responsible for engineering the secession against the will of the majority. He also kept Lincoln's declaration that the States repudiate their secessionist ordinances, disclaim the debts of the Confederacy, and ratify the Thirteenth Amendment.

Johnson's new amnesty exceptions resulted in the greatest emigration in United States history. Over ten thousand Southerners left the country for Mexico, Canada, and Brazil. The majority of these people were military leaders, government officials, and aristocrats. This sudden depletion of leadership would have dire effects in the coming reconstruction.

Before the announcement, Senator Sumner had a number of interviews with Johnson during the first month of his presidency. Along with Chief Justice Chase, they urged Johnson to support immediate Negro suffrage. The president listened repeatedly to the Senator and assured him "there is no difference between us." When Johnson issued his proclamation for the reconstruction of North Carolina, making no provisions for suffrage; Sumner and the Radicals were stunned to learn about it through the newspapers. Johnson intended to restore the States on his own authority without calling Congress into a special session and hand them a fait accompli by their next legislative session in December.

Johnson lacked Lincoln's political sagacity when functioning as a party leader nor did he give much thought to preparing public opinion. Throughout the summer and fall, Radical leaders, such as Davis, Stevens, Sumner, and Wade, lobbied him to slow the Reconstruction efforts and give Congress an opportunity to participate, but the president cold-shouldered them. Once Johnson made a decision, he would never revisit the subject nor take responsibility for the consequences. The reaction to Johnson's Presidential Reconstruction was not surprising. Democrats and Conservatives were lavish with praise. After four years of war, the nation was tired of fighting and bickering. Republican newspapers, aware of the possible split in the party that was occurring, criticized the Radicals for their opposition.

One man who was particularly upset by Johnson's proclamation was Congressman George Boutwell of Massachusetts. As one of the chief proponents of Negro suffrage, he favored the "suffrage-before-restoration" formula and disagreed with Johnson's idea that a State had a right to readmission without congressional approval. After conferring with the president, Johnson assured Boutwell that no reorganization of other States would occur until the experiment in North Carolina was complete, declaring the measures "only tentative" and "experimental."

This assurance calmed Boutwell's immediate fears but he warned Johnson that a continuance of the policy would divide the Republican Party. Boutwell later noted, "I did not then realize that my closing observation was an encouragement to the president to pursue the policy against which I was protesting." Johnson quickly violated his pledge, announcing the reorganization of seven more Southern states in June and July.

Johnson was not a true Republican Party man. Although he owed his presidency to the Republican Party, he enjoyed keeping his lone wolf status and playing both sides against each other. As a War Democrat, he came into the Republican-Union to expand the party's base in the South. As Governor of Tennessee, Johnson had constantly battled a hostile legislature, and as Military Governor, he had ruled without a legislature. He was not a man who relied on diplomacy but on bullheaded determination to achieve his goals. What Johnson wanted most was to be president elected in his own right. How successfully he achieved reunification with the South would determine his goal.

Prominent Democrats praised the new president and pledged their support. The war had split the party, and the conservative Democrats remaining did not want to give up their power positions and work under the old Whigs and Republican leaders. Neither did they want to join hands with the Copperhead wing of the party whom they blamed for their downfall. With Johnson committed to the reunification of the South, Democrats felt the resurgence of their party and rallied to Johnson's standard.

Throughout this summer honeymoon period, he flirted with top Democrats over publicly committing himself to the Democratic Party. He convinced them that it was in their best interests to back his policies for the speedy restoration of the South. The sooner the restoration of the South, the sooner the Democrats would be back in power. In return, the Democrats wanted him to dismiss both Seward and Stanton, the prime Republican leaders in the cabinet, and he gave the impression he would do so as soon as it was practical. However, he was not ready to split from the Republicans at that point. The moderates of the Republican Party pledged their support for his program and preserved Republican unity for the time being.

New York Democratic leader, Samuel Barlow, became aware that Johnson had an insane backup plan to create his own personal party if he could not get what he wanted from the Republicans and Democrats, but he was not overly concerned. A veteran of party politics, he foresaw Johnson's coming clash with the Republicans, and he was willing to play along and bide his time. He was confident that when the conflict occurred, either Johnson would be forced to join the Democrats on Barlow's terms or he would be left "powerless outside of it". Unfortunately, the window of opportunity to create a coalition of disparate members of the two main parties would close quickly. In the summer of 1865, however, in the glow of peace and with Congress not in session, all seemed possible, and Johnson was the master of his future.

Montgomery Blair, working to reunite Johnson with the Democrats, wrote Barlow assurances of Johnson's real position. He would be stiff on the punishment of traitors only for the present to prevent a break with the Radicals. He committed himself against interference for suffrage in the South and meant to restore the Southern states to their old places in Congress, which would assure the dominance of the Democratic Party.[175]

Troubles with the Reconstruction program started early that summer when Treasury Secretary McCulloch complained that he could not find enough qualified Southern whites to fill the revenue offices. This was due in large part to Johnson's additional fourteen exemptions to Lincoln's amnesty offering. To remedy this situation, Johnson began issuing pardons in wholesale lots. This sudden granting of pardons was definitely an out-of-character change for the man who promised to make treason odious and punish traitors by breaking necks. Stanton was worried. Was somebody compromising the president? To find out, he asked the head of the Secret Service, Lafayette Baker to look into the situation.

Baker began investigating the pardon brokers who were fast becoming the most important people in Washington. One broker in particular had ready access to the White House; a woman of easy virtue, Mrs. Lucy Cobb. Suspicious that Mrs. Cobb was making money by selling pardons, he set a trap for her. Using one of his detectives to impersonate an ex-Confederate, he applied for an amnesty. He then paid Mrs. Cobb for her services and received a receipt. She then was able to get an audience with the president who referred it to the attorney general. Mrs. Cobb received the pardon for her client with a minimum of investigation. Once Baker had the evidence, he arrested Mrs. Cobb and warned the president "a system of manipulation and corruption are being practiced by persons holding official positions under the government in connection with the procuring of pardons".

Baker's implication that pardons were being granted for sexual favors gives added credence to the theory that Booth was able to obtain his travel passes using the same method. For his part, Johnson did not appreciate Baker's efforts to save him from the pardon brokers, nor was he pleased about being the subject of an investigation. However, since Baker was under the protection of Stanton's war department, Johnson waited two years before dismissing him for insolence and maintaining an espionage system in the White House. When the lobbying methods of the women involved became public knowledge, Johnson's "problem child" Robert took the fall for being seduced by the female brokers and allegedly influencing his father.

More trouble arose when it became obvious that Johnson's wholesale pardon program was strengthening former rebels, returning them to power. Johnson was issuing pardons on an average of 100 per day to individuals officially excluded from his May 29 Proclamation. In only six months after Appomattox, Johnson had granted paroles to several members of Jefferson Davis's cabinet including Davis's Vice-President Alexander Stephens.[176]

The same men who had brought the nation to civil war began encouraging the harassment of federal soldiers and offering the protection of southern courts. Former rebels initiated scores of suits against federal military personnel asking damages for soldiers' actions made under martial law during and after the war. Army officers told the war department that they were now fearful of financial ruin for exercising their assigned functions. In the state courts judges, jurors, and claimants were white men, and almost all were former rebels. What soldier or white Unionist or Negro, could expect fairness from this group?

In April 1865, Stanton and the senior army officers offered Johnson the same support given to Lincoln, assuming that he would back up the army and employ the powers of his office to protect military personnel who were performing duties to which he had assigned them. However, Johnson seemed to have a disregard for his soldiers. For a man who had stepped into the presidency under the most inauspicious of circumstances, he was moving recklessly at a most rapid pace showing an alarming lack of discretion. He was not listening to congressional leaders and seemed much to prefer working with Southern aristocrats. Stanton kept a close watch over the new president, his character and purpose was coming under increasing scrutiny.

Blairs vs. Stanton

One cannot discuss the administration of Andrew Johnson without including the influence of the Blair family. The Blairs had been prominent players in the politics of the United States since the Andrew Jackson administration. Lincoln said of them: "The Blairs have to an unusual degree the spirit of clan. Their family is a close corporation and Frank is their hope and pride."

Francis Blair, Sr. (Father Blair as Lincoln called him) was a prominent newspaperman in Frankfort, Kentucky, when he started the *Washington Globe* in 1830. Under his leadership, the *Globe* became the official house organ of the Democratic Party. He became a leading member in Jackson's Kitchen Cabinet of advisors, and some considered him the power behind the president. Blair's position of influence ended in 1845 when new President James K. Polk told him that if he did not step aside, another paper would become the official organ of the party. This action forced him to sell his interest in the *Globe*. Bitter at the treatment of the Democrats and of his political exile, Blair would preside at the 1854 convention that would form the Republican Party.[177]

The Blair family evolved into a powerful ruthless clan of political insiders with particularly strong links in the key Border States. Francis Blair Sr. had grown up in Kentucky and built a home in Maryland. His sons Montgomery and Frank Jr., began their professional careers as lawyers in Missouri where Montgomery was a U.S. Attorney. Montgomery moved back to Maryland, but his brother Frank stayed in Missouri where he became an influential politician playing a large role in preventing the State from seceding.

As the 1860 election approached, the Blair family were the kingmakers in the Republican Party. Montgomery Blair controlled the delegates from Maryland, and his brother Frank, the delegates from Missouri. Political rivals of Salmon Chase of

Ohio and William Seward of New York, the Blairs threw their support to Lincoln. In exchange for their support, Lincoln appointed Montgomery Blair Postmaster General and in August 1862, he promoted Frank Blair Jr. to brigadier-general of volunteers and then to major general in November 1862.

Throughout the war, the Republican Party had been a coalition of moderates and left-wing radicals with each group jockeying for a position of power. In the fall of 1863, it became obvious that Salmon Chase was going to run for president against his boss. With the help and encouragement of the radicals within the party, he would have presented a very formidable challenge.

To counter this threat Montgomery Blair took action. Ever eager to do battle, he was once reputed to have said; "When the Blairs go in for a fight, they go in for a funeral"[178]. In October 1863, he made a speech in Rockville Maryland upbraiding the radicals in the party and Senator Charles Sumner of Massachusetts in particular.

Blair's speech was designed to drive a wedge between Chase and his supporters. He excoriated the ambitions of "ultra-abolitionists' who's despotic ambitions would be "fatal to Republican institutions'. He then praised Lincoln's efforts to rehabilitate the South by putting men loyal to the Union in charge of the rebellious states.

The speech was reprinted in newspapers and pamphlet form throughout the country. The sting of its criticism infuriated the radical camp but it eventually led to its desired effect. For the fourth time in his tenure as Secretary of the Treasury, Chase offered his resignation and to his surprise, Lincoln accepted it. Chase believed Stanton influenced Lincoln to accept the resignation, and he bitterly turned against his old friend.

Chase's bid for the presidency collapsed in early March 1864, when an ill-timed, and defamatory public attack on Lincoln backfired on the Chase candidacy. Left in a political limbo he grudgingly swung his radical supporters to Lincoln for the nomination. Lincoln later rewarded Chase's support by nominating him to the Supreme Court.

The radicals took their revenge against Blair by lining up behind a third party candidate, former nominee John C. Fremont, threatening the party unity needed to win the 1864 election. With the fall voting rapidly approaching, Lincoln felt it necessary to cut a deal with the radical wing of the party. They would end their support of Fremont's candidacy, and Lincoln would ask for the resignation of Montgomery Blair.

After the re-election of Lincoln and the embarrassment of Andrew Johnson's acceptance speech, the Blairs invited Johnson out to their Silver Spring home for some recovery time. Francis Blair insisted that Johnson was all right. "He hadn't said anything that was in bad sense only bad taste". After many long discussions, they found his views on the coming reconstruction remarkably similar to their own. With their own position of power within the Republican Party now lost, they longed for a person who could re-unite the Democratic Party to its old Jacksonian glory. In Johnson, they thought they had the man who could do that in 1868. Lincoln's assassination sped up that timetable.

The primary goal for the Blairs after Johnson took office was to get the president to remove Seward and Stanton from the Cabinet and replace them with conservative Democrats. Working with Senator Doolittle of Wisconsin, they hoped to elevate Grant to the position of war secretary where he would be in position to be elected president as a Democrat in 1868 should Johnson fail to get public support.

A major opportunity presented itself when Stanton repudiated the peace agreement between General Sherman's army and the Confederate's Joe Johnston. Sherman, who had contempt of all politics, stretched his authority from accepting a military surrender to negotiating an armistice. The excitable Stanton, mindful of the dictatorial threats that charismatic Generals such as McClellan and Hooker posed during the war, quickly and publicly rebuked Sherman feeling that unless powerful political opposition were taken, a military coup would be possible.

Sherman was not surprised at Washington's rejection of his agreement terms, but he bristled at Stanton's implication that he was not a loyal Union soldier. After Johnston surrendered on the same terms as Lee, Stanton's denigration of the popular general brought him widespread criticism. Montgomery Blair was the first to advise Johnson to replace Stanton. Even radicals like Ben Butler and Salmon Chase worked behind the scenes to seek Stanton's removal. Johnson's refusal to ask for Stanton's resignation sparked murmurs of damaging evidence he held against the president. These murmurs would get louder in the coming year.

The tragic death of Lincoln unified the country behind his successor. Based upon his performance as Military Governor of Tennessee, the consensus amongst the leading Republicans was that he would be firmer with the rebels than Lincoln would, and be a good president. Charles Dana wrote, "the probability of any serious division in the Republican party seems to be entirely removed by the accession of president Johnson. For the present he commands the undivided support not merely of the party, but of the country in general".

Great divisions of opinion surely existed in the Republican Party concerning how to go about readmitting the Southern States. Stanton was flexible to the details of reconstruction. The key was to be able to change the plan when it became obvious which parts were not working. His goal was to "unite the conflicting interests of the Republican Party" to form a consensus working agreement. He, like Lincoln, agreed that Congress held the final disposition of any plan so their cooperation was essential.

Stanton had no reason in April 1865 to believe that he and Johnson would eventually become political foes. When Johnson was Military Governor, Stanton worked to resolve issues between Johnson and the military commanders, but these were never very serious difficulties. Both he and Johnson had been War Democrats before they found a home in the Republican Party. To Stanton, the Copperheads, which now dominated the Democratic Party, were not only treasonous but dangerous to the continuity of the nation. They were already clamoring to cut back on the army appropriations, which would force a withdrawal of the military occupation and complete anarchy in the South.

Late in 1865, the Blair family and Manton Marble of the *New York World,* induced Joseph E. Maddox to sue Stanton for damages arising from his wartime arrest as a disloyal northern civilian. The suit was initiated to discourage army officers in the South from enforcing property confiscation and financially break Stanton. If Maddox won his case, the precedent would be set for similar verdicts against hundreds of lesser officers.

When Stanton and Grant learned that the Blairs were behind this plot, they were outraged that men who were now the president's chief advisers, would involve the army as a part of a personal vendetta. Neither Stanton nor Grant could believe that the president was privy to the plot but Johnson ordered the southern state courts to hold off the many damage suits pending against military personnel until settlement of the suit.

Caleb Cushing, Maddox's attorney brokered a compromise dropping the suit against Stanton. Grant and Stanton quickly took advantage of Johnson's Reconstruction proclamations and sanctioned the use of martial law in order to protect army personnel against suits originating in the former Confederacy. However, this was only a stopgap measure. If the president would not protect the soldiers from legal harassment, Congress would have to do so.

Representative Thaddeus Stevens (Pennsylvania)

The Republican floor leader and chairman of the Ways and Means committee, Stevens had a clubfoot and always wore a thick black wig to cover his bald head. He was a legal scholar, zealot for liberty, an astute parliamentarian and had an extremely sharp tongue. Sarcastic and bombastic he was strongly abolitionist, defended runaway slaves for free and fought tirelessly for racial equality.

He led the opposition to Johnson's policies in the House of Representatives and was the prime instigator of the impeachment proceedings. His final act was to be buried in a remote cemetery that did not have racial barriers.

Start of an Uncivil War

In the summer of 1865, a personality change seemed to overtake Johnson as the rich and famous from all over the South came to him to beg their pardons. New York politician Chauncey Depew wrote that their flattery offered to the man who once made their clothing "captivated him and changed his whole attitude towards them". A group of men called upon Johnson to say that once he was a class different from themselves and that therefore they had never recognized him socially. Now he became the supreme ruler and accorded social recognition. They accepted Andrew Johnson as their equal. Was this the reason for such an abrupt personality change?

Not likely, Johnson was above all a political animal. The opportunities to expand his power and become unbeatable in the 1868 were clearly visible. Southern leaders hoped to recoup their power through their friend in the White House. By complying with the president's demands to ratify the 13th amendment, repudiate their war debt, and annul their ordinances of secession, they hoped to maintain their civil power, withdraw the military occupation, and throw the party of Lincoln out of power. If these Southerners could gather the votes of the regions they represented and the president could gain the votes of the Copperheads in the North, Johnson realized that he could win the presidency on his own terms. The flattery offensive of the Southern aristocrats stroked Johnson's ego to the point that he was considering turning his back on the people who had put him in the president's chair.[179]

Front and center of this effort was Montgomery Blair. He sought to divide the Republican coalition between the Radicals or 'ultra abolitionists' and the Lincoln Unionists. The Radicals had forced Blair from the Lincoln cabinet, and he not only hated them for it, but also hated the cause for which they fought. The Negro question was delaying the grand coalition of the parties that the

Blairs were visualizing. To solve this problem the Blairs resurrected their idea of war with Mexico as the ideal answer. By invoking the Monroe Doctrine, the U.S. could invade Mexico and remove Napoleon III of France's puppet monarch Maximilian I. Once the Emperor was deposed, Blair envisioned Mexico as "a home for our negroes…where we can send some 100,000 black soldiers to take possession permanently & send their families to join them thus opening the way to the separation of the races and disposing them on the soils adapted to their special natures".[180]

Johnson was in full agreement with the Blair's social position. He was determined to keep this social order in the South. As a Congressman, he once stated that if blacks were given the right to vote, that would "place every splay-footed, bandy-shanked, hump-backed, thick-lipped, flat-nosed, woolly-headed, ebon-colored Negro in the country upon an equality with the poor white man."[181] However, rather than adopt Blair's Mexican proposal and rush the country into another war, Johnson was content to let Secretary of State Seward negotiate a solution to the Mexican situation. This action put Seward in the cross hairs of Blair family.

As Johnson continued his charm offensive with the former rebels, he forced Thaddeus Stevens and the Radicals to watch from the sidelines. At this point, the South's greatest fears were property confiscation and interference with their handling of the Negroes. Stevens was aghast as he watched Johnson forfeit all his bargaining power and receiving nothing in return. Stevens wrote the president asking him, "…can you not hold your hand and wait the action of Congress and in the meantime govern them with military rulers? Profuse pardoning will greatly embarrass Congress if they should wish to make the enemy pay the expense of the war or a part of it."

Johnson arrogantly ignored Stevens' letter and did not even bother to give him the courtesy of a reply. This purposeful snub further strained relations within the party.

Another of the issues that showed his change of heart was the fate of Jefferson Davis. Johnson's cabinet had split on the issue of a civil or military trial for Davis. Attorney General Speed, whose decision for a military trial for the Lincoln assassination brought an abundance of criticism from the press, decided to change positions and argue for a civil trial. Johnson who received similar criticism privately from high-ranking Democrats concurred. However, civil courts were not yet open in the state of Virginia. Johnson had not restored the writ of habeas corpus due to hostilities still present in the area. Since there was no indication when they would be, it was impossible to bring Davis to trial. Although Stanton argued that "the murder of Union prisoners of war by starvation and other barbarous and cruel treatment" and "the crime of inciting the assassination of Abraham Lincoln" could be interpreted as violations of the laws of war and subject to trial by military court, Johnson would not be moved.

As the deadlock continued and relations between Johnson and Congress got more strained, some of the extreme Radicals began to entertain the Beverly Tucker thesis that linked Johnson to the assassination conspiracy since he was the greatest beneficiary. How else could one change their opinion so drastically that treason against the United States should not be a "most odious crime" but merely a political difference of opinion?

Historian William Cooper pointed out that "Johnson needed Davis in prison to show that he held the head of the Confederacy accountable," although it was becoming clearer every day that Johnson did not intend to actually prosecute him. Politically, Johnson could not afford to let Davis go free, and the Republicans and their allies were unwilling to do so.[182]

Robert E. Lee and the officers of the Confederate army were the men Johnson wanted to bring to trial for treason. Unfortunately, the paroles given to them by their surrender precluded this action. This led to the first confrontation between U.S. Grant and Andrew Johnson. Johnson was determined that Lee and his brigadiers had to face punishment. Grant insisted that the terms of Appomattox had to be honored.

> "When can these men be tried?" asked Johnson.
> "Never," Grant replied "Unless they violate their parole."
> Johnson, always quick to anger, became upset and demanded,
> "By what right a military commander interferes to protect an arch-traitor from the laws?"

Grant, who rarely lost his temper, became livid. He told the president that as the responsible commander in the field he had an obligation to destroy Lee's army. "I have made certain terms with Lee, the best and only terms. If I had told him and his army that their liberty would be invaded, that they would be open to arrest, trial, and execution for treason, Lee would have never surrendered, and we should have lost many lives in destroying him. My terms of surrender were according to military law, and so long as General Lee observes his parole, I will never consent to his arrest. I will resign the command of the army rather than execute any order to arrest Lee or any of his commanders so long as they obey the law."[183] Faced with alienating the most popular man in the country, Johnson backed down.

The results of Johnson's wholesale pardons became obvious in the Southern State elections in the autumn of 1865. Rather than selecting officeholders among men who stayed loyal to the Union, Southerners elected their wartime leaders and unpardoned rebels to Congress and local offices. Apparently, the South believed that with Johnson in the White House there would be no consequences from the rebellion. Not only did they elect leaders distasteful to the Republican moderates, but in Louisiana the Democrats called for compensation for the slaves and restitution of confiscated property. In addition, the enactment of "Black Codes" by Southern state legislatures clearly discriminated against Negroes in many aspects of the law and upset the majority of Republican moderates in Congress.

The Southern states were visibly taking advantage of Johnson's policies and proclamations. Johnson himself was appalled. "There seems in many of the elections something like defiance, which is all out of place at this time," he protested. To right the ship he might have refused to permit them to take office and call for new elections. He might have even concluded that his attempt at political reconstruction was premature and that federal control would have to continue for a while longer. However, Johnson could never admit a mistake. Instead, he decided to legalize the elections by issuing special pardons in wholesale lots to the elected unpardoned rebels – to delegates to state conventions, to governors, to members of the legislature, etc. Confederate military leaders merely had to call on the president or write him a letter to get a pardon. Altogether, Johnson had granted some 13,500 special pardons. To Johnson each pardon represented a political IOU that he would cash in when he ran for election in 1868. To the North the pardons begged the question, for what did 350,000 Union soldiers sacrifice their lives? [184]

The political issues in the summer and fall of 1865 were who would govern the South, and how would the Negroes be handled. Between the dissolution of the Whigs and until the election of Lincoln, the Democratic Party had enjoyed almost single party status throughout the country. The Republicans had no base of power within the Southern States; if the Democrats could defeat the Negro suffrage issue, they would control the South and once again become the majority party. The Democrats in mid-1865 had begun a political propaganda campaign with their friends in the newspapers. Revisionist historian Eric McKitrick described their strategy this way: "They proceeded to give names to the Republicans which did not as yet fit, blaming them for plans which they had not as yet laid, and predicting consequences which very few Republicans wanted to occur. But with their allies in the press they believed that the more 'radical' these alleged schemes might seem to be, the greater the advantage the Party would gain."[185]

The first political blow towards achieving these ends came on August 26, 1865, when Montgomery Blair gave a scathing attack on the Republicans and in particular Stanton, Seward, and Holt. In this speech he accused the then Secretary of War Holt and former Attorney General Stanton of undermining President James Buchanan's efforts to placate the South. He also accused Seward of deceiving the president in the pre-Sumter days, and in an effort to push for a Mexican war he charged Seward with suborning American interests to that of Napoleon III.

In all, he blamed the entire war on Seward, Holt, and Stanton. The Blairs hated Stanton, because they felt that his briefing of the incoming Secretary of State Seward on the secession crisis made him a duplicitous character, one who was looking to improve his position through deceitful tactics. In other words, they thought he was a man very similar to the Blairs themselves. It is interesting to note that at the time of the secession crisis, Blair wrote, "if Buchanan had the nerve of Andrew Jackson the Southern movement would have been nipped in the bud".

Blair's broadside fell flat and generally regarded as a clumsy attempt to rewrite history in favorable terms for the Democratic Party. However, its real purpose was to spread doubt among motives of the leaders of the Republican Party and to return to the Blairs the political influence they lost. Even Gideon Welles, Blair's greatest ally in the Cabinet, regretted the bitterness that Blair used to assault Seward and Holt. The Radical press as well as other newspapers severely criticized Blair.

Throughout the summer and fall, Stanton continued to get distressing reports from his Generals concerning the problems in the South. Personally, he favored the granting of limited Negro suffrage as Lincoln had suggested to Governor George Hahn of Louisiana. Due to the difficulties of administrating that policy, however, he changed his opinion. Stanton distrusted the black man's ability to function as a voter and officeholder and by no means did he appreciate a freedman as a social equal. However, he was now inclined to the belief that Sumner had been prophetically correct on the need for the Negro to vote in the South if the North's victories were to be perpetuated. Furthermore, after his conference with Congressional leaders on the Presidential Reconstruction Plan he realized that Congress would never approve any program that did not have some form of Negro suffrage. [186]

He was not happy about secessionists returning en-mass to the government He was not sure about the kind of ties that the president was seeking to bind the rebels to the nation, and he wondered whether Blair had had the "left handed assent of Johnson to make the attack" on him.

But Stanton worried most over Johnson's inconsistencies and snap decisions. His ordering of an expedition of troops into Indian country without notifying Stanton or Grant was one such decision. Before the war, Southerners in Buchanan's cabinet sent the army to the far reaches of American territories leaving Washington defenseless. That was a painful memory of anxious days for Stanton.

As far as the president's flirtation with the Democratic Party, Stanton concluded that Johnson was "trying to ride two horses and he probably means to join the party which finally wins." If true, and Johnson hoped to go along with the prevailing wind once its strength and direction were clear, then it seemed to Stanton it was his task to help steer events so that the president would tack the right way. Whether or not the black man voted in the South would determine the issue.[187]

Montgomery Blair

Postmaster General under Lincoln, he was despised by radical Republicans. The president asked for his resignation in September 1864 when Lincoln needed to appease the John Fremont faction of the party and keep the radical favorite out of the presidential race.

Journalist Noah Brooks said of him that "he was a restless mischief-maker and like his brother Frank he was apparently never so happy as when he was in hot water or was making water hot for others. John Hay echoed this saying; "What injured him are his violent personal antagonisms and indiscretions."

The Surratt Problem

On September 16, 1865, John Surratt, hiding near Montreal, made his move. With the help of two priests, Surratt (using the alias of Mr. McCarty) took a tug to the steamship *Peruvian* and entered the cabin of Lewis McMillan, the ship's doctor. McMillan kept him locked in his cabin until the ship sailed. Once at sea, Surratt began to talk openly with his host, admitting that he was a Confederate spy. Among the stories, he told the Doctor was that he had killed three escaped Union prisoners in cold blood as well as a Union spy. He also told him that over the course of the war he had transferred $100,000 from Secretary of State Judah Benjamin to the Confederates in Montreal.

Upon docking in Liverpool, McMillan went straight to the American consul, Henry Wilding, and told him of the adventures of his traveling companion. After taking his deposition, Wilding wrote to the secretary of state to let him know that Surratt was in Liverpool and awaited instructions. After discussing the matter with Holt, Stanton, and Johnson, they decided to take no action regarding Surratt. William Hunter, the acting Secretary of State for the recuperating Seward wrote to Wilding, "It is thought advisable that no action be taken in regard to the arrest of the supposed John Surratt at present".

Any number of reasons could have influenced the Johnson administration to take this course. First, and most important, was the timing. Johnson's reconstruction program would soon be coming before the Congress. Putting John Surratt on trial at this time would divert too much attention from the critical issue at hand.

Secondly, Johnson's disregard for mercy in the case of John's mother, Mary, brought a great deal of public wrath upon him. To bring Surratt to trial would reopen those wounds at a time that Johnson needed all the public support he could muster. Even worse, the country was at peace. It would now be impossible to bring Surratt before a Military Commission. An acquittal in civil court for the same crime that his mother hanged for would renew criticism that the conspirators did not get a fair trial.

Lastly, Surratt was a wild card. How much he knew of the Lincoln plot and whom he could implicate was unknown. Stanton was aware that he was the Confederate courier who transferred money and information between Secretary of State Benjamin and agents in Washington, New York, and Montreal. However, with his mother executed, Stanton did not have any means to get him to turn states-evidence against the Confederate hierarchy. In fact, Surratt may have been privy to the previous relationship between Booth and Johnson, and keeping that quiet was a top priority.

Mary Surratt

Five out of the nine members of the Military Commission recommended that Mary Surratt be shown mercy "due to her sex and age". President Andrew Johnson rejected the argument saying that "her sex and age didn't make her less guilty".

When the political winds changed, he was later to claim that he was never shown the formal petition on which he commented. On July 7, 1865, Mary Surratt became the first woman in American history to be executed.

The Radical Agenda

Before the opening of the 39th session of Congress, Senator Charles Sumner paid a visit to President Johnson in hopes of avoiding a split in the Republican Party. Sumner was one of the most brilliant and articulate men in the Senate. He could also be pompous, overbearing, and insistent. With a personality like Lincoln who could admire a man's well-thought-out position and filter out his personality quirks, Sumner was highly regarded and esteemed. Lincoln did not deprecate Sumner's agitation for an immediate emancipation policy, even though it did reflect upon the course of the administration. On the contrary, he welcomed everything that would prepare the public mind for the approaching development. Despite their many disagreements, the two men remained close friends. On one occasion Lincoln told Sumner, "The only difference between you and me is a difference of a month or six weeks in time."

Unfortunately, the personalities of Johnson and Sumner were similar in that neither could see the other's side of the argument and neither was able to compromise. Sumner felt that the path that Johnson was pursuing had "thrown away the fruits of the victories of the Union Army and the Rebellion is not yet subdued." Sumner's prime complaint was that within the North Carolina and other proclamations, Johnson had not enfranchised the Negro nor had he any plans to do so.

For three hours, both men went back and forth. Finally, Sumner realized "with the painful conviction that the president's whole soul was set as a flint against the good cause, and that by the assassination of Abraham Lincoln, the Rebellion had vaulted into the presidential chair". He warned Johnson unless he changed his view on the Negro suffrage issue, he and his friends would make war on him in Congress. As he took his leave, he discovered with disgust that the classless Johnson had used his hat as a spittoon.

On December 4, 1865, the first day of the new session, the clerk of the House, Edward McPherson began to call the roll, purposefully skipping the names of all the rebel states. When Northern Democrats protested, Thaddeus Stevens rose to remind members that until the House organized itself with the election of the Speaker, no acknowledgement of any protests or points of order were possible. Upon the organization of the House, Stevens immediately called for a joint committee to investigate the conditions in the South and for Congress to refuse to seat any members of the former Confederate States until those conditions were determined. The resolution was quickly approved.

Congress was acting within the power given to them by the fourth section of the fourth article of the Constitution, which provides that the United States shall guarantee to every State in the Union a republican form of government. A Supreme Court decision made more than twenty years before in the case of *Luther vs. Borden* stated that under this article the decision rests with Congress to decide if the government is republican or not.

By moving on the first day, Stevens stole a march on the president and set the tone for the resistance that would come. Stevens had convinced his fellow Republicans that after four years of war the rebel states "should not be allowed to waltz back to their seats of power" without the approval of the loyal states. The sharing of the responsibility between the House and Senate in this matter was unprecedented, and the Joint Committee of Fifteen would take control to formulate a Congressional reconstruction policy.

On the second day of the 39th Congress, Johnson in his annual message announced the process of reconstruction was complete. The Southern states restored, federal courts, customhouses, post offices were open, and it was now the duty of Congress to seat Southern senators and representatives. As to the issue of black suffrage, he asserted that he gave it very serious consideration but emphasized that the Constitution left the matter of voting qualifications to the individual states, so he was unable to give the vote to the black freedman. Thus, he declared victory for his reconstruction effort, patted himself on the back, washed his hands of Negro suffrage, and was ready to celebrate Christmas.

The political point of his address gave the Republicans the choice of leaving the South out of the Union and keeping the country divided or reunify the country and accept the former rebels as Congressmen. Johnson believed that politically it was in the best interests of the Republicans to accept the results of his Reconstruction policy.

Public reaction to the speech was overwhelmingly positive. Johnson was praised not only by newspaper editorials but also by letters and local politicians of every stripe. Most expected acceptance of the president's program within 90 days. Despite proclaiming his good news, Johnson continued his military rule and did not annul the suspension of the writ of habeas corpus. Since, the president did not take these steps; it was obvious that the cessation of hostilities proclamation was at best premature.

Johnson felt that he was at the height of his popularity and was certain that Congress would buckle to the pressure of his will. However, the Radicals led by Stevens were not about to bend when they felt that the sacrifice of the Union soldiers were being wasted.

On December 18, Stevens countered Johnson on the issue of readmitting the Southern States by proposing the Radical plan for reconstruction. The main points were:

- Reduce all States that participated in the rebellion to territories. Pay no attention to their ratification of the Thirteenth Amendment since they have no intention of living up to the spirit of the Amendment.
- By constitutional change, base the number of House representatives upon actual voters rather than population.
- Pass measures to ensure the freedmen equal civil rights and give a homestead to every Negro.
- Give the Negro the right to vote.

Before the Congress adjourned for the holidays they heard more from Stevens in the House and Sumner in the Senate who read for them letters they received detailing the outrages that were occurring to the Negroes in the South. The Radicals insisted that the pardoned rebels who now controlled the Southern States were still unrepentant secessionists who would begin a new rebellion at the first opportunity.

General Carl Schurz, was sent to investigate the situation for Johnson and concurred with this assessment. His report of one hundred and five printed pages also contained official documents and formal statements from nearly all military officers in the Southern States.

Among their conclusions was that the Southerners were persecuting Northern settlers and keeping Negroes in a state of involuntary servitude by use of the Black Codes.
Schurz stated that these laws codified "the idea that although the former owner has lost his individual right of property in the former slave, the blacks at large belong to the whites at large." The Negro had now become "the slave of society". The Radicals contended that there was no excuse for these codes. The purpose for them as stated by James G. Blaine was to prove that the Negro "was fit only to be chattel" and that he had lost rather than gained by his emancipation.

To counter Schurz's disturbing report, Johnson sent Grant on an eight-day tour of the South, and Grant sent back a two-page opinion report of the situation. He saw few people, reported no facts, and gathered no testimony. Stanton warned that sending Grant's report to the Congress would have disastrous results. Johnson ignored the advice and asked the Congress to accept Grant's report rather than Schurz's. Sumner was outraged.

On December 20, he made a speech and declared Johnson's message as "whitewashing". Sickened by the "outrages where human rights are sacrificed and rebel barbarism received a new letter of license" he compared Johnson's message to Franklin Pierce's letter on the Bleeding of Kansas that helped precipitate the war

In the view of the Radicals, eight months of Johnson's reconstruction program produced an unrepentant post war South that had restored the rebels to power and returned the freedmen to a near-slavery condition. Still there was optimism that if Johnson would work with Congress to enact legislation to protect the Negroes, the reunification would be successful. However, Democrats and Southerners urged Johnson to strike a blow at the Radicals who refused to seat the Southerners and prevent their majority in Congress. Advisors such as Blair and Welles advocated that if he wanted to form his own party he would have to marginalize the influence of the Radicals. Johnson agreed. A showdown on Negro suffrage would be his battleground. He believed that Northern whites would not support dividing the nation over the fate of the Negroes.

Despite the differences in how each side saw the world, the largest contingents in Congress were Republican moderates who were anxious to cooperate with Johnson. The Radicals were a small minority of men shunned in their own party. All Johnson needed to do was work with the moderates to ensure the safety of the Negroes in the South and Johnson would have controlled the Congress. However, Johnson was never able to play well with others.

Congress accepted Schurz's conclusions and declared against admitting members under Johnson's provisional governments. Furthermore, they declared that the rebellious states could not reenact their former slave constitutions and that insurgent leaders could not participate in public affairs. This declaration was binding on all departments of the government including the executive branch.

Rather than working with Congress to amend the deficiencies of the program, Johnson decided to push his program down the throats of the majority party in his patented incendiary style. He denounced the Congress as a "usurper" and "dictator".

Stanton strongly advised the president against his reaction. Although the North Carolina proclamation had been mostly Stanton's work, he realized that it was always subject to the approval of Congress. When Johnson decided to avoid the Negro question, he abandoned one of the prime principals of the proclamation. Stanton decided that his best course of action was to work with the majority of the Congress and try to maintain both the Union and a rational form of reconstruction.

General Carl Schurz

General Carl Schurz was involved in the German revolutionary movement before immigrating to the United States in 1852. He became active in Republican politics and supported the antislavery movement. Lincoln appointed him U.S. Minister to Spain (1861-1862). His ability to recruit German-American soldiers got him named to be brigadier general of volunteers, and then major general of the XI Corps. He was elected to the U.S. Senate from Missouri (1869-1875) and was appointed secretary of the interior (1877-1881).

Chapter 9

The Counter-Revolution of 1866

No Place for Moderation

In January 1866, Lyman Trumbull, the chairman of the Senate's judiciary committee, was preparing two bills. The first was to extend and expand the Freedmen's Bureau. The second was a Civil Rights bill that would put teeth into the Thirteenth Amendment, grant citizenship to the former slaves, and eliminate the Black Codes. Trumbull, one of the most able lawyers in the country, realized that the Southern legislatures had effectively annulled the effect of abolishing slavery by enacting the Black Codes and continued slavery under a different name. Unless Federal law protected Negroes, the black race would never be freedmen.

Taking Johnson at his word that he wished to see reform take hold, Trumbull conferred with the president offering to make any changes before presenting the bills to Congress. The president had none to offer, bringing a sigh of relief to the moderates since the majority of the Republicans (including many Radicals) wanted to avoid a direct conflict with Johnson. They were now confident that they had performed the necessary steps to avoid one.

The Freedmen's Bureau, was established during the Lincoln administration. Its purpose was to address and supervise all relief and educational activities relating to refugees and freedmen. It issued rations, clothing, and medicine within the States that were under reconstruction. The Bureau also assumed custody of confiscated lands or property in the former Confederate States, Border States, District of Columbia, and Indian Territory. This department had no budget of its own but was part of the war department.

Stanton championed the bill wanting the Bureau expanded to hear court cases involving freedmen rather than have them tried by the biased civil courts of the South. Soldiers and civilians, including Negroes, who asserted that justice was unobtainable in southern state courts could transfer any suits pending against them to the Freedmen's Bureau paramilitary tribunals or to federal civil courts. In the former, martial law prevailed. In the latter, Congress had prescribed that all federal court personnel, jurors, attorneys, and claimants, had to swear an ironclad oath of past loyalty to the Union

Meanwhile, the Democrats were waiting for a signal from Johnson that he was ready to separate himself from the Republicans and join with them in forming the "Andy Johnson Party". Some thought it would mean the removal of Stanton and the nomination of General James Steedman of Ohio. Letters of recommendations for Steedman from top Democrats came pouring into his office at the end of January. The *National Intelligencer* newspaper, the prime press outlet for the administration, hinted that the separation would be coming soon.

Instead, Johnson chose to reject the Freedmen and Civil Rights bills to separate himself from the party that put him into power. Not only did he veto both bills but he also harangued specific members of Congress by name with an angry tirade. He declared, "We are now almost inaugurated into another rebellion!" Like a drunken man challenging everyone in the bar, he denounced Thaddeus Stevens, Charles Sumner, and named them as traitors opposed to fundamental principles of government and even declared that efforts were being made to have him assassinated!

" ..*if my blood is to be shed because I vindicate the Union and the preservation of this government in it's original purity and character, let it be shed; let an altar to the Union be erected and then, if it is necessary, take me and lay me on it....*"

As he continued his diatribe, he became more and more inflammatory. It was the demagogic Johnson with a new enemy in his sights.

The long knives were now out in the open. Johnson's denouncement of the traitors on Washington's Birthday created a sensation, and the Congress circled the wagons to protect their own. *The Nation*, a moderate publication declared, "anyone whose moral sense was not offended by it the minute his eye lighted on it was past redemption". In four years of war, Lincoln had never used such language even in denouncing the Confederacy. Edwin Godkin of *The Nation* wrote, "The appearance of the president at the windows of the White House to accuse prominent members of another branch of the government of the foulest crime of which a man can be guilty is something new and alarming in American history."

In Congress, rumors began that once again he was intoxicated when he made the speech. In fact, some said, he was inebriated the entire week, which was why he vetoed the Freedmen's bill. Whenever his name was mentioned on the floor, objections would be made concerning his position so that his title became "Vice-President acting as President". His messages would be pushed aside without being read, and the Clerk would read editorials aloud that berated the president to the delight of the House. Johnson's vitriolic attack rather than isolate the Radicals actually enhanced their prestige. His rant was instrumental in rescuing Sumner in his contested re-election bid for the Senate.

Thaddeus Stevens was not the type of man to let Johnson's charge of treason go unanswered. Rather than responding with fiery oratory, he used his caustic wit and sarcasm to lampoon the president. Noting that the president had the habit of blaming Radicals for all his faults and then changing the official record of his comments, Stevens took up Johnson's side.

Why the fuss? he asked his fellow representatives. Johnson made no such speech, and he was glad he had the opportunity to exonerate the president. "It's all part of the running contrivance of the Copperheads who have been persecuting our president since the 4th of March last." To prove his point he read a newspaper account of the president's drunken inaugural speech. This, Stevens roared in mock outrage, was typical of the "slanders" our president has suffered. This recent attack was simply more of the same. Therefore, he concluded, the speech made on Washington's Birthday must obviously never have happened. "It is not possible, sir, and I am glad of this opportunity to relieve him from that odium."

The Northern Press reacts to Johnson's veto of the Civil Rights Bill.

The House laughed heartily at Steven's mocking of the president, but the veto of the Civil Rights Bill infuriated Trumbull and the rest of the moderates who had gone out of their way for sixteen weeks to mend fences only to have the ground pulled out from under them. In Johnson's cabinet, only Welles opposed the bill. The proposed legislation affirmed equality of civil rights among all classes of people and equal punishment under the law. Trumbull, stated that "he never indicated to me, nor so far as I know to any of his friends, the least objection to any of the provision of the bill until after it's passage".

The machinery used to enforce the law came from the old Fugitive Slave Law. Johnson vetoed the bill on a States Rights justification. He had no objection to the enforcement of the Fugitive Slave Law, but turn it on those who would mistreat a person based upon their race and he found it "fraught with evil". After analyzing Johnson's objections, Trumbull declared, "The president's facts are as bad as his law." As the *Washington Daily Chronicle* put it, the Congress acted in the interests of Blacks while the president acted in the interest of their oppressors. For the first time, there began serious talks of impeachment.

Charles Sumner led the charge from the Senate. He proclaimed,

> "This is one of the last great battles with slavery. Driven from the legislative chambers, driven from the field of war, this monstrous power has found a refuge in the executive mansion, where, in utter disregard of the Constitution and laws, it seeks to exercise its ancient, far-reaching sway. All this is very plain. Nobody can question it. Andrew Johnson is the impersonation of the tyrannical slave power. In him, it lives again. He is the lineal successor of John C. Calhoun and Jefferson Davis; and he gathers about him the same supporters."

The March 27 veto effectively ended Andrew Johnson's affiliation with the party of Lincoln. Governor Oliver Morton of Indiana warned Johnson that failure to sign the Civil Rights Bill would produce an irreparable rupture between the president and the Republicans. Johnson stated that he intended to build a new party that would assure the triumph of his policy. To this, Morton replied, "all roads leading out of the Republican Party lead to the Democratic." Soon afterwards, Morton, hitherto a Johnson supporter, opened a successful campaign in Indiana for the United States Senate, running as a Radical.

Johnson's position forced the moderates and radicals to unite to save their party and their country. Both vetoes were overturned. This overturning of a presidential veto was almost unprecedented. Before this point only six times in the history of the country had Congress successfully overridden a presidential veto. Congress also passed a Thaddeus Stevens resolution declaring that no representatives of the rebellious States should be received in Congress until that body decided that such States were entitled to representation.

Johnson's veto of the Civil Rights Bill told the party moderates that Johnson could not be trusted. It was apparent that there would be no compromising with Johnson on the reconstruction issue; he would denounce every bill that passed Congress and then veto them. Rather than risk other presidential vetoes, and stretch out the process indefinitely, Republicans decided to bypass the president entirely by amending the Constitution. The Fourteenth Amendment went into the planning stage.[188]

On April 2 in an attempt to undercut the lawmakers, Johnson issued an executive order declaring the rebellion over and the insurrectionary States back in the Union as before, with all the rights powers and privileges as loyal states.

A disenchanted Stanton wrote to Philetus Sawyer of Wisconsin:

> "If President Johnson can put flesh on the bones and blood in the veins of three hundred thousand men and return them to their families, he can make this nation think he is right; if not he never can. A year ago we had a million fighting men in the field and the same sentiment and influence that sent them there will return them again, before the people will see the political power of this nation placed in the hands of the rebellious states by Andrew Johnson or any other man."[189]

The president's proclamation sent panic through the army in the south. A week later, Grant sent out a confidential message to his military commanders. He cautioned them to exercise restraint in dealing with the state governments and civilians but also authorized them to employ martial law whenever they felt it necessary, despite the president's statement that peace was at hand. He also informed them that the Freedmen's Bureau was exempt from presidential jurisdiction; since in his opinion, the Bureau was Congress' creation.

On May 1, Memphis, Tennessee, erupted into three days of rioting. White mobs including off duty policemen tramped through Black sections of the city killing 46 people and burning homes, schools, and churches. Memphis officials did nothing to curtail the uprising, leaving the army to put down the violence. Grant recommended that the leaders of the riot be taken into custody until local officials agreed to press charges, but Johnson refused to intervene. Local law enforcement was a State matter.

It became apparent to Grant that Johnson was not interested in protecting the freedmen from white terrorism. He told the *New York Times* that those sections of the South that had not felt the war directly "are much less disposed to accept the situation in good faith than those portions which have been literally overrun by fire and sword. A year ago they were willing to do anything; now they regard themselves as masters of the situation".[190]

Indeed, with the power of the executive branch of government on their side along with the support of the Copperheads in the North, the newly empowered former secessionists now felt that they could dictate the terms of the peace to the Union. Stanton and Grant now shared the view of most army commanders assigned to the South that former rebels were incapable of true reformation.

In Pulaski Tennessee, six young Confederate veterans 'hungering and thirsting' for amusement formed a "secret society" in the law office of Judge Thomas M. Jones. They took their name from the Greek word "Kuklos" or circle. The Klan soon found their amusement in terrorizing the Negro community. They set out at night on raids to burn houses, destroy crops, and lynch "uppity" Negroes who demanded their rights. Within two years, the Ku Klux Klan had killed thousands of former slaves.

On April 30, a joint committee proposed the Fourteenth Amendment to the Constitution consisting of five sections. The design of the amendment was to grant citizenship to and protect the civil liberties of recently freed slaves. It did this by prohibiting States from denying or abridging the privileges or immunities of citizens of the United States, depriving any person of his life, liberty, or property without due process of law, or denying to any person within their jurisdiction the equal protection of the laws. It also reduced membership in the Congress proportionately for States who denied the vote to eligible citizens as well as denying former members of Congress the right to serve if they had broken their oath to serve in the rebellion. Finally, it repudiated the debts incurred by the Confederate States.

Heralded as the official peace treaty between the North and the South, the amendment reversed the original policy of the Constitution, which left it to each State to decide exclusively for itself whether an individual could become a citizen and vote in elections. Congress would not only decide the qualifications for citizenship but would assume protection of a citizen's due process rights granted by the Bill of Rights. This usurpation of *States Rights* made it unacceptable to the old Confederacy.

Johnson polled his cabinet for their opinion. Stanton did not give his assent, because he was opposed to a section that proposed to "exclude all States lately in rebellion from representation in Congress till July 4, 1870". He felt that it was unwise that Congress tie its hands for more than four years in advance. But, in his opinion, the legislature had a right to participate in the reconstruction process (which was not Johnson's view), and there was adequate room for compromise. Johnson told friends in the press about the results of the meeting, including Stanton's negative view of the amendment. The pro-Johnson press twisted the opinion to say that Stanton had actually agreed with the president's stance.

Meanwhile, the Union Democrats of Missouri, under the direction of Father Blair, made a public endorsement of Frank Blair, Jr. for secretary of war. This was Johnson's way of pressuring Stanton not to oppose his position thus driving a wedge between the Republicans.

Stanton's influence with Congress was as powerful as it had been during the war years when he served as the administration's "point man" defending accusations from the congressional Committee on the Conduct of the War. Stanton was trusted and respected by House and Senate leaders. He became an effective advisor to both the Congress and the president advising both sides as to what would be acceptable and what would not. Lincoln frequently signed documents without reading them as long as Stanton, a master of details, affixed his signature.

Stanton realized that the army was all that was holding the South in the Union. If he chose to resign his position, there would be no counterbalance to Johnson withdrawing the troops or reducing their number to an ineffectual level. Winning the war was a long arduous process, but any mistakes in this reconstruction process would sow the seeds for another armed conflict. Stanton was determined that if he could not move Johnson in the right direction, he would move Congress.

Secretary Seward was also trying to maintain good relations with Congress. When approached for his opinion on the amendment, he penciled in suggestions for revision leaving intact the important first and second sections. The amendment then passed the House without the clause that Stanton opposed. The *New York Times* declared that if Congress would accept this proposal as its answer to the reconstruction problem, it would enhance party peace and national unity. It passed through Congress and forwarded to the States for ratification in June. Johnson, with no official input allowed on amendments, declared that the amendment passed without executive approval.[191]

The Counter-Revolution of 1866

By this time it was clear to all that Johnson was not Lincoln. Obstinate, inflexible, and owning the most uninhibited tongue of any previous White House occupant, Johnson was unwilling to compromise on anything. On the freedmen's rights issue, Johnson's racial antipathies were not something he could put aside. He felt that the freedmen were best off by leaving them to the tender mercies of their former masters. Being a Jacksonian Democrat, he did not feel the need to compromise with the Congress on areas that infringed on his narrow views, so his opposition to the Fourteenth Amendment was expected. He voiced his opinion clearly in a statement to his secretary Colonel Moore, "Sir I am right, I know I am right, and I am damned if I do not adhere to it". Politically, he did not believe that a majority of white voters would support equality for Negroes. Therefore, he made the decision that his opposition would become the primary issue of the upcoming Congressional elections.

There is no doubt that Johnson wanted to be president in his own right. The adulation of the Southern delegations and the urgings of the Blairs fanned his ambitions. In retrospect, adviser and supporter Gideon Welles felt that this was Johnson's greatest mistake. Had he devoted himself to enacting Lincoln's reconstruction principles rather than following his own ego, he may have made better decisions and not alienated so many people.

However, Johnson needed to be the center of every storm. He built his entire political career upon the energy that his controversial positions generated. He was a living defiance to the dominant southern belief that leadership belonged to the plantation aristocracy. To him 'compromise' meant 'betrayal'. The purity of his mission was what mattered and no one could alter his course.

Senator Charles Sumner (Massachusetts)

Strongly opinionated and an absolute abolitionist, Charles Sumner had the ability to craft political incorrectness into an art form. He was severely beaten on the Senate floor by South Carolina Democrat Congressman Preston S. Brooks on May 21, 1856 for his views.

Sumner and Lincoln disagreed on reconstruction issues but both respected each other. Lincoln was able to manipulate the old bachelor by allowing him to lobby his wife. He was a frequent visitor to the White House and often escorted Mary to the opera or theatre whenever Lincoln was too busy.

Honest, obnoxious, cultured and highly educated; Sumner was Andrew Johnson's leading foe in the Senate for his Reconstruction program.

A Party of His Own

The effects of the war changed forever the relationship of the government and the economy. When the Southern Democrats abandoned their seats during the secession crisis, the North took political advantage of the situation passing laws meant to stimulate capitalistic growth in the country. These included higher tariffs to spur industrialization, restoring aspects of the centralized banking system destroyed by the Jackson Democrats of the 1830's, the Homestead Act, and loans to build the first transcontinental railroad. Had the southern Democrats occupied their seats these acts would have never been enacted into law. Now, in order to re-occupy their seats they would have to accept this economic new deal along with the dreaded Thirteenth Amendment.

The Thirteenth Amendment abolishing slavery throughout the country was an economic disaster for the South. This loss of "human capital" represented a confiscation of about three billion dollars from the war torn Southern economy.[192] Furthermore, the Fourteenth Amendment, giving the former slaves the right to vote, would give blacks the majority of political power in several Confederate States. The thought of whites subjected to laws made up by blacks was abhorrent to Southerners, and the president concurred. Johnson could do little about the economic consequences of the Thirteenth Amendment, but the threat to the social order created by the proposed Fourteenth Amendment had to be opposed.

By late spring, Johnson felt that by taking his case to the people, he could not only stop the Fourteenth Amendment at the State level but also have the Radicals voted out of office. To accomplish these tasks he decided that he was going to form his new political party, with the help and sponsorship of the Blairs. The party would be dedicated to his ideas on reconstruction and any former Lincoln cabinet members who did not agree with him could hand in their resignations.

In May 1866, a political club called the "National Union Club", a non-partisan group, organized themselves in Washington. Its purpose was to form a new party with Johnson as the head hoping to attract Democrats and Republicans under Johnson's standard. They arranged to greet the president and his Cabinet on May 23 with the idea of forcing Cabinet members to reveal their positions. They hoped to get Stanton to embarrass himself by revealing the wide differences he had with the president and justify in the public mind the need for his removal.

Stanton was ready. Reading from prepared remarks and appealing to patriotism, he explained his views and emphasized the powers of Congress giving his enemies nothing that would justify Johnson removing him. Attorney General Speed, Secretary of the Interior Harlan, and Postmaster General William Dennison handed in their resignations rather than work outside the Republican Party.

Johnson tried to attract Democrats to his banner by replacing Republican beneficiaries of patronage with Democrats, but to the out of power Democrats it was never enough to gain much support. The Peace Democrats and War Democrats badly divided the Party during the war, but now the separate factions were coming back into the fold. With the certain prospects of controlling the South once readmitted into the Union, why would they want to follow Johnson?

Johnson's new policy of rewarding his supporters with patronage whether they were Democrats or Republicans and removing those who didn't agree with him drove the Conservative Republicans further into the Radical camp. Senator John Sherman, brother of General William Tecumseh, was infuriated. Differences of opinion on public policies were one thing, but "turning out good men merely because they adhered to their party convictions is simply an unmitigated outrage". Johnson had poisoned his own well as far as Republicans were concerned. The chances of success for his new party were slim.

Stanton decided to remain silent on the issue of supporting Johnson on the formation of a new party. He realized that to surrender his cabinet position and allow Johnson unsupervised use of it would result in a racial bloodbath in the South. Johnson's fanatical opposition to the Fourteenth Amendment further led Stanton to believe that once Johnson gained Democratic support, he might use the army to unseat the Republican majority. This use of the army was not a farfetched scheme. If Frank Blair, Jr., had gotten control of the War Office, he undoubtedly would have used it for the new party's benefit. He indicated as much in a letter to his father in regards to his State of Missouri:

> ...if we had the president's active cooperation- If he would turn every Radical in the State out of office (which it seems his cabinet will not allow him to do) and if he could give us some man in the place of Genl Pope who would not allow the militia to overawe our people, we could clean out every Radical now in Congress from this State. I know such a thing is impossible with Stanton as Secretary of War- impossible with Seward and the rest of the scoundrels the president has about him.[193]

Politics, they say, make strange bedfellows, and the relationship of Stanton and Johnson proves the validity of this statement. When Gideon Welles, Johnson's most reliable 'yes' man, discovered that Stanton was opposed to the formation of the new party, he immediately informed Johnson. Although, he said, it pained him to counsel Johnson concerning one of his colleagues; he frankly told the president that the administration could "not get along this way". "No, it will be difficult," was all Johnson said, leaving Welles in a state of incredulity.

Stanton was walking a critical line in the summer of 1866. His president was openly trying to destroy the party that had put him into power. He was maneuvering to make it impossible for the army to protect the freedmen and maintain control in the Southern States, and he was openly challenging the authority of Congress to pass laws that were different from his own reconstruction program. As an advisor to the president, Stanton continually counseled to cooperate with the Congress and though he tried to appear as a neutral, it was clear that he was acting with the Radicals. Yet, Johnson still refused to ask Stanton to resign his post.

Many historians agreed with the Blairs' conclusion that Johnson's unwillingness to fire Stanton illustrated Johnson's weakness of character. However, up to this point, Johnson was willing to take on the entire Congress and risk his presidency hoping that the voters would support his program. Neither was Johnson a fool. He knew where Stanton stood in relation to his policy and his influence in the legislature. There was no deception on the part of Stanton, despite the efforts of Pro-Johnson historians to make us believe so. Welles, Blair, and other confidants to Johnson constantly advocated firing Stanton, reminding Johnson that Stanton was not on his team and pointing out his "treachery".

The Counter-Revolution of 1866   295

One of Johnson's chief defenders, Treasury Secretary McCulloch described the relationship in his memoirs. Stanton "attended Cabinet meetings, not as an adviser of the president but as an opponent of the policy to which he had been committed, and the president lacked the nerve to dismiss him. The failure of the president to exercise his undoubted right to rid himself of a minister who differed from him upon very important questions, who had become personally obnoxious to him, and to whom he regarded as an enemy and spy, was a blunder from there is no excuse. In this crisis of his political life, Mr. Johnson exhibited a want of spirit and decision which astonished those who were familiar with his antecedents".

Johnson's strategy at this point was to do his best to embarrass and isolate Stanton in cabinet meetings forcing him to resign. He obviously felt it was in his own best interests not to fire him.

On July 14, Governor Parson Brownlow of Tennessee, a rival of Johnson who was anxious to bring his State back into the Union, asked General George Thomas for military assistance to compel the attendance of the Democratic members of the legislature in order to muster a quorum to ratify the Fourteenth Amendment. Thomas refused to interfere in a State matter so Brownlow used his sergeants-at-arms to round up the legislators, obtain his quorum, and ratify the amendment. The next day Stanton showed the telegram to Johnson who agreed with the decision that the military must not interfere with the civil government. On July 19, Brownlow signed the legislation, and Tennessee, Johnson's home State, became the first to return to the Union under the dictates of Congress.

Stanton Remains Untouchable

The New Orleans Riot of July 30, 1866 may have brought Johnson to the breaking point with Stanton, but it still did not push him over. The president's May 1865 amnesty proclamation and wholesale distribution of pardons re-enfranchised Confederate veterans. By the end of the year, the former rebels enacted Black Codes to ensure white dominance of the liberated black laborers. Under Johnson's restoration of white "home rule," former Confederate soldiers controlled the city government of New Orleans, suppressed the black vote and allowed Democrats to retake power.

Since Congress had yet to approve the State constitution of Louisiana, former governor George Hahn and Unionists moved to reconvene Louisiana's constitutional convention to enfranchise blacks in Louisiana and prohibit the former Confederates from voting. Their intent was to revise the State's constitution and make it acceptable to Congress.

Johnson told the Louisiana delegation that this would be an extremely bad time to take such an action. However, the Free-Soilers who wrote the Louisiana constitution in 1864 took advantage of a clause to reassemble the Constitutional Convention. Delegates proposed establishing a new state government based on Lincoln's original premise of a loyal electorate and fairness to Negroes. With the prospect of a biracial democracy, blacks in New Orleans rallied in support of the conventioneers.

On July 27, at a public meeting, the convention adopted the black suffrage amendment to the constitution. The convention's next step was to submit the amended constitution to a vote of the people, and if ratified submit it to Congress for approval.

The Counter-Revolution of 1866

On the July 28, the mayor of New Orleans and the lieutenant governor (Democrats) proposed to General Absalom Baird, the acting Federal commander and Johnson's handpicked head of Louisiana's Freedmen's Bureau, that they felt the convention was illegal and they were going to arrest the delegates. General Baird objected to the mayor's action feeling that the delegates had the right to assemble and telegraphed Stanton as follows:

> *A convention has been called, with the sanction of Governor Wells, to meet here on Monday. The lieutenant governor and city authorities think it unlawful, and propose to break it up by arresting the delegates. I have given no orders on the subject, but have warned parties that I should not countenance or permit such action without instructions to that effect from the president. Please instruct me by telegraph.*

Again, Stanton did not respond to this telegram. Since Johnson recently advised him not to have the military interfere with civil authorities, he gave Baird no permission to impede or obstruct the convention.

On the same day, the lieutenant governor and the mayor telegraphed President Johnson:

> *Radical mass meetings composed mainly of large numbers of Negroes last night ending in a riot; the committee of arrangements of said meeting assembling tonight. Violent and incendiary speeches made; Negroes called to arm themselves. You bitterly denounced! Governor Wells arrived last night, but sides with the convention movement. The whole matter before the Grand Jury; but impossible to execute civil process without certainty of riot. Contemplated to have the members of the convention arrested under process from the criminal court of this district. Is the military to interfere to prevent process of court?*

The president replied the same day:

> *The military will be expected to sustain and not to obstruct or interfere with the proceeding of the court. A dispatch on the subject was sent to Governor Wells.*

The president did not tell Stanton of the reply nor did he issue any military orders directly to General Baird. The mayor gave the police their orders.[194]

On July 30, a white mob primarily made up of ex-Confederate soldiers attacked the convention of Freedmen. When the New Orleans police force intervened, they joined the assailants in the slaughter. Union troops finally arrived to provide order but it was too late. Of the 38 conventioneers murdered, 34 were Negroes. Of the 146 wounded, 119 were black. The news coming right before Johnson's National Union Convention had a devastating impact on the North. People were horrified to read of former Confederates wantonly murdering helpless blacks. To many this was the proof that the South was unrepentant for the war and that Negroes needed protection. It also brought fears that hostilities between the two regions would flare up again.

Two weeks after the riot, Johnson learned of the message from General Baird to Stanton asking if he had any special instructions as to how to handle the upcoming convention. Stanton gave no orders to Baird, nor did he show the telegram to Johnson. Had he done so, Johnson said he would have directed the military not to offer protection to the Freedmen, and the convention would have dispersed, thus avoiding any possible confrontation.

Stanton replied that there was no indication that any confrontation was in the offing since the president did not share his information with him. Thus, he had no reason to contradict the president's own instructions given the previous week. Baird believed that the convention to be legally authorized and Stanton agreed that the Freedmen had a right to assemble. Neither man knew the president had a secret conversation with the city officials, and did not suspect that the city police were going to kill convention members. Stanton's decision not to give any extraordinary guidelines to Baird was in keeping with the policy that Johnson had proclaimed.

Johnson could not publicly censure Stanton without admitting that his policies in the South worked only when the rights of Negroes were suspended. Johnson compounded the situation by expressing absolutely no sympathy for the murdered victims. Anxious to find a scapegoat he launched a vile attack on the Radical members of Congress in an attempt to blame them for instigating the melee. He also attempted to control the political damage by publishing an edited version of the riot by General Sheridan. This condensed version totally misrepresented details by censoring the part that severely rebuked the police. He released the entire report after Sheridan sent an indignant protest.

The riot hastened the coming of Military Reconstruction. Carl Schurz wrote to his wife;

> "Have you read of the disturbances in New Orleans? Several of my friends and acquaintances were killed or severely wounded in them. Isn't it frightful to think that the president himself should have encouraged such misdeeds? And yet there are men who force their way in to kiss his hand! The federal officers are attempting here also to organize a Johnson party."[195]

The massacre in New Orleans led Radicals to believe that the South was intent on ignoring the Civil Rights Act of 1866 giving Negroes the right of suffrage. They proposed putting the suffrage principle into the Fourteenth Amendment so that it would become enshrined in the Constitution. This action would effectively overturn the *Dred Scott* decision and prevent the Supreme Court from ruling the Civil Rights Act of 1866 to be unconstitutional.* Schurz began to talk of a fifteenth amendment which would enforce upon the rebel states the necessity of giving their former slaves the right to vote *and* provide a system of common school education for all.

General John Pope summed up the feelings of the army officers with a speech risking his professional career by assuming a public position. He argued that if the "military power is suspended" in the South, "at once the old political & personal influences will resume their activity." Stanton and Grant approved its text hoping that Pope's words of warning would alert the North that the president was putting the nation on a disastrous course.

Five weeks after the riot, Johnson excused the slaughter on the ground that the Freedmen had denounced him and that the conventioneers were insurgents and traitors.[196]

Privately he blamed Stanton

---

* the *Dred Scott decision* declared that African Americans were not and could not become citizens of the United States or enjoy any of the privileges and immunities of citizenship

President Andrew Johnson

The Lincoln-Johnson ticket was the political equivalent of a shotgun marriage. Neither man liked the other very much but both used the other for political gain. Neither exchanged congratulatory telegrams on their nominations and there was very little communication between them afterwards.

Several times, Lincoln had avoided a conference requested by Johnson. Johnson met with Lincoln only once after the inauguration, on the day of the assassination.

The Critical Election

The campaign of 1866 was a referendum vote on the Fourteenth Amendment as the document to end the war. Although radicals Stevens and Sumner thought the amendment was only a step towards "complete justice", most Republicans and a majority of the Northern people thought it was fair settlement. The riots in Memphis and New Orleans belied Johnson's claim that he had reconstructed the Southern States. The North came to the realization that until the Negroes had the right to vote and the rebels disenfranchised there would be no peace. Future President, Rutherford B. Hayes of Ohio wrote his friend Guy M. Bryan of Texas telling him *"if we carry these elections, this plan contains the best terms you will ever get."* "Don't let Andy Johnson deceive you," he added. "He doesn't know the Northern people."[197]

Politically, Johnson's actions, statements, and supporters led to charges that he was in league with the traitors that they had fought a war to defeat. His stubbornness to rigid Constitutional theories, his harangues against Congress, and his open encouragement of the rebel states to resist ratification of the Fourteenth Amendment put his opposition into a perspective that the voters could understand. Thad Stevens said, "You all remember that in Egypt. He sent frogs, locusts, murrain, lice, and finally demanded the first-born of every one of the oppressors. Almost all of these have been taken from us. We have been oppressed with taxes and debts and He has sent us worse than lice, and has afflicted us with an Andrew Johnson."

In August, the National Union Convention made up of white southerners, northern Democrats, presidential appointees and moderate Republicans, assembled in Philadelphia to endorse Johnson's reconstruction efforts. The goal was to marginalize the Radicals influence by repudiating the proposed Fourteenth Amendment and form a new political party, headed by Johnson.

The Counter-Revolution of 1866

The convention began with Union General Darius Couch of Massachusetts marching arm in arm with Governor James L. Orr of South Carolina, symbolizing the reunification achieved under the president. However, despite the fervid oratory by many speakers the goal of creating a new 'Andy Johnson' party failed.

Johnson realized that his third-party movement lacked local support and grass-roots organization. Later that month, Seward received an invitation to speak at the dedication of a memorial to the late Senator Stephen A. Douglas. Sensing an excellent opportunity to make a stumping tour for the new party, Johnson decided to accompany his secretary of war state. The tour would hit the main cities of the North; Philadelphia, New York, Albany, Niagara, Detroit, to Chicago. It would then go down to St. Louis, Louisville and back to Washington. The president headed the delegation that included Seward, Grant, Admiral Farragut, and other local and military leaders to add luster to Johnson's appearance. Johnson supporters called it the "swing across the circle" and it was a complete disaster.

Throughout the journey, Johnson used his Tennessee rabble-rouser style of stump speaking abandoning all the dignity that comes with the presidency. A senator cautioned him, not to "allow the excitement of the moment to draw from you any *extemporaneous speeches*" but it was to no avail. Johnson never understood that the President of the United States needed to be a uniter not a divider.

His speeches were rambling, bitter, and self-pitying. He continued to use the phrase "Hang Thad Stevens" as his battle cry. It was the infamous Washington Birthday speech at every stop. Many newspapers again speculated that he was intoxicated. James Russell Lowell wrote, "What an anti Johnson lecturer we have in Johnson! Sumner has been right about the cuss from the first. …" He sparred with hecklers, excused all that was being done in the South by the former Confederates, and denounced Congress, charging it with trying to break up the government and even denying its lawfulness.

By denying its lawfulness, he inferred that any laws they enacted did not bind him. He had already asked the new attorney General Henry Stanberry for an opinion as to the legitimacy of the 39th Congress. Rumors circulated that Johnson planned to recognize a Congress made up of Southern representatives and cooperative Northern Democrats. In fact, he posed the possibility to Grant to gauge his reaction. Grant spoke plainly: "The army will support the Congress as it is now and disperse the other."[198]

Johnson's greatest weakness was his insensitivity to public opinion. He was unable to understand the northern mood in 1866 and worse; he was openly defiant of it. He believed all white men shared his racial views. His antics gained no support from the electorate and greatly weakened his cause by the violence of his language and manner. The governors of Indiana, Pennsylvania, Ohio, Illinois, Michigan, and Missouri all avoided greeting him. In Battle Creek, Michigan, he spewed a stream of curses at the crowd when someone called, "Three cheers for Thad Stevens!"

Grant, who did not enjoy his part of this dog and pony show, began drinking and became too "ill" to make appearances. He finally was able to leave the campaign halfway through the tour because, as he stated, he did not "care to accompany a man who was deliberately digging his own grave".[199] When his name was used in the campaign as supporting Johnson, Grant quickly responded that no man was authorized to speak for him on political matters.

With his campaign going badly, was Johnson perhaps planning a coup d'etat? Generals Grant and Sherman seemed to think so. Sherman was second in popularity only to Grant and sympathetic towards the president's problems. Johnson hatched a plan to send Grant on a diplomatic mission to Mexico and insert Sherman as general-in-chief ad-interim. With Grant gone, Sherman would be duty bound to obey Johnson's direct orders bypassing Stanton. Alternatively, he was prepared to offer Sherman the secretary of war position and dismiss Stanton. By replacing Stanton with a war hero, he would minimize the public fallout. Either way he would break up the Stanton and Grant relationship and gain control of the army.

However, Sherman would not take the bait. "This is some plan to get Grant out of the way, and to get me here, but I will be no party to such a move," Sherman wrote to his wife. Johnson was pressing to deploy troops in Maryland to support the white supremacist government. The governor threatened to replace registrars who refused to add un-qualified ex-rebels and asked Johnson for help. Johnson asked Grant to send troops to prevent violence, but Grant refused saying it would give the impression of supporting one faction over another.

On October 23, Johnson invited Grant to attend a cabinet meeting showdown. When asked if he was prepared for his mission to Mexico, Grant reminded the president that he had previously communicated to him that he felt that his present duties could not allow him to leave, and he did not wish to go. Johnson growled to his Attorney General asking if there is any reason why General Grant should not obey his orders. Before he could answer, Grant immediately rose from his seat and told the president in slow measured tones that he was obliged to carry out the president's military orders, not his diplomatic ones. Grant, who was famously described as a man who had a facial expression that looked as if he had decided to drive his head through a brick wall, and was about to do it, stared hard at the president and said, *"No power on earth can compel me to it."* The president backed down and decided to send General Sherman in his place.[200]

Grant told Congressman Boutwell that in early autumn, 1866, Johnson asked him, "If I should have trouble with Congress, which side would you support?" Grant replied, "That would depend upon which side the law was." From this conversation, Boutwell concluded that "Johnson made a serious and persistent attempt, in the autumn of 1866, to send General Grant to Mexico. . . without any sufficient and honorable reason." [201] Boutwell feared a presidentially inspired military coup to revolutionize the government in favor of the rebel states.

As the election approached, the debates over the opposing plans for reconstruction were intense on every stump spot and in every newspaper. Excitement ran extremely high during the campaign for members of Congress in 1866. The people listened and decided. Johnson's party suffered a humiliating rout. The Republicans won over a two-thirds majority in both houses of Congress. [202]

The *Nation* summed up election results in this way: "The first point which has unquestionably been passed upon is that the people will not trust the South, or its ally, the Democratic party of the North, to rule in our government. The second is that the South shall not be restored unconditionally to its privileges in the Union. The third is, that Congress, and not the Executive, is to name the conditions of restoration. The fourth that the conditions already proposed are abundantly liberal to the South."[203]

The overwhelming victory of the Republicans, combined with the illness of his wife, compelled Stanton to make plans to leave office in December when Congress reconvened. The Fourteenth Amendment was only three states away from ratification. All Johnson needed to do was support the will of the people, and the Southerners would have complied. However, the self-righteous Johnson had neither the intention of supporting the amendment nor the will to cooperate with Congress. Stanton was disheartened that Johnson's annual message to the Congress did not endorse the amendment or give any other hope of change.

Secretary Seward wrote and offered him a conciliatory message to give to Congress that he promptly rejected for a more confrontational one. Even though the voters of the country overwhelmingly rejected Johnson's policies and left him as a man without a party, Johnson would not change his tone or position. Nor would he try to seek an arrangement with Congress. The 'Great Plebeian', who enjoyed lecturing others that his power came from the common people, would now govern against their expressed will. The lines were drawn. Any hint of compromise would be regarded as weakness.

Due to Johnson's obstinacy, Congress decided to call itself into special session. It decreed that the Fortieth Congress (elected in 1866) would begin on March 4, 1867, rather than the normal time of the following December. The purpose was to prevent Johnson from pursuing his own policies in between sessions. The Congress took this action at the urging of Grant and Stanton although it did not require much persuasion. This was an unprecedented step, and many Johnson's supporters deemed it illegal. Friends of Johnson asserted that since this Congress was an illegal body, the president should use military force to dissolve Congress and call for new elections.

In October 1866, Congressman Boutwell hypothetically, spelled out Johnson's strategy in an article in the *Atlantic Monthly*. Boutwell prophesized that the president would refuse to recognize the Fortieth Congress and summon a new Congress with fifty persons claiming seats from the ten unrepresented states. If the Republicans denied these seats, Boutwell surmised, "the supporters of the president, aided directly or indirectly by the army and police, would take possession of the hall, and organize the assembly by force."[204]

Stanton feared that Johnson was contemplating just such an action. This talk combined with Johnson's attempt to move Grant to Mexico just before the election strengthened Stanton's suspicions. In early December, he invited Boutwell to the war department for a private meeting.

Stanton told Boutwell that his article had "disturbed the president," but that Johnson had not abandoned his scheme for the reorganization of Congress. Stanton shared his fear that Johnson might attempt to re-establish the government by assembling a Congress composed of members from the seceding states and Northern Democrats. He told him that he was more concerned about the fate of the country than at any time during the Civil War. Johnson was now a desperate politician, issuing military orders without talking to Grant or the secretary of war.

Stanton's greatest worry was that the president would send Grant away from Washington and take over direct control of the army.

Fearing a military coup the Republicans worked quickly. In order to protect the army from Johnson's meddling, Speaker Colfax put into the appropriations bill three clauses that compelled the president to disband the militias of the Southern States, submit all military orders to go through the Commanding General, and specified that the president must not move Grant out of Washington without Congressional consent. Congress attached this rider to the Military Appropriations Bill for 1867-68. Johnson was again furious by the Congressional interference of his Constitutional powers, but the alternative was to veto the bill and effectively disband the army. Other members of the cabinet felt that he had no choice but to sign the bill as written. The public reaction against him would be bitter and Congress would override his veto. He reluctantly agreed to sign the bill, but under protest.

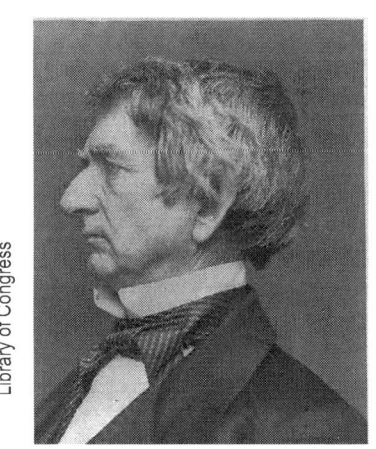

William H. Seward's wounds were first feared to be mortal but he made an amazing recovery and returned as Secretary of State under President Andrew Johnson. During Johnson's term, Seward became instrumental in avoiding war with Napoleon III of France over Mexico and obtaining a settlement with England for the damages caused by the Confederate warships provided by Great Britain. He also showed his foresight in being able to purchase Alaska from Russia in 1867.

William Henry Seward

Return of the Surratt Problem

John Surratt was unaware that the government did not want him captured as he traveled to London, Paris, and Rome. In Rome, he met up with a Dr. Neve of the English College. After staying with him for a time, Surratt decided to volunteer to become a Zouave and enlisted in the army of the Papal States under the name of John Watson. At this time, the newly formed Kingdom of Italy reduced the Papal States to Latium, the immediate neighborhood of Rome. The Papal army was a multi-national force made up by Catholics from all over the world. There, an old war acquaintance, Henri Beaumont de Sainte Marie recognized Surratt. Sainte Marie, familiar with Surratt and knowledgeable about the reward for his capture, reported his location to Rufus King, the American Minister to the Papal States on April 21, 1866.

At the time, there was no extradition treaty between the Papal States and the United States and it was contrary to Vatican policy to turn over suspected criminals when there was a possibility of the death penalty. However, King was able to secure the release of both Surratt and Sainte Marie from Cardinal Antonelli, the Papal Secretary of State.

Politics played a big role in these negotiations. The newly formed Kingdom of Italy was a threat to overrun the Papal States. Only the French army stationed in Rome kept the invaders at bay. No one knew how long Louis Napoleon would support the Pope. Napoleon's take-over of Mexico during the Civil War had put the United States and France on a course towards war. Secretary Seward was trying to evict French troops without starting another conflict. Pope Pius IX confidants asked King that if the Pope was compelled to flee the Papal dominions, could he find protection in the United States? Seward agreed and had a ship made ready.[205]

Seward's decision would have caused a political storm if it became public. Know-nothing anti-Catholic bigotry was still bubbling in the country. Michael O'Laughlin, Dr. Mudd and the Surratts were Catholics leading some to believe that the assassination was part of plot by the Catholic Church to take over the country.

However, with the critical elections of 1866 fast approaching, the last thing the Johnson administration wanted was to extradite John Surratt. The Radicals were fanning rumors implicating Johnson in Lincoln's assassination. Johnson believed that if Surratt was captured "such a person and in such a condition might make almost any statement". As a consequence extradition negotiations dragged on till after the elections. Once the paperwork was complete, Antonelli decided to have Surratt arrested before the extradition request of the State Department was forwarded. However, Surratt made a daring escape, leaping down a thirty-five foot drop to a narrow mountain ledge and into the Kingdom of Italy where he eluded capture from the pursuing Zouaves.

Surratt then surfaced in Naples telling police he was an Englishman escaping from a Roman regiment where he had been under arrest for insubordination. Naples was not part of the Papal States and not interested in returning deserters. Taken to the British Consulate Surratt claimed protection as a Canadian.

On the evening of November 11, Surratt, traveling under the alias of John Agostina, boarded a steamer, bound for Alexandria, Egypt, his third-class fare paid by "some English gentlemen". Rufus King, still on the trail, learned that he was aboard the TRIPOLI and cabled United States Consul William Winthrop at Malta, the ship's refueling point. Winthrop was unable to stop the ship and Surratt was able to continue his voyage unmolested.[206]

The great escape ended when the *Tripoli* docked at Alexandria on November 23. Authorities quarantined Surratt along with 77 fellow third-class passengers. Four days later, United States Consul-General Charles Hale confronted Surratt who now insisted his name was Walters. Unfortunately, Surratt was the only one aboard wearing a Zouave uniform, so Hale arrested him and reported his capture to the secretary of war state. Seward sent the *U.S.S. Swatara* to Alexandria, and on December 21, 1866, the final conspirator was in custody.

John Surratt in a Zouave uniform

John Surratt was tried by a civil court and received a deadlocked verdict from a largely southern jury, which included fellow conspirator Richard Smoot's brother. Fearing that he could be re-tried again at any time he decided to remain quiet about what he knew of the assassination.

He admitted his role in the abduction plot but not in the assassination. He blamed his mother's execution on the 'perjured' testimony of his friend Lewis Weichmann and claimed ignorance of his mother's plight.

Before he died in 1916 at the age of 72 he burned a manuscript detailing his side of the story, leaving no written record for history.

Chapter 10

The Implosion of 1867

The First Impeachment Review

On January 7, 1867, the House adopted a resolution, introduced by Representative James Ashley of Ohio, instructing the Judiciary Committee to inquire into the conduct of Andrew Johnson for evidence of high crimes or misdemeanors that could lead to his impeachment. The main charges investigated were that Johnson had illegally returned property to Southern rebels, he abused his pardon power towards enemies of the United States, he abused his veto power, and the implication of his involvement in the plot to assassinate Lincoln. As long as this committee was active, Johnson could not move against Stanton. However, if Stanton held his secret during these sessions, it would look like political sour grapes to implicate Johnson afterwards. When the committee finished their work, he would be able to free himself from the War Secretary.

Although his party lost the election, the president's lobbying effort against the Fourteenth Amendment appeared to be successful. Texas, Georgia, North Carolina, Arkansas, Florida, South Carolina, Alabama, Virginia, Mississippi, and Louisiana had all rejected the amendment by February 1867. The rejection of such a mild treaty to unify the nation again pushed moderates into the Radical camp. Future President James Garfield said, "...the last one of the sinful ten has at last with contempt and scorn, flung back into our teeth the magnanimous offer of a generous nation. It is now our turn to act. They would not cooperate with us to rebuild what they destroyed. We must remove the rubbish and rebuild from the bottom."

Meanwhile the Supreme Court was readying its decision involving the question of martial law. Martial law was the only legal protection the army in the South had from the persecution of its citizens. The biased civil courts were routinely letting offenders go with no more than a "disturbing the peace" offense. The Court's decision in the Milligan case concluded that martial law was unwarranted wherever civil courts functioned. This gave Johnson the confidence to continue his war with Congress and put the army in an impossible situation. In an attempt to resolve the problem, Congress asked the president for any facts which came to him with regards to the failure to enforce the Civil Rights Act. When Johnson turned the problem over to his cabinet, Stanton responded with a report from Freedman bureau chief General Howard using local newspaper accounts to show over 440 murders. Johnson was again infuriated with Stanton believing he was adding unnecessary fuel to his fight with Congress. However, Congress was already receiving many letters from the South detailing the murder and mayhem that were taking place upon Negroes and soldiers.

To remedy the situation Congress began efforts on what became known as the Reconstruction Act. Working closely with Grant, the bill divided the South into martial districts under the command of five generals, named by the president. Loyal unionists, black and white, were to rebuild the State governments while the electorate would create new State constitutions and ratify the Fourteenth Amendment. Once completed the States delegates would regain their seats in Congress.

Grant worked closely with General Sherman's brother Senator John Sherman of Ohio who sponsored the bill in the Senate, making certain that the act would provide for suffrage as well as an exit strategy for the military occupation. Previous to this point Grant was skeptical over the wisdom of enfranchising the Freedmen but the obstinacy of White Southerners for the Black Codes combined with the increasing violence convinced him that suffrage was required. This was the first public indication that Grant was leaning towards the Radical position.

The bill was remarkably similar to the reconstruction proposal that Stanton had made and Johnson had rejected in his first cabinet meeting almost two years before. Welles howled to Johnson that Stanton was the architect of this scheme and was deeply involved with the Radicals. Yet to his frustration, even though Johnson assented to all his observations Welles wrote, "he still hesitates, fails to act retains bad advisors and traitors".[207]

The Blairs believed that the president should not only veto the bill, but if it passed, he should refuse to execute it. Seward advised Johnson against Blair's opinion. Impeachment inquiries were already beginning in the Congress and further defiance could tip the scales and wreck the government.

Although Stanton worked with the Radicals, he was not one of them. When Thaddeus Stevens pushed his Military Reconstruction Bill, which would have reduced the Southern states back to a territorial status, Stanton stood against it. He advised the president that the Stevens proposal was one that would end in noise and smoke.
He believed that Steven's proposal to confiscate land from Southern whites and distribute it among the Blacks was not only wrong but would lead to large-scale guerrilla warfare in the South. He believed that the existing governments were lawful, the reconstruction was proper, and he was opposed to the bill. Even Welles concurred with his opinion.

Nathanial Banks, former Governor of Massachusetts, advised Johnson that in his view there should be someone in the Cabinet who could be a channel of communication between the President and Congress. The president rejected this advice. He gave thought to changing the holdovers of the Lincoln administration by appointing Grant as secretary of war, Admiral Farragut as secretary of the navy, and Charles Adams as secretary of state. However, he said, "Such a course would occasion harsh feelings on the part of some Cabinet officers who would be relieved, and to some of whom he was very much attached." Johnson was 'very much attached' to Seward and Welles. Obviously, he was fearful of "harsh" feelings with Stanton. [208]

In a cabinet meeting on February 22 to discuss the Reconstruction Act, Stanton stood alone in advising the president to approve the bill. He saw nothing in the act for Johnson to veto. Considering what measures the Congress could approve for dealing with the situation in the South, the act was a moderate process. However, once again, Johnson was angling for another fight with Congress even if it provoked impeachment. He vetoed the act, and once again, Congress overrode his veto.

Congress also passed a bill regulating the Tenure of Civil Officers. This bill was the response to Johnson's scheme of the Blairs to purge Republican officeholders and appoint conservative Democrats in their places.

Johnson had replaced almost seventeen hundred postmasters simply for political revenge. Postmasters were the heart of the political patronage system. The intent of the Tenure bill was to thwart Johnson from using his patronage power. It was a purely political law that allowed the president to remove officeholders only with the Senate's consent. When the Senate was not in session, the president could suspend an officer and give his reasons to the Senate within twenty days of its reconvening for a final disposition. The act referred specifically to Cabinet members who were to hold their positions "during the term of the president by whom they were appointed, and for one month thereafter, subject to removal with the advice and consent of the Senate". This clause prevented Johnson from removing the remaining Lincoln appointees (Stanton, Seward and Welles) from office. The main beneficiary of this clause was Stanton, the sole voice of reason within the Cabinet.

During the debate of the bill on the floor of the House, Congressman John Bingham warned that President Johnson would commit a high crime and misdemeanor if he removed a "competent and faithful officer…for corrupt and personal ends". The Democrats howled that Bingham was threatening the president. Bingham denied the accusation saying that he was merely "affirming a self-evident truth".[209]

When Johnson asked for advice from his Cabinet on the Tenure Bill, Stanton joined with the rest of the Cabinet in advising its veto. Welles pushed himself to the front of the line decrying that the member for whom it was framed was not worthy to be an adviser of the president.

Stanton advised that it was the president's duty to defend his power from usurpation. During the war, the inability to discharge inept officers hampered Stanton. He realized that it would be hypocritical of him to endorse a legislative restriction on not only the president's power but also his own as secretary of war.

Seeing a chance to pit Stanton against the Congress, Johnson asked him to compose the veto message. Stanton balked citing a lack of time and rheumatism. Seward then offered to write the veto on the condition that Stanton would assist him. Stanton concurred, and both men wrote the veto.

Anticipating that the veto would be overturned, Frank Blair Jr. advised Johnson to circumvent the intent of the Tenure Bill by making a clean sweep of all cabinet incumbents before returning the veto to the Congress. Johnson agreed, but as long as the Impeachment Committee was calling witnesses, he could not afford to betray Stanton's trust. However, he felt that Stanton's opposition to the bill would make it easier to remove him once the Impeachment Committee had finished.

On March 4, the Thirty-Ninth Congress ended, and the Fortieth Congress convened. All eyes were on Johnson. Would he follow and enforce the laws of Congress? His first move was to consult with Grant whose task under the Reconstruction Law was to recommend generals for the five Military District Commanders. Johnson promptly accepted Grant's recommendations. He appointed John Schofield to the first district (Virginia), Daniel Sickles to the second (Carolinas), John Pope to the third (Georgia, Alabama, Florida), Edward Ord to the fourth (Arkansas and Mississippi), and Philip Sheridan to the fifth (Louisiana, Texas).

Grant was still the popular hero, but not trusted by some of the Radicals. Johnson felt that if he could woo him over to the Democratic side, he would be helpful in future fights with Congress. Sickles, Pope, and Sheridan were certainly not people of whom Johnson would normally approve, but he would bide his time and dismiss them later.

The Blairs were also hoping that Grant would become the 1868 Democratic presidential candidate. Grant was a Democrat before the war, and he married the daughter of a Maryland slaveholder. The Blairs were willing to sacrifice their greatest desire, Frank Jr. as president, if Grant would accept the nomination. However, Grant remained noncommittal.

The Second Reconstruction Act passed Congress on March 23. This one made up for a deficiency in the first act by providing for the registration of voters who could swear to past loyalty. Registrars appointed by the military commanders would be responsible for verifying the claims. Once the registration of voters was complete, the act called for conventions and ratification by a popular majority. Johnson issued another veto and Congress again overrode it.

However, Johnson decided to cool down the hatred of political extremism. He was keeping a close eye on the Impeachment Committee. If he did not heat up the rhetoric or do anything to provoke Congress, impeachment would die a natural death. Besides, he saw a loophole in the Act that he would exploit when the Congress adjourned.

In an attempt to limit his commander-in-chief functions, the Reconstruction Act created a second army in whom the Military Commanders had the power to interpret the Reconstruction Law over their assigned territories. However, the president could remove them if they failed to carry out their responsibilities set by Congress. Johnson interpreted this as the Congress having bypassed Stanton and Grant, giving him the responsibility to remove commanders who did not interpret the law as Johnson interpreted the law.

General Sheridan was the first to take advantage of his new powers. While Congress was still in session, he removed the State and municipal officials who he felt were responsible for the New Orleans riot. Johnson quickly asked his Attorney General Stanberry if a District Commander had the power to remove civil officials and ordered Sheridan to cease and desist from further removals until Stanberry could issue his opinion. Grant gave Sheridan the order through traditional channels, but he also issued Sheridan a warning through private channels that his action displeased the administration, and there was talk of removing him. He assured Sheridan that he and Stanton would resist the move but "suggested" that he hold off on any further actions.

Grant's unofficial channels of communication were the key to offsetting the president's recklessness. The military men that he recommended for the District Command posts were all men with whom he had a solid relationship and would trust his advice. Stanton would give him an advanced warning about what was coming, and he would pass it along to the commanders.

On June 3, the Judiciary Committee voted 5-4 not to impeach the president. Feeling that the tension had been relieved, the Congress decided to adjourn until July 4, despite the protests of Grant and Stanton to stay in session and keep Johnson in check. Congress believed they had effectively blocked the president's power to control the army in the South. He could no longer replace Grant as he had recently tried to do by sending him to Mexico, or to bypass him and Stanton as he had done at New Orleans just before the riot. The Tenure of Office Act protected Stanton in the war secretary's position so the Republican majority in Congress felt comfortable enough to adjourn.

The Implosion of 1867

The preceding three months proved to be the calm before the storm. Attorney General Stanberry gave his opinion on the Reconstruction laws. Not surprising the opinion was very narrow and limited the powers of the District Commanders. Johnson's goal was to get a united cabinet to agree with the opinion that his interim "State Governments" in the South could annul and overturn the acts of Congress. This action would in effect establish State sovereignty over the victory of the Union army. Anticipating opposition from his Secretary of War, he asked Attorney General Stanberry to prepare a "string of questions" to corner Stanton into complying with the cabinet position.[210]

The purpose of this showdown was to either coerce Stanton into submitting to the president's position or to force him to resign. The Cabinet meetings lasted from June 18 through June 20 with Johnson and Stanberry hammering Stanton that the president by his authority of commander-in-chief had the authority to supervise the District Commanders and they were legally bound to carry out his instructions. By their interpretation of the law, the president could rectify any act of the Generals if they went beyond their powers. This included the power to suspend or abolish state laws or fire state officials.

Stanton stood alone tenaciously countering their opinion point by point. His fine legal mind for details was more than a match for the twisted self-serving logic of Stanberry and Johnson. He knew that Congress would not stand for interference and earnestly tried to dissuade the president from adopting Stanberry's extreme view.

Stanton informed the president that under the Military Reconstruction Act, the District Commanders were the ultimate authority in the territories they governed. Congress conferred their powers and the commanders were responsible only to the Congress for their actions. The president could not exercise oversight powers under his authority of commander-in-chief "any more than he could take upon himself in his own person any other duty of military service vested in a specific officer by law; as for example the duties of the quartermaster-general, surgeon-general or commissary-general".

Johnson was not interested in views with which he did not agree, and he was confident that with the unanimous opinion of the cabinet he could have his orders to the District Commanders supersede the will of Congress. At the end of three days of debate, Johnson was ready to issue his orders to the military commanders and suggesting that a preamble saying that he and the cabinet agreed on their interpretation.

Stanton quickly corrected the president on that point.

"Did not a majority vote constitute agreement?" asked Johnson.

"Not in the cabinet," replied Stanton. "The cabinet is merely an advisory body and the head of one department could not be bound by the opinions of other cabinet officers whose responsibilities were in other areas of government."

Seward concurred with Stanton on this point, and the frustrated Johnson told Stanton and Stanberry to write the preamble together in a language with which they could agree.

Therefore, the great debate within the cabinet ended with Stanton still heading the war department and not relenting to the pressure applied to him. Johnson leaked his accounts of these cabinet meetings to friendly newspapers. When Southerners heard Stanberry's interpretation, they felt emboldened to increase their harassment of Union soldiers and freedmen. Meanwhile, Stanton advised Grant on how his commanders could skirt the opinions of the Attorney General.

With the committee shut down and Congress on holiday, Johnson decided to launch his new offensive. On June 20, 1867, Johnson issued orders that registrars had no power to challenge a man's oath of loyalty. If suspected of swearing false oaths to qualify for voting, the proper recourse was to bring perjury charges in Southern state courts. Furthermore, he curtailed the powers of commanders to remove civilian officials who failed to cooperate in administrating the law. This interpretation gave the Johnson backed governments control over the elections and maximized the white vote.

The South was already taking measures to head off Negro suffrage by whippings. A conviction of a petty crime was punishable by a public whipping, which would disenfranchise a man from voting. North Carolina was now beginning to whip Negroes by the hundreds. General Dan Sickles infuriated by this practice forbade public whipping in the State. When the Governor protested to the president, Johnson immediately revoked Sickles' order, and the whippings continued.

Once again, Congressional resentment against Johnson raged. Grant and Stanton helped prepare a bill based upon Stanton's counterpoints in the Cabinet meetings. This bill became the basis for the Third Reconstruction Act when it returned in July after its recess. The act defined the intent of the Reconstruction Acts and completely reversed Johnson's order and Stanberry's interpretation. It specifically gave the military commanders independence from the president and recognized the army in the South as under the control of Congress.

Despite Grant's urging to reduce the president's ability to remove military commanders, Congress decided to go on hiatus. In order to keep a vigilant eye on Johnson, Benjamin Butler prevailed upon the House to adopt a resolution authorizing a new investigation to look for evidence concerning the assassination. Before Congress adjourned on July 19, Butler's committee was established and told to be ready to report when Congress reconvened in December.

The Butler Committee

Lafayette Baker, former head of the Secret Service, dismissed by Johnson for uncovering the Pardon Broker scandal had written a book, *The History of the Secret Service*. Within the book, he referenced Booth's diary, taken from his body at Garrett's Farm. News about the previously unknown diary created a sensation. The judiciary committee of the House, then in session, seized upon this news and asked Baker to take the stand and repeat his statements under oath. Congress subpoenaed the war department to produce Booth's diary. When the committee showed the diary to Baker, he claimed that someone had "cut out eighteen leaves".

In the heat of the Washington summer, ex-General Benjamin Butler assembled his committee to study the activities of Andrew Johnson. Butler enjoyed the role of the antagonist and the attention it brought him. Butler claimed in Congress that Johnson had been involved in the conspiracy to murder Abraham Lincoln. The Booth Diary gave him ammunition. Among the passages sensationalized was Booth's lament after his first failure to cross the Potomac:

After being hunted like a dog through swamps, woods and last night being chased by gun boats till I was forced to turn wet cold and starving, with every man's hand against me, I am here in despair. And why; For doing what Brutus was honored for, for what made Tell a hero. And yet I for striking down a greater tyrant than they ever knew am looked upon as a common cutthroat. My action was purer than either of theirs. One hoped to be great himself. The other had not only his country's but his own wrongs to avenge. I hoped for no gain. I knew no private wrong, I struck for my country and that alone.

A country groaned beneath his tyranny and prayed for this end. Yet now behold the cold hand they hand they extend to me. God cannot pardon me if I have done wrong. Yet I cannot see any wrong except serving a degenerate people. The little, the very little I have left behind to clear my name the Government will not allow to be printed. So ends all.

For my country I have given up all that makes life sweet and Holy. Brought misery upon my family, and am sure there is no pardon in Heaven for me since man condemns me so. I have only heard of what has been done (except what I did for myself) and it fills me with horror. God try and forgive me, and bless my mother.

Tonight I will once more try the river with the intent to cross; though I have a greater desire and almost a mind to return to Washington and in a measure clear my name, which I feel I can do. I do not repent the blow I struck. I may before God but not to man.

Butler asked the open-ended question: "Who it was that could profit by assassination (of Lincoln) that could not profit by capture and abduction?" He followed this with another rhetorical question: "Who it was expected by the conspirators would succeed to Lincoln, if the knife made a vacancy?" He also implied that Johnson had been involved in tampering with the diary of John Wilkes Booth. "Who spoliated that book? Who suppressed that evidence?"

Had Butler investigated a little harder, he might have indeed uncovered suppressed evidence. In answer to a question, Assistant Secretary of War Thomas Eckert testified that Atzerodt had made a statement "taken by one of McPhail's men by the name of Smith" which Eckert presumed "was in the war department files". This statement was the "lost" confession that should have been in the Department files but was not.[211]

Butler's open-ended questions generated a great deal of headlines and gave Johnson an opportunity to embarrass his War Secretary by openly speculating that Stanton got rid of the pages to conceal his guilt in railroading Mrs. Surratt to the gallows. Stanton was not about to get in a mud throwing match with the president and refused to make any comment on the charge. When called to testify, he denied removing any pages. Since the book was already almost one and one-half years old by the time it reached Garret's Farm, there was no way to prove that Booth himself had not torn out the pages over that time. At this point, it was only Baker's assertion that someone had partially destroyed the book and so the matter ended. Butler did not even bother to write a report on the committee's work.

Yet one is left to wonder what Booth meant when he wrote that he had *"a mind to return to Washington and in a measure clear my name, which I feel I can do."* Was he saying that he could name names and prove that he was acting in the interests and orders of his country, or was this merely the bravado of a desperately hunted man? Since he knew of the Torpedo plot, it seems likely that many Confederate operatives were glad Booth was dead.

At this point, the president realized that so long as Stanton and Grant were working together the army in the South was out of his control. In his view, the army controlled the South, and they were enforcing the 'illegal' Congress's reconstruction acts for the benefit of Negroes. Stanton stood in the way of his directly influencing the commanders of the military districts and Congress was supporting him.

Recognizing that Stanton was advising and influencing Grant, he felt that if Stanton was gone he could control the General himself and use him to his own advantage. Due to the Tenure Act, Johnson understood that the most he could do was suspend Stanton until Congress reconvened in December. By the time Stanton returned to the scene, he hoped to have driven a wedge between the two. After consulting with Stanton enemies, Welles, Chase, and the ambitious Montgomery Blair, Johnson decided to ignore the advice of Seward over risking a possible impeachment and proceed with his plans.

The problem he faced was that he could not dismiss Stanton on job performance issues since he was the only one enforcing the laws of Congress. He couldn't dismiss him because of political differences due to the Tenure Law. That left him with only one choice. He'd smear Stanton's character and dismiss him on integrity grounds. The headline making posture taken by the defense attorneys in the John Surratt trial gave him an opportunity to exploit this strategy.

Partisan feelings were running high that summer during the sixty-two days of the John Surratt trial. Due to the Supreme Court's decision in the Milligan case, Surratt was being tried in a Maryland civilian court rather than a military commission. The defense introduced Booth's diary into the testimony as proof that Surratt knew only about the kidnapping plot. Only Booth knew of the assassination plot. In an attempt to initiate sympathy for his client, defense attorney R.T. Merrick, implied that Surratt's mother was a victim of murder by the military commission, and there never had been a recommendation for clemency.

On August 1, he demanded that prosecutor Edward Pierrepont produce the mercy document. Pierrepont requested the record of the conspiracy trial and showed the recommendation to the defense, proving that Andrew Johnson had signed her death warrant in spite of pleas for mercy[212].

When the public learned that Johnson had ignored the Military Commission's petition for mercy in the trial of his mother Mary Surratt another political storm erupted. Johnson's enemies seized this issue saying that Johnson had 'blood on his hands'.

However, the devious Johnson devised a way to cover his tracks. Once again, he would use his subversive rhetoric to hang an unpopular decision on the neck of his Secretary of War. Johnson called in his secretary Colonel W.S. Moore and asked him to prepare a note for Secretary Stanton and to keep it on hand.

> *Sir: Public considerations of a high character constrain me to say that your resignation as Secretary of War will be accepted.*
>
> *Very respectfully yours,*
> *Andrew Johnson*
> *The President of the United States*

Johnson then called for the documents of the conspiracy trial including the clemency petition. After reviewing the documents for a few days, he initiated his plan to attack his enemies and claim the moral high ground.

Even though *The New York Times* reported the existence of the document on the day of the execution, implying that Johnson also knew of its existence, Johnson publicly asserted that Judge Advocate Holt had never shown him the petition for clemency. By virtue of Stanton, being Holt's superior and officially responsible for his actions he was thus betrayed by Stanton. He implied that Stanton "railroaded" the execution of Mary Surratt. Johnson would now abdicate all responsibility and attempt to play the part of an innocent bystander to the execution of Mary Surratt.

By moving against Stanton in this fashion, Johnson was taking a risk. However, Johnson seemed to have no conscience or fear of consequences. He was a man with power but no honor. To Johnson the end justified the means. He calculated that if Stanton revealed the passes while negative publicity roiled around him, he would look like a desperate man attempting to extricate himself from the devious web of deceit that Johnson was accusing him of spinning. If by chance the passes would suddenly appear from another source, he would deny them as a clever forgery foisted by an evil man.

On August 5, with the negative publicity now in place, Johnson instructed his secretary Colonel Moore to re-date the dismissal notice and deliver it to Stanton. Stanton replied:

> *Sir: Your note this day has been received, stating that public consideration of a high character constrain you to say that your resignation as Secretary of War will be accepted.*
>
> *In reply I have the honor to say that public consideration of a high character, which alone have induced me to continue as head of this department, constrain me not to resign the office of Secretary of War before the next meeting of Congress.*
>
>   *Edwin M. Stanton*
>   *Secretary of War*

Johnson frowned as he read Stanton's letter. Stanton would neither resign nor get into a mud-slinging contest with the president. This left Johnson no other option but to suspend him and await the verdict of the Senate. He then said to Moore, "The turning point has at last come. The Rubicon is crossed. You do not know what Mr. Stanton has said and done against me."[213]

According to Moore, "The president very emphatically declared that he had never seen the recommendation. He was positive that it had never before been brought to his knowledge or notice, and explained to me the circumstances attending the signing of the order to carry into effect the sentence of the commission. He distinctly remembered the great reluctance with which he approved the death warrant of a woman of Mrs. Surratt's age, and that he asked Judge Advocate General Holt, who originally brought him the papers, many questions, but nothing whatever was said to him respecting the recommendation of the Commission for clemency in her case. He had been sick, but when he had signed the papers his mind was as clear as it's ever been...and he felt satisfied that it had been designedly withheld from his knowledge".[214]

To keep the pot boiling on August 10, Johnson released to the *New York Times* the details of a story told to him from a woman representing herself as the wife of Sanford Conover.

The woman claimed that certain parties had held out promises and assurances of a pardon on condition that her husband would do certain things. Conover described elaborate efforts of the Impeachment Committee Chairmen James Ashley and Benjamin Butler to have him fabricate testimony of Johnson being involved in the assassination plot.

In exchange, they would get him a pardon. Their scheme was to have Conover prove that Booth and Johnson corresponded with each other and that the Booth planned the assassination to occur at the second inauguration. Johnson became intoxicated to steel himself for the murder that he was expecting at any moment. Unfortunately, Conover could not sell this story to Butler's committee, so now he was double-crossing them by appealing directly to the president.

While the public and newspapers were sorting out that story, another story surfaced on August 15 charging that two Democrats had offered witnesses a bribe to swear falsely that Holt and Conover induced them to commit perjury.

These planted stories caused quite a furor in the press and helped muddy the waters of the Impeachment Committee's work.

A political general and military politician, Butler gained fame by marching his regiments through Maryland to the capitol shortly after the attack at Fort Sumter.

Described as a politician "'who could strut while sitting down" he was anxious to bring about the impeachment of Andrew Johnson. He formed a Special Committee to investigate the matter certain that Johnson was somehow involved in Lincoln's death. His committee discovered the existence of Booth's 'diary' but was unable to substantiate any involvement by Johnson.

Benjamin Butler

Over the Rubicon

On Sunday, August 11, the president summoned Grant and offered him an interim appointment as war secretary while continuing as commanding general. Grant felt he had no choice but to safeguard the army and the nation by taking the position. Stanton had already encouraged him to do so rather than let Montgomery Blair have the office. That evening Grant appeared at Stanton's house and asked for a private audience. After fifteen minutes, Stanton told his wife that Johnson would suspend him from his office in conformity with the tenure law.

Regardless of the two and one half years of turmoil between them, Stanton found it hard to believe that Johnson would force him from office. His seven years in government service had ebbed away his personal savings, and he had made no plans for his future. Needing a rest from the heat and pressure of Washington, he relaxed at the home of Congressman Hooper at Cape Cod. Despite his lack of ready funds, he turned down the opportunity to make speeches. His host gave the reason for this, as "there are things he does not wish to say nor omit to say".[215]

Stanton was apprehensive about how Grant would act. He was still a Democrat who thought and acted in harmony with the president at the close of the war. However, since the disastrous "swing around the circle", he performed directives from the White House only after coercive pressure. He still maintained cordial relations with Johnson, but he kept his plans and thoughts to himself.

Thurlow Weed, close advisor to Seward, felt that the president had lost all hope of reconciliation, and it was best that his friend leave the sinking ship before he too, was publicly disgraced. Seward was frustrated. The president often ignored his advice on domestic affairs, and his loyalty to him probably cost him his last shot at the presidency in 1868. Yet, he was still influential in foreign affairs and was busy trying to avoid a war in Mexico with France over their installation of Maximilian as emperor. However, with the Blairs still clamoring for his head and with rumors that he would be next, he submitted his resignation on August 23. Johnson wisely asked him to remain to minimize the fallout from the Stanton suspension.

Grant was the pivotal piece in this struggle. Keeping his opinions to himself and his options open, he ran the war office on the same principles as Stanton. However, if he decided to stay on as the head of the war department, at Johnson's request, his popularity and control of the army would add to Johnson's political strength, and the Tenure Law would be of no value.

Emboldened by Stanton's departure, Johnson then ordered the firing of Generals Philip Sheridan and Dan Sickles. Sheridan's firing was in retaliation for his dismissal of the governor and attorney general of Louisiana as well as the mayor of New Orleans and the judge who freed all the perpetrators of the New Orleans riot. Sickles' offense was refusing civil courts' writs of habeas corpus for Southerners convicted for killing Union soldiers in military tribunals.

Grant vigorously opposed the firings fearing that a new revolution could erupt as a result. Francis Lieber, a law professor at Columbia College and frequent advisor to the war department opined, "the Governors at the North may have to call for armed Loyalty to sweep down on Washington & Maryland".

Partisan feelings were so high that at the cabinet meeting to discuss the action, only the loyal Welles agreed with the president. Even Stanberry opposed the move stating it would surely lead to impeachment since it would clearly indicate the intention of the Executive to hinder the execution of the reconstruction laws. Johnson ignored the advice.

Grant by virtue of his position as Interim War Secretary, gave the unintended public impression that he supported the dismissals. He understood that his position of power in this cabinet post was debatable and its tenure tentative. However, as commanding general, Grant considered himself independent of the president by virtue of Congress' enactments. He continued to send secret messages to his commanders, supporting them in their actions and keeping them informed of pending actions. The army would wait until Congress reassembled in December 1867, when the Senate would judge whether Johnson had acted rightly in suspending Stanton.

Johnson knew that by having Grant replace Stanton his popularity would deflect much of the criticism. He also believed that he could tarnish Grant's reputation in the eyes of the Republicans making him less likely to be the Republican presidential nominee in 1868, thereby increasing Johnson's own chances for a Democratic bid, which he greatly desired.

Johnson regarded Grant as a political neophyte whom he could maneuver into a position where Grant would either use his popularity to support him or dissipate it before the next presidential election. William C. Church biographer of Grant described the relationship in this manner: "An ambitious and intriguing politician, Johnson was more than a match for the single minded soldier in artfulness and craft. By various subtle methods he sought to entangle the General in his controversies with Congress." [216]

Grant wisely kept silent. Any disclosures of his views would garner him a slew of political enemies who would endeavor to destroy any hopes he had of being a presidential candidate. Blair, seeing a chance to influence Grant, prepared an article in the *New York World* advocating his nomination on the Democratic ticket. The *New York Times* remarked that Montgomery Blair was "buzzing about General Grant like a bee in a tar barrel – seeking private interviews, and holding private conversations".[217]

Stanton was also gaining the benefits of silence. His martyred status gained him support from many quarters. Johnson's action had the effect of thumbing his nose at Congress and the nation. Confident that they would fight on his behalf, Stanton refused to wage a war of words with Johnson, nor would he divulge anything embarrassing. He would let the Senate defend him when it was in session.

Toward the end of the summer of 1867, James G. Bennett of the *New York Herald* became hysterical at "The Fate of the Republic" which would be either "Despotism or Anarchy." Both Congress and the president, said he, were trying for dictatorship. "The contest between the rivals," he commented, "trembles on the brink of open war." [218] The reason for Bennett's warning of doom was the rumor that the president would proclaim a pardon to all rebels to prevent disfranchisement by the registration officials in the five military districts.

On September 7, Johnson issued a second amnesty proclamation narrowing the number of excepted classes to 3 and reducing the number of those still unpardoned to about 300.

Coming on the heels of his suspension of Stanton, Democrat and conservative newspapers created a furor over his amnesty action declaring that the president intended to use the army to reopen the registration books and to force the insertion of disfranchised southerners therein, then to disperse Congress, and to set up a military dictatorship supported by Copperheads and rebels. Johnson's own newspapers as well as rebel and Copperhead papers urged the president to take this step of revolution and disperse Congress by force, as Cromwell did Parliament, and as Napoleon I. did the French Legislature.

This call for a second civil war brought a great deal of apprehension to the Republicans in Congress, as well as the nation. But, rather than calm the waters he was stirring, Johnson enjoyed the feeling of renewed power. As long as Congress remained adjourned, he was oblivious to the consternation of the country and would dare Congress to impeach him.

General Edward Ord	General Daniel Sickles	General John Pope	General Philip Sheridan

The whole force of the Reconstruction policy of Congress lay in the power of the District Commanders to remove civil officers who opposed or obstructed the new law. These commanders reported directly to Grant who reported directly to Congress bypassing the president.

Johnson had the power to fire the commanders if they were not following the law. Johnson took advantage of this power to fire Generals Pope, Ord, Sickles and Sheridan because he did not agree with the law, especially the registration of Negroes to vote.

His action continued to embolden the former rebels that he returned to power and encourage the disenfranchising of the Negro freedmen.

The Second Impeachment Effort

In his annual message to the Congress on December 3, Johnson once again ignored the advice of Seward. Rather than appealing to the moderates by offering an olive branch, he decided to throw down the gauntlet. Using Seward's draft of the message, Johnson then added his own quarrelsome personality blaming Congress for the failures of reconstruction and again denouncing the overriding of his vetoes. The key point of the message occurred when he referred to charges that he planned to subvert the government. He declared that, if Congress passed a law producing immediate and irreparable injury to the organic structure of the government, he would have to "save the life of the nation at all hazards".

Thurlow Weed thought that if Johnson had left out the threat of using arbitrary force to save the nation from Congress, the message might have had a reaction that would have stimulated debate. However, Johnson once again stimulated opposition to himself by using the threat of force.[219]

With Johnson's new threats ringing in their ears, Congressman Boutwell presented an argument for the "broad view" of congressional impeachment power. Congressional conservatives held that the president could be arraigned only for criminal violations, while Radicals like Boutwell maintained that "misdemeanors" should be applied in a political rather than a criminal sense. Boutwell argued that Johnson had expanded his powers to the point that his "capacity for wrongdoing" put the country at risk. Boutwell confessed that he would be inclined to allow Johnson to complete his term were it not for the disastrous consequences of his continued tenure.

Before the seating of the new Congress, Johnson called his Cabinet for advice. Anticipating impeachment for his actions Johnson asked each member for their opinion on a number of questions: Could the president be removed upon any other basis than that prescribed by the Constitution? Could he be suspended from office during the trial? If Congress should pass a law to suspend him during trial, should he vacate?

Despite Johnson's provocative actions, the House Committee tabled the impeachment recommendation. Feeling vindicated, Johnson told his secretary Moore that the time for defense was past, and he was ready to begin a new offensive on Congress. He then promptly dismissed General Pope and General Ord as Military Commanders and confidently predicted victory in the Senate sustaining Stanton's firing.

Johnson was whistling past the graveyard with that prediction and he knew it. In his message to the Senate justifying Stanton's dismissal, he gave the following rationale as his argument.

1. Johnson portrayed Stanton as a conspirator who issued secret orders to nullify the president's Reconstruction plan despite the fact that Stanton was the original author.
2. Stanton advised the president to veto the Tenure of Office Bill and then took advantage of it to stay in office.
3. Johnson blamed him for not preventing the New Orleans riot, and for not "exculpating" the president from responsibility for the insurrection.
4. Finally, Johnson considered his letter refusing to resign as defiant in tone.

It is curious that Johnson did not charge that Stanton conspired in withholding from him the Mary Surratt clemency plea. If there was ever justification for a firing, withholding information that would cause the death of someone should rank as number one. The reason he did not is because an independent investigation by Congress would not only have proven it false, but may also have uncovered the secret of the passes.

Johnson was too wily a politician for that. He was getting the mileage he wanted out of smearing Stanton and Holt with a baseless political charge. As long as his friends in the press believed and promulgated the story, he was satisfied. There was no way he wanted to have an official investigation into the matter.

Stanton, in his defensive rebuttal wrote;

1. His outline for the Reconstruction program as well as Johnson's statements at the time described the Southern governments as provisional and "subject to the controlling power of Congress". His outline included a provision giving the Negroes the power to vote, which Johnson ignored. Stanton always followed the laws set down by Congress and copies of his orders proved that fact.
2. He agreed with Johnson that he advocated a veto of the Tenure of Office Bill, but believed that now that it was law, all are required to obey it.
3. As for the riot in New Orleans, Stanton did not feel that there was any reason at the time to change the existing instructions that General Baird was working under. Since the president felt all was normal in the country, why should Stanton suspend the constitutional right to assemble? Giving the president political cover by exculpating him from responsibility was not the job of the war secretary. Besides, Johnson had already exculpated himself by blaming Congress.

4. As for being defiant in his refusal to resign, Stanton pointed out that he had merely used the same language as the president in his original request.

Although Stanton had a point-by-point defense of all the charges, he did not bother to send his reply to Capitol Hill. The Senate was scrutinizing Johnson's actions as president on a daily basis. His case against Stanton was dead on arrival.

Anticipating Stanton's reinstatement by the Senate, Johnson prepared another plan. He had his secretary Colonel Moore prepare a letter of dismissal for Stanton to be ready for signature as soon as the Senate acted. According to Moore: "The president expressed the opinion that perhaps it would be well for the Senate to reinstate the secretary, as he could at once be removed, in the meantime General Grant be gotten rid of; indeed both would be disposed of, so far as the war department was concerned. 'Grant' (the president remarked) 'had served the purpose for which he had been selected, and it was desirable that he should be superseded in the War Office by another'."[220]

Johnson was ready to spring his trap on Grant. He believed he had an understanding that Grant would not surrender the office to Stanton when he returned but he would surrender the keys to the president. Thus, it would put Grant in the position of violating the order of the Senate. After reviewing the situation and talking it over with General Sherman, Grant recognized the position Johnson was putting him in and decided on a different tact.

On Monday, January 13, the Senate spoke returning Stanton to the War Office. The next day Grant wrote a letter of resignation from the cabinet and handed the keys to General Townsend who delivered them to Stanton. At noon, Grant went to deliver his letter at the White House. There, the surprised Johnson gave him a tongue-lashing in front of the cabinet accusing him of plotting with Stanton and not warning him that he was giving up the War Office. Johnson then foolishly decided to embarrass Grant in public and show off his own self-righteousness by releasing his version of the details of the cabinet meeting to the press, thereby casting doubt on the General's loyalty. The Press reported that Johnson had "sworn and kicked the chairs around at a great rate" and that he and Grant almost came to blows. Picking a fight with arguably the most admired man in the country and then releasing details to the newspapers was not a good idea politically, but it was vintage Johnson.

Grant rightly believed that Johnson was trying to avoid the responsibility of resisting the reinstatement of Congress by forcing him to either remain in the War Office and violate the law or face the president's accusation of disloyalty for violating an understanding they had between them. Grant smartly sidestepped the trap.

Stanton was not planning to stay more than the rest of the week in office. Vindicated by the Senate, he collected his back pay and planned to leave Washington on a high note. Heeding his wife's pleadings, he intended to return to private practice. However, Republican leaders led by the moderate Trumbull pleaded with him to stay. There were rumors of Republican and Democratic military companies organizing to defend the Congress or the President.

Johnson's dismissal of Sheridan and Sickles as well as his public feud with Grant worried Stanton over what might happen if he abandoned the office to anyone Johnson might appoint. His patriotism and sense of duty told him that by giving up his office all the work that he had accomplished since 1861 would be lost. He decided to stay in office, and by doing so, became a pawn in the showdown between the president and the legislature.

By now, Johnson had given up on Grant. He had lost him to the Republicans. The next year, 1868, was an election year and Johnson still had his eye on the Democratic Party nomination. The president had a lingering hope that with the aid of a subservient secretary of war and new military commanders devoted to his cause, he might control the elections, defeat all movements for new state governments, and continue military rule until he could make another election campaign to reverse the policy of Congress.[221] Congress stymied this hope by passing another law, over the president's veto, putting into Grant's hands the executive authority that the reconstruction acts had given to the president. Thus, Johnson had lost his ability to fire Military Commanders and could no longer influence their decisions.

By the middle of February, Johnson was rapidly running out of options. He asked General Sherman to take over as war secretary again hoping that a war hero would limit the political fallout from releasing Stanton. Sherman turned Johnson down cold, refusing to climb over Grant's shoulders. Johnson then tried another tactic. He issued an order creating a new Military District the Army of the Atlantic consisting of Maryland, Delaware, Virginia and West Virginia commanded by Sherman with his headquarters in Washington. He sweetened the pot by offering him a Brevet General nomination. Sherman turned down both the command and the Brevet nomination and returned to his home in St. Louis.[222]

The Implosion of 1867

At the suggestion of Gideon Welles at 9:00, February 21, Johnson summoned Adjutant General Lorenzo Thomas to the White House and gave him two orders. Tell Stanton to vacate the War office and succeed him as secretary of war-ad interim. Welles and Johnson were confident that Stanton was a cowardly bully who would vacate the office without a fight. Once again, Johnson ignited a firestorm around himself without knowing how far or fast it would spread. Worse, by acting impulsively and alone, Johnson's allies in the Senate and House were caught completely surprised.

When word of Stanton's firing reached Capitol Hill, both houses of Congress erupted. This action, coming immediately after the creation of the new "Army of the Atlantic," finally convinced the Congress that the president's intentions presented a clear and present danger. The fear that Maryland would be the heart of a presidential *coup* was widespread because that state had just recently removed all disfranchisements from its constitution and Copperheads and former rebels now controlled the legislature. The House offered a resolution for impeachment of the president. The Senate went into immediate executive session, and by 3:00, Stanton's office filled with Congressmen urging him to stay until the Senate acted. Senator Charles Sumner sent him a famous one-word message, "Stick!"
By 10:00 p.m., the entire Senate had told Stanton to stay.

Stanton stayed. He decided to remain in continuous possession of the Department night and day for several weeks. That night Thomas boasted openly that if Stanton did not relinquish the office, he would take it by force. Rumor swept the city that Johnson was contemplating civil war and intended to expel Stanton with a detachment of Marines.
General Grant posted guards at the war department based upon information that a secret military force in Maryland officered by former Confederates had been formed. To Grant this sounded like the Ku Klux Klan may attempt to take the war department and force Stanton out. Grant was taking no chances.

The next morning the newspapers were howling with the news of the new rebellion. Johnson's organ, The *National Intelligencer* proclaimed: "We are in the midst of a revolutionary crisis ... We ... have the second rebellion — the rebellion of Congress against the Constitution." The *New York Tribune* compared Johnson's attempted eviction of Stanton to Bonaparte's *coup d 'état* of November 9, 1799 while The *Cincinnati Commercial* quoted a list of telegrams offering money and men to both the President and Congress.

By the time Johnson finally lit the match to the combustible bitterness he had compiled he was already a political corpse. His constant vetoes, in order to protect white supremacy in the South and the use of executive power to obstruct reconstruction implementation, alienated potential allies and forced non-Radicals into the Radical camp.

Johnson's action and the reaction of Congress, again divided the country into two camps. One side was willing to go to arms to protect the Congress, the other willing to go to arms to protect the president. One more spark may well have reignited the war.

Because the non-Radicals were reluctant to impeach Johnson as evident by the two unsuccessful impeachment votes, the megalomaniac mind of Johnson interpreted these results as a sign of weakness and decided to violate the Tenure of Office Act.

At that point moderate and conservative Republicans finally heeded Thad Stevens as he moved from group to group repeating his mantra, "Didn't I tell you so? What good did our moderation do you? If you don't kill the beast, it will kill you."

The Implosion of 1867

A long-time opponent of impeachment, Judiciary Committee Chairman James F. Wilson, said: "Guided by a sincere desire to pass this cup from our lips, determined to drink it if escape were not cut off by the presence of a palpable duty, we at last find ourselves compelled to take its very dregs." The president finally pushed Congress to the wall and on Wednesday, February 24, the House voted 126 - 47 to impeach Andrew Johnson.

Thaddeus Stevens urges congressmen to vote for the impeachment of Andrew Johnson.

"Let them impeach and be damned!" was Andrew Johnson's response to the official notice of impeachment

Chapter 11

Epilogue

A Deal is Struck

Johnson's one vote triumph in the Senate to save his job was a costly victory and had a long lasting effect upon the South. The Southern Unionists were now in fear of their lives. "It is with sadness we learn that the greatest traitor of the century is acquitted," Daniel Richards wrote to E.B. Washburne from Florida. "News of the failure to convict Johnson will be like Greek fire throughout the entire South. May God save our country from the consuming conflagration. The eyes of the rebel sparkle like those of the fiery serpent. They hope they have found their 'lost cause' and think they see it. I am not certain but they are right." From South Carolina, Sumner heard that since the acquittal, Union men had been in deadly danger, and that one of the Republican members-elect of the state legislature had been brutally murdered. The cause for Congressional Reconstruction had suffered a severe reversal in the South.[223]

Johnson's victory implied that one-third of the Senate did not want him removed based upon his philosophy and job performance. Democrats made it a point to proclaim that they were only defending the president on principle, not because they backed him politically. Gideon Welles believed that the Democrats were hoping that the impeachment procedure succeeded anticipating that public opinion would turn against Grant and the Republicans in the 1868 election.

The impeachment of a president is a political trial decided not on the evidence presented, but on the deals made behind the scenes to the senators who will decide the result. One of Johnson's counsels, William Evarts, realized that the actual issue was not what Johnson had done as much as the fear of what he would do if he were acquitted. Evarts went to a group of moderate Republicans and offered them a proposition.

What if the president nominated as secretary of war a man that the Senate could confirm, who would be fully on board with Reconstruction as defined by the Congress? The man Evarts proposed was General John Schofield, a close friend of Grant who thought the president's actions highly irregular. Other concessions included no further Attorney-General interpretations of the Reconstruction Acts, no more efforts to test their constitutionality, and no more attempts to interfere with Grant.

Lead counsel and former Attorney General Stanberry managed to finally put a muzzle on Johnson and persuade him that Schofield's nomination and acceptance of Evarts' proposition was all that stood between him and conviction. Johnson surrendered by sending Schofield's name to the Senate nominating him as secretary of war one day after the impeachment trial began. Being close to the end of his term, some moderates, such as Lyman Trumbull, William Fessenden, and James Grimes, felt it better to contain the beast rather than kill him. Some felt that removing Johnson by impeachment might ruin not only the Republican Party but also the nation. Only by acceding to this deal was Johnson able to escape the humiliation of removal from office. His one vote victory finally convinced him that any deviation from his promises would certainly bring about another impeachment and a conviction. Never in American history had a president thrown away so much support in such a short amount of time.

Another factor that played into Johnson's acquittal vote by moderate Republicans was, in part, to block the presidential ambitions of Benjamin Wade. Elected from Ohio, Wade was the President Pro-Tem of the Senate in 1868. Because Johnson had no vice-president, under the rules of presidential succession at the time, Wade would have replaced the president had the Senate voted to convict Johnson. Many members of the Republican Party viewed Wade as an arch-Radical that no one could work with. Future President James Garfield warned that Wade was "a man of violent passions, extreme opinions and narrow views who was surrounded by the worst and most violent elements in the Republican Party". Wade's ascension to the presidency would have given him the powers of presidential patronage and would have made him a formidable rival to U.S. Grant in the race for the Republican Party presidential nomination that year. *The Detroit Post* summed it up succinctly: "Andrew Johnson is innocent because Ben Wade is guilty of being his successor."

The agreement between Johnson and the Republicans did not restrain him from voicing his displeasure with Congressional acts. He vetoed the bill that would have readmitted Arkansas, the Omnibus bill that would have readmitted all the states except Virginia, Tennessee, and Mississippi; and a bill that would again extend the Freedman's Bureau – all were overturned. The Senate retaliated by turning down most of the appointments made by Johnson for various Federal offices.

Senator Edmund G. Ross (Kansas)

Senator Edmund Ross had no sympathy for Andrew Johnson, yet he cast the deciding vote against his conviction. He believed that if a president could be forced out of office based on partisan disagreement, the presidency would then be under the control of whatever congressional faction held sway.

Ross became the principal target of abuse from the press, the public, and his fellow Republican legislators. Neither he nor any other Republican who voted to acquit Andrew Johnson were reelected to the Senate.

The Making of the President 1868

The mood of the country was one of fatigue. After four years of war and three years of political gamesmanship, they were tired. They were glad to hear that in the middle of the impeachment trial, the Republicans held their presidential convention and nominated U.S. Grant as their presidential candidate. The people could finally see the end of the bickering in sight. Johnson realized that the only hope for vindication of his philosophy was to be elected president in his own right. He still entertained thoughts of being the Democratic nominee but the impeachment proceedings ended his public backing by the Blair family.

Frank Blair Jr. in a letter to his father finally threw up his hands: "…Consider for a moment what would have been the position of affairs if instead of Andy Johnson we had a man of military experience and approved leadership in the White House? Would he have been impeached? Would Grant and the army have disobeyed his orders? But nobody expected Andy to resist. Nobody wants him to resist and nobody would help him if he did, and simply because he has shown himself to be incompetent." [224]

After five days of wrangling at the Democratic convention, members of the New York delegation planned to nominate Chief Justice Salmon Chase in an effort to split the Republican Party. However, Clement Vallandigham, the old Copperhead from Ohio, wanted nothing to do with his fellow Ohioan. Before Chase's name was brought to the floor, Vallandigham made an emotional plea for Horatio Seymour of New York. Seymour had twice declined the nomination but Vallandigham convinced the convention to make him their unanimous choice, an offer he couldn't refuse. Before Seymour could decline the nomination for the third time, he was quickly hustled out of the hall by the

Blair family, who were then able to get Francis Blair, Jr., nominated for vice-president.

Blair's acceptance speech set the new segregationist tone for the Democratic Party that would continue for decades. "My fellow citizens, I have said that the contest before us was one for the restoration of our government; it is also one for the restoration of our race. It is to prevent the people of our race from being exiled from their homes—exiled from the government which they formed and created for themselves and for their children, and to prevent them from being driven out of the country or trodden under foot by an inferior and barbarous race."[225]

Bitter at the rejection and subterfuge of the Democratic Party leaders, Johnson went back to the White House and continued to bark his defiance at the work of Congress. On Christmas Day, 1868, he took one last shot at outraging the lawmakers by issuing pardons to the remaining prisoners of the Lincoln assassination; Dr Samuel Mudd, Edman Spangler, Samuel Arnold, and the perjurer Sanford Conover. (Michael O'Laughlin had died in his Fort Jefferson prison.) He also extended amnesty to all former insurgents including Jefferson Davis. The "Canadian Confederates" *were not* exonerated.

As a politician, Johnson was not finished at the end of his term. In 1874, he made a successful run for the Senate from Tennessee. Although most of the Radicals were gone, it was high drama as Johnson joined the body that came within a vote of ending his presidency early. Among his visitors and well-wishers was his old bodyguard William H. Crook who later wrote of their conversation:

"'Crook,' he said, 'I have come back to the Senate with two purposes. One is to do what I can to punish the Southern brigadiers. They led the South into secession and they have never had their desserts. The other is to make a speech against Grant.' He made it in less than two weeks from that evening. It was a clever one, and bitter. ....*He was the best hater I ever knew.*"[226]

Johnson's internal hatred came out again two days before he died, as he talked about his presidency on a train ride with friends. He continued to demonize the deceased Stanton even claiming that Stanton had committed suicide when he realized the error of his ways. He again blamed Stanton and Holt for the execution of Mary Surratt. He believed that he was right and that was all that mattered to him. He lost sight of Lincoln's vision and wanted only to punish his opponents. If he had been willing to compromise, he would have easily isolated the Radicals and would have probably been re-elected. He said that he hoped a calm and correct historian would say one hundred years later that, "He pursued the right course" rather than he accomplished his goals.

A certain school of thought believes that since Johnson was essentially following Lincoln's policies; Lincoln's second term would have resulted in the same failure as Johnson. This equivocation is hardly the case. Lincoln wanted loyal unionists in southern governments before he would recognize them. Johnson was willing to pardon the supporters of the war and keep them in power.

In Lincoln's last speech, he advocated the radical position of Black suffrage. Johnson would not even consider it. Lastly, Lincoln was a far more flexible politician who could isolate enemies or charm them. He showed a high degree of insight in pursuit of his goals. Johnson treated anyone who did not agree with him as a mortal foe. These large differences dispute the notion that Lincoln's failure was inevitable.

In biographer Hans Trefousse's opinion, "Johnson had restored hope to Southern racists and undermined the process of reconstruction so that it could not succeed afterward. From his own point of view, he had been successful. He had preserved the South as a 'white man's country'." As the South continued in its segregated policies for the next hundred years, politically correct historians gave him the praise he desired.

President Ulysses S. Grant

General U. S. Grant was the country's greatest hero and courted actively by both parties to be their presidential candidate. Andrew Johnson saw him as a formidable rival and a political neophyte. He was determined to either have him publicly support his policies or politically damage him in order to enhance his own candidacy.

Grant managed to avoid doing both, sidestepping the traps Johnson set for him. He survived the Johnson Presidency with his reputation enhanced and in 1868 at age 46 became the youngest man elected to the presidency.

The Fate of Jefferson Davis and the Canadian Confederates

Since the May 1865 proclamation and the criticism of the military tribunal, Johnson was reluctant to issue a military trial for Davis. He made the excuse that Davis would not receive a fair trial and pointed to the perjury of Conover as an example. However, Conover's testimony was only linking Davis to the Lincoln assassination. There was other evidence available if they wanted to try Davis only for treason. This was the position Stanton had belatedly come to in 1866. The problem with a trial for treason was that the Constitution required that treason be tried in the State in which the crime was committed. This, according to Attorney General Speed, meant the Federal Circuit Court in Virginia, where any jury impaneled there would undoubtedly acquit the Confederate president. However, since there were no civil courts' operating in Virginia, Davis was imprisoned in a legal limbo for over two years.

The state of Virginia was in the federal judicial district of the Chief Justice of the Supreme Court, Salmon Chase. Chase would not hold court there until martial law was no longer in effect. Chase felt that a court under the martial law could only act with the sanction and supervision of the military power, and he would not hold court until these conditions had changed.

On August 20, 1866, Johnson finally restored the writ of habeas corpus throughout the Union by presidential proclamation. Attorney General Stanberry proposed the release of Davis from military custody and transferring him to the United States marshal in Virginia.

Stanton advised against this proposal for two reasons. The first was that Stanberry had not prepared a valid indictment against Davis and was not ready to go to trial. Second, there was no court available to bring Davis to a prompt trial, so there was no purpose in releasing him from military custody. At this time, Johnson was taking his "swing around the circle" and did not want to stir up any more hatred in the North by releasing Davis from military custody. Johnson refused Stanberry's recommendation.

For his part, Davis looked forward to his trial. By making his defense in a civil court, he would get the chance to vindicate the South by arguing the constitutional case for the right to secede. The government would not risk losing in court what was won on the battlefield. Lincoln's original position of "shooing" the rebels out of the country seemed to be the best solution. Johnson would later confide to his secretary that the greatest disappointment of his presidency was the failure to hang Jefferson Davis for treason.[227]

Once Davis was remanded to a civil court, he was allowed to leave the country on his own recognizance. Chief Justice Chase noted that the Fourteenth Amendment excluded Davis from certain rights of citizenship, and since he had already received punishment the case, he could not be tried ex post facto. Johnson's universal amnesty proclamation entitled him to a full pardon, if Davis asked for one. Jefferson Davis could have even returned to the Senate from the State of Mississippi, but he could not bring himself to ask for the Federal pardon he needed to take his seat. Asking for the pardon would have been an admission of guilt that he was not prepared to acknowledge. Instead, he wrote his own account of the Civil War in which he justified the righteousness of his lost cause.

It is curious to note that in his ten volumes *Rise and Fall of the Confederate Government,* his most trusted advisor, Judah Benjamin--the man who held the positions of Attorney General, Secretary of War and Secretary of State--is mentioned only as being a part of the original cabinet. The historical record is clear that Davis turned to Benjamin in all critical moments and was clearly his most admired counselor. Other administration members as well as Davis' wife Varina frequently noted his reliance and dependence upon Benjamin. Perhaps they had a falling out after the war and Davis wanted to keep Benjamin's influence at a distance. Whatever the reason, he said nothing more about the man. Davis died in New Orleans in 1889 at age 82.

For his part, Benjamin was an intensely secretive man, burning all letters to him immediately after reading them. He told a biographer "I have never kept a diary or retained a copy of a letter written by me. No letter addressed to me by others will be found among my papers when I die." He made good his boast. Later in his life, he sought out any correspondence that he wrote and destroyed it. At his death his biographer, Pierce Butler said, "he did not leave more than half a dozen pieces of paper".[228]

One letter he did leave behind was one to Davis in which he said he would defend him against attacks on his character, but he would not discuss any issues regarding the Confederacy. "I freely confess that it is not agreeable to mix in any way in controversies of the past which for me are buried forever."[229]

It is also curious that, Johnson adamantly refused to withdraw his proclamation of May 1865 implicating Jefferson Davis and the Canadian Confederates in the assassination conspiracy. Too much intelligence pointed to a larger Confederate plot. He knew that Booth was not acting alone, and although he could not hang Davis for his acts, he was not going to absolve his agents.

Sanders and Tucker both declared bankruptcy while living in exile in London. Even though Judah Benjamin, Clement Clay, and Jefferson Davis had the means to help their former confederates, none had the desire to lend a hand. Sanders returned to New York in poor health and died broke in 1873. No "Sons of the Confederacy" attended his funeral.[230] Tucker returned to Washington in 1872 after an absence of fifteen years becoming a lobbyist. Although some remembered him, he was never able to regain the trust he once enjoyed. He died in Richmond on July 4, 1890,

Jacob Thompson, the espionage mastermind of the Confederate apparatus in Canada, denied all involvement in the plots to burn northern cities and incite copperhead uprisings. He fled to England at the end of the war after depositing Confederate funds into Liverpool banks. As the custodian of Confederate funds, Thompson became a rich and important man. In England, Thompson and his wife were received by the Prince of Wales and his mother, Queen Victoria and spent a year traveling through Europe. After passions cooled he returned to the United States and lived an easy life in Memphis until his death in 1885

General Sharpe's intelligence from England showed that cash advanced for the Canadian operation came from drafts drawn by Judah Benjamin on the British business house of *Fraser, Trenholm & Company* thus providing an embarrassing link to England in the assassination plot.[231]

Trenholm, who assumed the secretary of the treasury position for the Confederacy from July 1864 to April 1865, became fabulously wealthy during the war running the Union blockade. Whether he was a Southern patriot or a Daddy Warbucks scoundrel is open for interpretation.

Imprisoned at Fort Pulaski, Georgia, the Federal government confiscated most of his property with the rest litigated away. He later became the model for Margaret Mitchell's dashing Rhett Butler in her novel *Gone with the Wind*. He died at his home *Ashley Hall* in Charleston in 1876 and buried at Magnolia Cemetery.

In the summer of 1868, Seward sent Reverdy Johnson to England to come to an agreement for the claims against the Confederate raider ship *Alabama* and other British made Confederate ships. *Fraser, Trenholm & Company* financed these ships and made in the *Laird & Company* shipyards. Although England's official position was neutrality during the war, government officials were willing to look the other way on this blatant violation of neutrality despite the protests of the American ambassadors.

When Seward reviewed the treaty, he was perplexed. Rather than providing compensation for the losses caused by these ships, the treaty stated that claims of citizens of both nations would be settled on an equal basis. Nowhere in the treaty was there an admission of British guilt or responsibility or an expression of regret. The entire treaty was contrary to Seward's instructions.

However, President Johnson sent it to the Senate hoping for a quick approval. The Senate rejected the settlement by a vote of 54-1. Two years later, under the implied threat that if compensation were not forthcoming, war would follow, Britain finally expressed regret in the Treaty of Washington and provided a settlement of $15,500,000 to the United States. The treaty was one of the first applications of Britain's 'appeasement' policies that helped to cement the confidences of the two English-speaking nations and would eventually lead to their wartime alliances in the following century.

Edwin Stanton

Throughout the impeachment trial, partisanship was the order of the day. Army agents spied on defense witnesses who arrived in Washington and tried to rush them to the Senate before they could be defiled by communication with the White House. Grant openly supported anti-Johnson sentiment among the senators after testifying at the trial.

On the other side, Johnson was indulging in surreptitious surveillance over Stanton. He employed an army officer on war department duty who transmitted full reports on the Secretary's actions to the White House. Johnson knew how strained Stanton's nerves were and believed that the Secretary was cracking as the weeks passed.[232]

No matter how the trial ended, Stanton was determined to leave. Although Senator Benjamin Wade, who would have succeeded Johnson upon conviction, asked him to stay on as war secretary, Stanton refused. He felt that with Grant now firmly in the Republican camp and still in control of the Army that Johnson could make no further moves to hinder reconstruction. He needed rest, recuperation, and time to restore his personal fortune that had dissipated in his eight years of government service.

He turned down the opportunity to become a senator from Pennsylvania to go into private practice with his son, but his health was steadily in decline. Long a sufferer from asthmatic disorders complicated by the extensive hours and the inclement climate of Washington, the boundless energy he had as war secretary had deserted him.

He took on high profile, large fee cases that required travel and research that weakened him further. With no interest in returning to public service, he continued to take on cases when his health permitted. As a reward for his services, President Grant nominated him and on the same day, the Senate confirmed him to become a Supreme Court Justice. He died four days later on December 24, 1869, before he could take office or write his memoirs.

Many of his political enemies (Johnson, McClellan, Chase, Welles and the Blairs) left behind bitter feelings in writing towards him, but Stanton never bothered to respond. Stanton was meticulous in understanding the details of every issue, never letting them sidetrack him from the larger goal. Impervious to criticism or the feelings of others, he was satisfied in his accomplishments and content to let history decide his fate. His reputation came under assault after his death by people who took Johnson's side in their dispute. Depicted by some as a power-hungry bureaucrat out to sabotage or take over the presidency, Stanton became a villain to a new audience of Americans one generation after his death.

Unlike others in Lincoln's circle such as McClellan, Chase, Seward and the Blairs, Stanton had no designs to become president or even run for political office. He was a no-nonsense, results-oriented secretary of war who took over a corrupt ineffective department at a desperate time and turned it into the most efficient and powerful department in the cabinet. General Joe Hooker called Stanton the "greatest genius; a man who could argue a case before the Supreme Court and direct an army in the field. He would work night and day - it finally killed him. He was equal to ten generals in the field."[233] Scrupulously honest, his agents returned over one million dollars fraudulently obtained and left office much poorer than when he entered.

Epilogue

U.S. Grant had the innate ability to size up the people he met and express his thoughts with both directness and simplicity. With regards to Stanton he said: "Stanton's reputation rests a good deal on his quarrel with President Johnson, and in this his character is treated unfairly. Stanton's relations with Johnson were the natural result of Johnson's desire to change the politics of his administration and Stanton's belief that such a change would be disastrous to the Union. … Of course, a man of Stanton's temper, so believing would be in a condition of passionate anger. He believed that Johnson was Jeff Davis in another form, and he used his position in the Cabinet like a picket holding his position in the line." [234]

Grant's analysis is convincing. Stanton did hold to his position rather than move to Johnson's white supremacy standpoint and keep the Negro as a sub-citizen. His mistake was in believing that Johnson would not move against him. After four years of war, he desperately wanted to leave Washington and move on with his life, but felt duty bound to continue rather than let Johnson's policies precipitate another conflict.

Covering up for a president's misjudgments is an unstated part of the job description for a cabinet member, and Stanton did it remarkably well. Johnson not only took advantage of it but even accused Stanton of disloyalty for not doing it in the case of the riot in New Orleans. With a more scrupulous man as president, the secrets Stanton kept should have easily secured his position for as long as he wished. Welles's diary tells us that Stanton's actions should have forced his removal years before Johnson acted, but he was always hesitant to move against him.

Perhaps the sudden death of sentry Silas T. Cobb on November 9, 1867, at the ripe old age of 29 emboldened Johnson to make his fatal move against the then suspended Stanton. The timing of Cobb's death came at a critical and fortuitous time for the embattled Johnson.[235] Combined with the death of Browning the testimonies of the two young men became forever frozen in time. Statements to the contrary would be regarded as mere hearsay. When Johnson finally moved forcefully against Stanton, he did so in a heavy-handed and careless manner, without proper political preparation. It cost him dearly.

Stanton never wavered from the principles that he and Lincoln held together. Together they poured over numerous reports from provost units on duty in the South and discussed the proper approach to reconstruct the Southern States. Together they concluded that a nucleus of loyal Southerners could sustain itself as the true state government when combined with the muscle of the war department. The assassination of Lincoln and the policies of Andrew Johnson irreparably changed that strategy.

The victorious prosecution of the war was by no means a predestined certainty. The Confederacy had their opportunities, but the Union was able to commit not only all their Northern resources to the fight but also Southern resources (freed slaves) which eventually made the critical difference. The ability to marshal all these resources was due in large part to Stanton's administrative prowess. Without his assistance to the Thirteen, Fourteenth, and Fifteen Amendments, the history of the country and even the admiration that we hold for Lincoln would have been markedly different.

Edwin Stanton

At the time of Stanton's appointment, field commanders such as Generals Fremont and McClellan had strong political backing and were virtually independent from the Secretary of War and the President. Stanton worked quickly to prevent further degradation of civilian authority. He found material for the fronts, ended the corruption within the Department of War, advised the president, sustained the generals, and worked with legislators to keep the needed public support for the war.

Appointed to the Supreme Court in 1869, he died before taking office.

Collateral Damage

The life of Mary Todd Lincoln was never able to recover from the assassination. Plagued by the knowledge that her husband attended the play solely due to her instigation, she was unable to cope with her feelings of guilt developing what we now call an obsessive-compulsive disorder. Like Shakespeare's Lady Macbeth who obsessed about her guilt in the death of the king, her long grief and depression followed her for the rest of her life. She lost her son Tad in 1871 and lived in morbid fear for her last surviving son Robert. She relied upon her spirit mediums to keep her in touch with her family and lived in fear of poverty while going through extravagant spending sprees. She became so irrational that Robert could no longer handle her and had her committed to an institution.

After her release, she never forgave Robert and believed that he was trying to kill her for her money. She returned to Springfield to live with her sister. She secluded herself for the rest of her life, passing away in 1882.

Senator John Hale called in as many favors as possible to silence the rumors of a romance between Lucy and Booth. Her parents were shocked when Lucy told them of their engagement and denied it all to whoever asked. Booth's brother Edwin told his sister Asia of a heartbroken letter he received from the poor little girl to whom he promised so much happiness. Lucy had written that if necessary she would marry him at the foot of the scaffold.

Epilogue

After four years abroad, Lucy returned from Europe with the rest of her family and devoted the next four years of her life to the care of her ailing father. After his death in 1873, she renewed acquaintances with an old beau William Eaton Chandler. She had first met Chandler when he was a freshman at Harvard and she was twelve. Chandler later married the daughter of a New Hampshire governor and had several children. Now a widower and corporate lawyer they courted and married in 1874.

Chandler was a man much like her beloved father. Successful in politics, he served as Secretary of the Navy under President Chester Arthur in 1882 and as Senator from New Hampshire from 1887 – 1901. They had one child, a son born in 1885.

However, for Lucy, the light was gone from those blue-grey eyes. One of her stepsons described her as "a thoroughly unpleasant woman, in no way a sensuous woman." Washington society was full of evil whispers about her past romance with Booth, and she would always remain withdrawn from the social events that she used to thrive at as a younger woman. It became so painful for her that her widowed sister would later serve as the Washington hostess for the Chandler household. She died in 1915.

Although Secretary of State Seward and his son Frederick made miraculous recoveries from their injuries, his wife Frances and daughter Fanny did not. Six weeks from the attack, after serving as fulltime nurse for her family Frances collapsed and died at age 59. It was rumored that near the end of the assassination trial Secretary Seward was going to ask for Powell's pardon on the ground that it was not right that he should outlive his own murderer. The sudden death of Frances ended that hope. Her daughter Fanny took over as caretaker until she fell ill with tuberculosis the following year and died at the age of twenty-one.

Robert Lincoln became a successful lawyer and President of the Pullman Company. Due to his successes, he rose to the posts of Secretary of War and Minister to Great Britain. But he was never able to shake his feelings of guilt for turning down his father's invitation to the theatre that night leading to several nervous breakdowns. These feelings worsened the day he was with President Garfield when an assassin shot him on the train platform. Feeling he was cursed he vowed never to serve another President for the rest of his life. Robert made his last major public appearance on May 30, 1922, for the dedication of the Lincoln Memorial. He died in 1926 at the age of 82. His widow, Mary Harlan Lincoln decided to have Robert interred at Arlington National Cemetery rather than the family plot at Springfield because she felt that he was his own person and made his own history, independently of his great father. She decided that he should have his own place in the sun and not spend eternity in his father's shadow.

The assassination deeply affected Major Henry Rathbone and fiancée Clara Harris, the Lincoln's guests that night. They married in 1867 but he continued to replay the events of that night in his mind. Frequently, complaining of head and stomach pains, he resigned from the army and sought help overseas in European spas. President Grover Cleveland appointed Rathbone as his consul to Germany, but he became increasingly violent, even threatening his wife's life. On December 23, 1883, he went berserk and replayed the assassination. First, he shot his wife as Lincoln had been shot, then tried to stab himself to death as Booth had done to him. Clara died of her wound, but again Rathbone survived. Found guilty of murder he was committed to an asylum for the criminally insane. Rathbone died in the asylum in 1911. His last words were reportedly "The man with the knife! I can't stop him! I can't stop him!"

Epilogue

Because of his 'betrayal' of Booth, Captain Willie Jett was jilted by his sweetheart, ostracized by his friends, outlawed by his family, and finally obliged to leave his home in Westmoreland County. His loyalty to the Southern cause and the bullet he took in the abdomen defending his country gained him no favor. His choice was to die or protect John Wilkes Booth, and his neighbors believed that he chose poorly. He died of apoplexy at the age of forty-two in Williamsburg.

Not even Abraham Lincoln was allowed to rest in peace. At the close of the Civil War, between one-third and one-half of all U.S. paper currency in circulation was counterfeit. To counter this threat to the security of the nation's economy, Lincoln authorized the formation of the Secret Service. On July 5, 1865, it was created as a bureau under the Department of the Treasury to rein in the counterfeiting of the currency.

In the 1870's one of the nation's largest counterfeiting rings was headquartered in central Illinois. This ring suffered a severe blow when Ben Boyd, the gang's master engraver, was convicted and imprisoned. Realizing that Boyd was a unique talent that could not be replaced, Jim Kinealy, a saloon owner and ring leader of the group, decided to revive Booth's kidnap plot and steal Abraham Lincoln's body holding it as ransom until the government paid $200,000 in gold and freed Ben Boyd. It was almost a perfect crime since grave robbing was not covered under the theft laws of Illinois at the time. The Secret Service caught the perpetrators in the act convicted them of a misdemeanor to handle, move, disturb, embalm, or remove a dead body, without the permission of the coroner. They were sentenced to one year in Joliet Prison.

In 1901 in order to prevent a repeat of that crime, Robert Lincoln determined that the coffin be buried in a huge cage ten feet deep and encased in concrete with the Lincoln monument built above it. In order to put an end to the rumors that Lincoln was not buried in his tomb, his casket was opened one last time on September 26, 1901 and positively identified. Although dead for some 36 years, he was remarkably well preserved. This was undoubtedly due to the constant re-embalming efforts that he underwent in the twenty cities that his funeral train visited.

Lewis Powell's father and older brother George claimed his remains in 1871. As per his mother's dying request, they buried by her son by her side.

In January 1992, in the Anthropology Department of the Smithsonian Institution in Washington, DC, researchers found the skull of a young, white male. The inventory records of the skull described it as Number 2244; "Cranium of Lewis Payne (sic) Hung at Washington City for Complicity in the Assassination of Abraham Lincoln". Officials returned the skull to the family and interred it with the rest of his remains in November of 1994.

Mary Surratt's Grave Secret

It's generally agreed by historians, and confirmed by commission member Thomas M. Harris, that the "shooting irons" testimony by John Lloyd was the evidence that sealed Mary Surratt's fate. Her defenders have thus labeled Lloyd as a perjurer ever since. However, even though Atzerodt's lost confession backs up Lloyd's testimony, it doesn't necessarily prove her guilt. The commission also found Mary Surratt guilty because the conspirators used both of her properties as havens. She denied knowing Lewis Powell when he came to her door and lied about relaying the "shooting irons" message. Nothey, the man she was supposed to meet on her errand to Surrattsville, testified that he did not know she was coming to talk to him.

Indeed, it does seem odd that a staunch Catholic woman would leave on Good Friday, especially during the sacred 12:00 - 3:00 hours, for a four-hour buggy ride on the chance that the man she wanted to see would be available. Upon arriving in Surrattsville, Mrs. Surratt found that tavern keeper John Lloyd was not at home so she and Weichmann waited for his return. What puzzled the commission was why after coming all that way did she wait for Lloyd rather than go a little further down the road to the Nothey's house? As Weichmann later remarked, a three-cent postage stamp and a letter would have served the same purpose as her ride to Surrattsville for the task that she said she wanted to accomplish. The commission rightly concluded that her real mission was to pass a message to Lloyd not Nothey.

Logically, it is hard to justify Booth using Mary Surratt solely for the purpose of delivering field glasses and passing a message to get the rifles ready. The evidence suggests that he did not begin to finalize his plans until he learned of Lincoln's planned attendance to the Ford Theatre around noon. If in his escape plan, he made it as far as the Surrattsville tavern, why would he need the rifles? It's not likely that at that point he would anticipate a shootout with an approaching cavalry. What he really needed was a change of horses in order to keep his distance from any pursuers. Eli Huntt's house was five miles south of the tavern. If Booth intended to mislead his pursuers southward he needed to turn north at Surrattsville and take the road to the train depot at Annapolis Junction. Along with the 'shooting irons' message did Mary Surratt ask the intoxicated Lloyd to bring the horses to the tavern?

Lewis Weichmann, who witnessed the conversation between Lloyd and Mary Surratt, claimed that he heard none of it. Therefore, Lloyd's testimony is the sole source of what transpired. His admission of the 'shooting irons' message was the least self-incriminating story he could offer allowing him deniability of any knowledge of a larger plot.

Lloyd was very fearful of retribution if he said too much. When taken into custody by Officer George Cottingham, he wept bitterly and told him, "Oh my God, if I was to make a confession they would murder me!" Cottingham asked, "Who would murder you?" Lloyd replied, "These parties that are in the conspiracy." Lloyd then told him the story of the carbines and that Mary Surratt asked to have them ready. He did not reveal any other names or specifics but finished by wailing. "Mrs. Surratt, that vile woman has ruined me! I am to be shot! I am to be shot!"[236]

Epilogue

Mary Surratt gave many people the impression that she was incredibly naïve about the comings and goings of the suspicious people in her tavern and boarding house. However, to believe her requires a complete denial of the facts. She was an active southern sympathizer with a son (Isaac) serving in the Confederate army. She knew John worked for the Confederacy, that he took long trips to Montreal, escorted couriers to Richmond, and seemed always to have money but no real job. John Surratt tried to keep her in the dark, and she preferred to remain there rather than admit the obvious truth that was occurring in front of her. She frequently made excuses for him and passed information between him and other confidants like Booth. The shooting irons trip was not an isolated incident, just one more mission.

With John safe in Canada, she displayed an attitude common to southern women during the war, one of a self-righteous defiance. She took a calculated risk that by denying knowledge of the guns, it would have been merely her word against that of a drunkard and she would receive the benefit of the doubt. At worst, her gender should have allowed her to escape execution, an advantage that her son did not possess. Being a good mother, she chose to take the fall for her son.

From his prison cell, Lewis Powell, feeling remorse for his actions, said of Mary Surratt; "If I had two lives to give, I'd give one gladly to save Mrs. Surratt. I know that she is innocent and would never die in this way if I hadn't been found in her house. She knew nothing about the conspiracy at all." Powell then hedged his statement slightly saying she may have known something was going to happen but she didn't know what. [237] The second statement is probably closer to the truth. Especially if the account of Richard M. Smoot and his visit to the boarding house on the night of the assassination is true.

Smoot was a Maryland planter who worked with the Charles County underground. In a memoir written in 1904, Smoot felt comfortable enough to reveal his role in the kidnapping plot. Atzerodt identified him in statement #6 of his lost confession as the man who sold his boat to John Surratt, which was to be used to convey Lincoln to Virginia for $300. Smoot's memoir confirms Atzerodt's statement and reveals that Surratt still owed him $100 of that money.

With the balance long overdue, Smoot asked tavern keeper Lloyd where he could find Surratt. He advised him to see his mother at the boardinghouse in Washington. When he called upon her the Wednesday morning before the assassination and asked to see John, she gave him a "penetrating look of inquiry" and he fell under immediate suspicion. When Smoot told her of the object of his visit, "in an instant her whole demeanor changed and she extended a most cordial greeting.

She eagerly inquired if the boat was in place and easily accessible ... she whispered to me that if I returned to the house on Friday, I would most likely see John and the boys." On the night of the assassination (Friday) he called upon Mrs. Surratt hoping to collect the balance. He found Mrs. Surratt "in a state of feverish excitement. She then informed me that she was positive that the boat would be used that night, and that I would get my money in a day or two. She most earnestly besought me to leave the city and not be seen at her house again".[238]

Smoot's story infers that Mrs. Surratt knew of the kidnapping plot and was still expecting the president to be abducted not murdered. If she was positive the boat would be used that night, it's because that is what Booth told her. Booth did not reveal that his new plan was to assassinate not kidnap until his meeting with Powell, Herold and Atzerodt at approximately 8:00 that night. In any case, it leaves little doubt that she was involved with Confederate clandestine operations. This would also help to explain an observation made by Weichmann on their ride home that was not part of the court transcripts:

> When about halfway down, we saw a group of cavalrymen to the left, a short distance from the roadside...Stopping the buggy, Mrs. Surratt hailed a farmer, and desired to know what those soldiers were doing there. "They are pickets," he replied. She then asked if they remained out all night, and he stated that they were generally called in at about eight o'clock in the evening. "I am glad to know that," she said and drove on.[239]

With the pickets gone by early evening, she knew that road would be clear for Booth. Why else would she be glad that the soldiers would be gone by eight o'clock?

When Andrew Johnson decided to re-enter politics as a Democratic candidate for the House of Representatives in 1872, he realized that his constituents in Tennessee would not agree with his former stand that justice had been done for Mary Surratt. To counter this unpleasant fact he decided to re-circulate his charge that the vindictive Holt and Stanton were responsible for her death and that he was an innocent victim of their duplicity.

W. Scott Smith a newspaper reporter had an interview with Johnson on the matter and his comments appeared in the *Philadelphia Press* on December 12, 1881, six years after the former president's death:

"Talking of this matter of the Lincoln assassination, I remember asking Andrew Johnson, one day, when traveling through East Tennessee, at a time when he was running for congressman-at-large against Horace Maynard and Frank Cheatham. He was in a communicative mood and said. 'The true history of that case has never been told. It was represented in the newspapers that I refused to see Annie Surratt when she came to the White House the morning of the execution, asking for the pardon of her mother. The fact is that I never knew it was Miss Surratt, because a man named Mussey, who had general charge of the White House, came to me and said that a crazy woman was downstairs and wanted to see me, she would not give her name, but was crying and tearing her hair, and exhibiting all the evidence of insanity.'"

Once again, Johnson plays the innocent bystander, this time blaming his military secretary General R.D. Mussey for leaving him oblivious to all that was going on around him. Conveniently, for a man who told Colonel Moore that *"his mind was as clear as it's ever been"*, he does not mention the intervention of Mrs. Douglas who promised Anna Surratt to tell the president that she wished to see him.

That same evening after the executions, a Dr. Butler was at the White House by appointment with some Tennessee ladies who were friends of the president. When Johnson learned that Butler had been on the scaffold with Atzerodt, he asked him some questions about the hanging. He then remarked that his reason for refusing to commute Mrs. Surratt's sentence was "She kept the nest that hatched the egg". [240]

The reopening of this issue incensed Judge Joseph Holt. A deeply principled man who took great pride in building a reputation for honesty and integrity, he was again being slandered by the self-serving, obstructionist, drunken, demagogue from Tennessee.

As Judge Advocate Henry Burnett stated, "No graver charge could be made against a public officer than this against Judge Holt and, if true, no more cruel and treacherous betrayal of a public trust was ever committed by a man in high official position. It would be murderous in intent and effect. This charge rested, so far as human testimony went, upon the solemn assertion alone of President Johnson and, if untrue, was one of the most cruel wrongs ever perpetrated by one man against another. I came to the conclusion without any doubt that the charge made by Andrew Johnson was absolutely false".[241]

In February 1873, seeking further vindication for his position, Holt wrote the author of the clemency petition John Bingham. He inquired if he had conversed with Secretary of State Seward regarding the petition and asked if he would divulge the details.

Bingham stated that he called upon Secretaries Stanton and Seward and asked if the president reviewed the clemency petition before he approved the death sentence. Both men answered that the president had seen the petition, and it was considered by him and his advisers before approving the death sentence. Mr. Stanton and Mr. Seward stated that they were present when the president polled individual members of the cabinet regarding the prayer of the petition

However, Bingham had more to say. As he lay on his deathbed in 1900, Bingham told his physician John S. Campbell that he would tell him what Mrs. Surratt had privately told him during her incarceration. The revelation was of such a magnitude that Bingham went directly to Secretary Stanton to discuss it. They agreed that the *"evidence presented by Mrs. Surratt proved so shocking that its publication would threaten the Republic"*. Therefore, they decided on perpetual silence. At the moment of repeating what Mrs. Surratt had told him, he balked and decided to keep his pledge. He then said:

"The truth must remain sealed."[242]

This revelation could help to explain a controversial request by Stanton to prohibit conversation among the prisoners. An order from the war department and signed by Assistant Secretary of the Navy Gustavus Fox stated that all the prisoners shall "for better security against conversation…have a canvass bag put over the head of each and tied around the neck, with a hole for proper breathing and eating".

This order, barbaric by modern standards, is one of the reasons for a negative historical attitude of Stanton. However, the hooding of prisoners was not an unknown practice in the U.S. Navy at that time. This is probably why his most severe critic Navy Secretary, Gideon Welles, whose assistant signed the order, did not think it significant enough to protest it or even record it in his famous diary.[243]

It could also explain why Major Thomas Eckert, Stanton's top lieutenant and custodian of the physical evidence in the case was allowed to try and get a statement from all the condemned conspirators with the *exception of Mrs. Surratt*. What information could Mrs. Surratt possibly have inadvertently gleaned that would have "*threatened the Republic*"?

In order to persuade her to deliver his message to Lloyd, it is probable that Booth showed her the passes from Johnson and explained how he would make his escape. This is why she told Smoot she was positive his boat would be used that night.

How else could Booth reassure her that he could cross the bridge at night and get the guns? She had crossed the bridge enough times on her way to her tavern to know the bridge closed at 9:00. They were his trump card in convincing her that the trip to Surratsville had to be made that afternoon, Good Friday.

Epilogue

If Mary Surratt confided to Bingham the secret of the passes, it leads to an interesting conundrum. Did President Andrew Johnson cover-up his knowledge of the clemency plea, quash Judge Wylie's writ of habeas corpus, and ignore the pleadings of Anna Surratt, Mrs. Douglas and others to preserve justice in sanctioning Mary Surratt's execution, or to preserve his own secret?

The truth remains sealed.

President Dwight D. Eisenhower

Eisenhower used powers granted the president during Reconstruction to enforce court ordered desegregation in Little Rock Arkansas.

President Lyndon B. Johnson

Johnson used his political skills to change the Democratic Party's century old segregation policy and passed the Voting Rights Act in 1965.

A Century of Segregation

The South changed little in the one hundred years after the war. While the rest of the nation moved westward and embraced industrialization, the South remained largely a rural community with Negroes as second-class citizens. The Confederate military strategy of extending the conflict until the citizens of the North decided the fight wasn't worth continuing had failed, but it did succeed politically. In the disputed election of 1876 between Rutherford B. Hays and Samuel Tilden, a fateful deal was struck. Despite Tilden's victory in the popular vote the Electoral College votes of four states came into dispute. Both parties sent officials to those States to defraud the other party and ensure that their party won.

An ad hoc Electoral Commission created by Congress awarded all 20 votes to Hayes giving him the presidency by one electoral vote. Behind closed doors, the issue was settled when Southern Democrats agreed to stop their House filibuster blocking the final vote count, and give Hayes the victory. Sixteen years after the South refused to accept the legal election of Abraham Lincoln; they split with the Northern Democrats and forfeited what was very likely the legitimate election of Democrat Samuel Tilden to regain their Southern rights.

The complete details of the 'Bargain of 1877' have never been fully revealed but in return for the removal of federal troops in the Southern states and the return of Democrats to power in Louisiana and South Carolina, the Ku Klux Klan was disbanded and the use of terrorism to gain political control ended.[*] With the exit of the army, the power to enforce the fourteenth and fifteenth amendments left with them. The black codes were re-established and a large percentage of Negroes lost the right to vote in future elections.

---

[*] The Klan remained dormant until 1915 when it's glorification by the Hollywood movie *The Birth of a Nation* sparked a revival.

The political counter-revolution begun by Andrew Johnson had reached its conclusion. During the Grant administration, about 15% of the officeholders in the south were black. With this deal, the Democratic Party became the 'white' party of segregation and dominance in the South. "Jim Crow" laws were born and black officeholders disappeared. The "Solid South" became the bastion of Democratic Party power for the next hundred years.

Segregation became the law of the land in 1892 when the Supreme Court decision of *Plessy vs. Ferguson* cemented the concept of "separate but equal" in the South. Separate but equal also defined how the rest of the country viewed the South during this era. No Southern politician could escape the baggage of segregation to be considered presidential material, and the price to be paid for Southern support in the Congress was to keep the status-quo.

The wall of segregation cracked in 1954 when the Supreme Court struck down the "separate but equal" doctrine for public education in the *Brown vs. The Board of Education* decision. It declared the permissive or mandatory segregation that existed in 21 states unconstitutional. The decision cleared the legal barrier but the political battle for civil rights was just gearing up.

In 1957, President Eisenhower renewed his fight for Civil Rights legislation that would have guaranteed all the right to vote. A Civil Rights Bill had passed the House in the previous Congress but southern Democrats killed the bill using delaying tactics.

Eisenhower was shocked to discover that in Mississippi out of 900,000 eligible Negroes only 7,000 were allowed to vote. He investigated and found that the voting registrars were asking Negroes such questions as, "How many bubbles are there in a bar of soap?" In Louisiana, the registrars had closed their doors in the face of five thousand Negroes lined up to register; a local grand jury found "no case" against State officials.

The key figure in this legislation was Senate Majority Leader Lyndon Johnson of Texas. He received his position by the Southern bloc of Democrats in particular to obstruct civil rights legislation. However, Johnson was an ambitious man and wanted to make a run at the presidency in 1960. He knew that and he needed to be on the right side of this issue if he hoped to become the Democratic nominee.

The Eisenhower administration opened the issue to public debate and the astute Johnson realized that this time the Senate would have to act. The usual filibustering tactic would polarize the South and be devastating for the Democratic Party. He felt that the South was on the verge of an economic expansion, if their leadership would be willing to make some progress on civil rights. His Senate leadership position as well as his future ambitions was at stake.

Behind the scenes, Johnson promised the principal opponent of the civil rights bill the powerful Richard B. Russell of Georgia, that if he did not filibuster the bill, he would take the responsibility of neutering it with amendments and minimize its impact. He told Russell,

"These Negroes, they're getting pretty uppity these days and that's a problem for us since they've got something now they never had before, the political pull to back up their uppityness. Now we've got to do something about this, we've got to give them a little something, just enough to quiet them down, not enough to make a difference. For if we don't move at all, then their allies will line up against us and there'll be no way of stopping them, we'll lose the filibuster and there'll be no way of putting a brake on all sorts of wild legislation. It'll be Reconstruction all over again."[244]

The amendment that killed the effect of the bill was one that would assure a jury trial to anyone cited for contempt of court in a civil rights case. Since voting lists made up the jury lists and were virtually all white, the amendment had the practical effect of nullifying the bill. Legislatures knew it was highly unlikely that a Southern white jury would convict another white man of violating the rights of a Negro. However, the right of an accused to a trial by a jury of his peers was so deeply ingrained in the American tradition, and so sacred that it attracted support from Northern liberals.

The passage of the amended bill was a great victory for Johnson in that he managed to pass the legislation without splitting the Democratic Party. He assured the disappointed advocates of the 1957 bill that the passage was historically important because it was the first civil rights bill to pass Congress since 1875. "Once you break virginity," he drawled, "it'll be easier next time."

Eisenhower was incensed when presented with the emasculated bill on September 9 for his signature. He had already desegregated the District of Columbia, completed the integration of the armed forces and appointed progressive federal judges in the South. He had hoped that the 1957 bill would finally restore the vote to the disenfranchised blacks. However, the much larger political and moral showdown was already forming in Little Rock, Arkansas.[245]

Close associates of Governor Orval Faubus stirred up a mob to prevent integration of Central High School. Faubus promptly declared an emergency calling out the Arkansas National Guard and placing it around the school preventing the Negroes from entering.

Eisenhower warned Faubus that he was in direct defiance of a court order and demanded that Faubus change the guard's orders from preventing desegregation to enabling it. Faubus gave Eisenhower the impression he would change the National Guard's orders, despite warnings from U.S. Attorney General Herbert Brownell, that segregationists were not trustworthy enough to uphold the law. As Brownell expected, Faubus double-crossed Eisenhower challenging the president to act.

It had been eighty years since the government used federal troops to maintain order in the South and segregationists were agitating white mobs, conjuring up the ghosts of Thaddeus Stevens and Charles Sumner. Democrats such as Senator Richard B. Russell warned against using "strong armed totalitarian police-state methods" in Little Rock. Despite Southern pressure, Eisenhower declared that "mob rule cannot be allowed to override the decisions of our courts". As a General, Eisenhower had already broken the color barrier in the military by deploying black soldiers alongside whites to win the Battle of the Bulge in December 1944 and January 1945.

The president addressed the nation declaring, "the federal law and orders of a United States District Court …cannot be flouted with impunity; I will use the full power of the United States, including whatever force may be necessary to prevent any obstruction of the law and to carry out the orders of the federal court." Using legal powers from the Reconstruction laws, he sent the famed 101 Airborne Division into Little Rock. The same division, whose heroic stand at Bastogne a dozen years earlier had stabilized the Western Front for Eisenhower and the Allies.

In order to avoid a "brother against brother" confrontation, Eisenhower called the Arkansas National Guard into federal service and used them side by side with the paratroopers. The newly integrated Central High set a precedent for change. Segregationist southern governors could no longer use the state's armed forces to prevent integration. Segregationist forces never recovered from the defeat. The employment of federal troops by presidents of both parties was used to protect life and property during the racial unrest in the 1960's.

However, it was another accidental southern president, Lyndon Johnson, who was finally able to reverse the course taken by his namesake Andrew. Rising to the office after the assassination of President Kennedy, Johnson muscled through the opposition in his own party to enact a Civil Rights Bill in July, 1964. He had hoped that the passage of this bill would give America a respite from the continual conflict of race relations and the country would begin to assimilate the political and social impact. He began working on a Voting Rights bill that was to be ready by the spring of 1966. However, events in Mississippi and Alabama pushed him to accelerate that timetable.

On June 21, 1964, three Civil Rights workers who were registering Negroes to vote in Neshoba County, Mississippi, disappeared shortly after their arrest by the local police. The FBI began a search for the three men and started dredging nearby ponds, lakes, rivers, and swamps for their bodies. The search unexpectedly turned up dozens of unreported murdered Negroes within the county. Although unreported by the press, officials knew it would only be a matter of time. Finally, an anonymous tip led the FBI to an earthen dam where the workers bodies were discovered, ending the manhunt and the carnage discoveries.

In March 1965, civil rights leader Dr. Martin Luther King began a drive for voter registration in Alabama by leading a march from Selma to Montgomery. Governor George Wallace sent the

Afterward

State Police to break up the march leading to demonstrations throughout the country.

After sending federal troops to bring order to Alabama, Johnson presented the Voting Rights Act to Congress. In his twenty-four years in Congress, Johnson had accumulated a number of favors from legislators, and he was now determined to use them. Although bitterly opposed by the 'Dixiecrats' in his own party, the Republicans gave him the overwhelming support he needed to end the Southern filibuster and enact the bill into law

The 1965 Voting Rights act had the dramatic effect on the South that Negroes had long hoped to achieve. Similar to the 1957 Civil Rights Act that he had helped water down as a senator, it changed the political complexion of the South. The act outlawed literacy tests, poll taxes, and all other local obstacles that restricted people from voting.

Politically, the impact of the act had a ground shaking effect. By the next general election, African-Americans had become an important voting block in the old Confederate States. Due to the monopoly of organizational power the Democratic Party had in the South since the Civil War, they capitalized on the enlarged black vote to counteract the loss of Southern whites giving it a political gain because of the act.

Two technical innovations also came along at this time to help change opinions and revitalize the South. The first was national television that was able to present to Americans the deplorable conditions that the segregated South subjected Negroes. The second was air conditioning. Air conditioning allowed the South to industrialize in areas that was never previously possible. Its effect on the Southern economy was as great as the cotton gin had been 150 years before. Air-conditioned buildings in the summer to go along with their inexpensive labor market and mild winters made the South the ideal place for manufacturing expansion in the 1970's and 1980's.

But it was the fading warrior Thaddeus Stevens who foretold of these developments in his last speech on the House floor. In his final declaration of political faith, he told his colleagues:

"My sands are nearly run, and I can only see with the eye of faith. I am fast descending the downhill of life, at the foot of which stands an open grave. But you sir, are promised length of days and a brilliant career. If you and your compeers can fling away ambition and realize that every human being, however lowly-born or degraded by fortune, is your equal, and that every inalienable right which belongs to you also belongs to him, truth and righteousness will spread over the land, and you will look down from the Rocky Mountains upon an empire of one hundred million happy people."

Exactly one-hundred years after John Wilkes Booth's act, the United States had come full circle. The "house divided" finally fell and returned to the vision that Lincoln, Stevens, and the despised 'black' republicans had for it one century earlier. The counter-revolution that had begun with an assassination was finally over.

Bibliography

- **Ambrose, Stephen E**. *–Eisenhower soldier and President,* Simon & Schuster, 1990
- **American Art Association,** The political correspondence of George N. Sanders, (1914)
- **Armstrong,** Biographical Encyclopedia of Kentucky (1878)
- **Arnold, Samuel;** *Memoirs of a Lincoln Conspirator,* edited by Michael Kauffman, Heritage Books MD. 1995
- **Baker, Lafayette;** *Traitors & Conspirators of the late Civil War,* Philadelphia: Potter, 1894
- **Baker; Lafayette;** *United States Secret Service in the Late War,* Philadelphia: Potter, 1890
- **Bakeless, John;** *Spies of the Confederacy,* Philadelphia: Lippincott, 1970
- **Basler Roy;** *Collected Works of Abraham Lincoln Volumes I – VIII,* New Brunswick, NJ: Rutgers University Press, 1953
- **Bates, Homer David;** *Lincoln in the Telegraph Office,* University of Nebraska Press, 1995
- **Beale, Howard K**. *The critical year; a study of Andrew Johnson and reconstruction (More information?)*
- **Bishop Jim,** *The Day Lincoln was Shot,* Harper Bros, 1955
- **Brodie, Fawn M.** *Thaddeus Stevens Scourge of the South,* Norton, 1959
- **Brooks, Noah,** *Washington in Lincoln's Time* New York, Rinehart, 1958
- **Bryan, George;** *The Great American Myth,* New York, 1940
- **Boutwell, George S.** *Reminiscences of Sixty Years in Public Affairs.* 1902. Reprint. New York: Greenwood Press, 1968
- **Bowers, Claude;** *The Tragic Era,* New York, 1929
- **Burlingame, Michael, editor;** Walter B. Stevens, A REPORTER'S LINCOLN, UNIVERSITY OF NEBRASKA PRESS, 1998
- **Burnett, Henry Lawrence;** *Assassination of President Lincoln and the Trial of the Assassins,* manuscript in Goshen NY Library.
- **Butler, Benjamin F.** *Autobiography and Personal Reminiscences of Major-General Benj. F. Butler. Butler's book, 1892.* Thayer
- **Butler, Pierce**; *Judah P. Benjamin American Statesmen*; 1907; p346-347
- **Callahan, J.M.** *The Diplomatic History of the Southern Confederacy,* 1901, see note p.255
- **Castel, Albert;** *The Presidency of Andrew Johnson,* 1979
- **Chase, Samuel P.;** *Inside Lincoln's Cabinet The Civil War Diaries of Samuel P. Chase,* David Donald editor, 1954

- **Church, William C.**; *Ulysses S. Grant and the Period of National Preservation and Reconstruction*, New York [etc.] G.P. Putnam's Sons 1897
- **Clarke, Asia Booth**; *John Wilkes Booth A Sister's Memoir*, Terry Alford editor 1996
- **Conrad, Thomas N.**, *A Confederate Spy,* New York: Oglivie 1892
- **Conrad, Thomas N.**, *The Rebel Scout*, Washington: National Publishing, 1904
- **Cottrel John,** Anatomy of Assassination, 1966
- **Cox, Lawanda & Cox, John H.**, *Politics, Principle and Prejudice 1865-1866,* Macmillan, 1963
- **Craven Avery**, *The Coming of the Civil War*, University of Chicago Press, 1957 2nd ed.
- **Crook William H.**; **Gerry,** Margarita Spalding: *Through Five administrations; reminiscences of Colonel William H. Crook, body-guard to President Lincoln*, New York, Harper & Bros
- **Davis Burke,** *The Long Surrender,* Random House Publishing Group 1989
- **Davis, William C.**, *Jefferson Davis The man and His Hour,* Harper Collins 1991
- **Doster, William E.** : *Lincoln and Episodes of the Civil War.* New York: Putnam, 1915
- **Douglas Frederick** : *The Life and Times of Frederick Douglas.* London 1882
- **Dickenson, John.** *Andrew Johnson*, 1808-1875, chronology, documents, bibliographical aids
- **Dunbar, Rowland.** *Jefferson Davis Constitutionalist*, Vol VIII, Jackson, Dept of Archives, 1923
- **Eisenschiml, Otto**: *Why was Lincoln Murdered?* Halycon House NY, 1939
- **Evans, Eli**; *Judah P. Benjamin The Jewish Confederate;* New York, 1988
- **Flower, Frank A.**; *Edward McMasters Stanton;* Springfield Publishing, 1905
- **Giblin, James Cross**; *Good Brother, Bad Brother;* Clarion, New York, 2005
- **Good, Timothy**: *We saw Lincoln Shot;* University Press Jackson Mississippi, 1995
- **Goodwin**, **Doris Kearns:** *Lyndon Johnson and the American Dream* ; New York: St. Martin's Press, 1991
- **Gorham, George C**.: *Life and Public Services of Edwin M. Stanton*, Vol. 2, NY 1899
- **Grover, Leonard**; *"Lincoln's Interest in the Theatre,"* Century Magazine (April, 1909),
- **Hay, John**; *Lincoln in the Civil War in the Dairies of John Hay*; New York, 1939

Bibliography

- **Hanchett, Dr. William;** *The Happiest Day of His Life*, Civil War Times Illustrated :December, 1995
- **Hanchett, Dr. William;** *The Lincoln Murder Conspiracies;* University of Illinois Press, Chicago, Urbana :1983
- **Hamilton Howard,** *Civil War Echoes: Character Sketches and State Secrets,* Washington, DC, Howard Pub. Co. 1907
- **Hamand, Lavern M**. *"Lincoln's Particular Friend"* in *Essays in Illinois History.* (1968)
- **Harris Wiliam C.,** *Lincoln's Last Months,* Cambridge, Mass. : Belknap Press of Harvard University Press 2004
- **Headley, John W**. *Confederate operations in Canada and New York.* NY: Neale, 1906
- **Hendrick, Burton J**. *Statesmen of the Lost Cause.* Boston, 1939
- **Hendrick, Burton J**. *Lincoln's War Cabinet* .Brown, 1946
- **Hesseltine William B.,** *Ulysses S. Grant, Politician* ,New York, 1935
- **Higham, Charles**. *Murdering Mr. Lincoln,* Beverly Hills, 2004
- **Hunt, H. Draper**. *Hannibal Hamlin: Lincoln's First Vice President,* Syracuse Press, 1969
- **Jones, Thomas A**. *J.Wilkes Booth,* Chicago, Laird & Lee, 1893
- **Kauffman Michael,** *American Brutus*, Random House NY, 2004
- **Kinchen, Oscar A**. *Confederate operations in Canada and the North,* North Quincy Mass: Christopher Publishing house, 1970
- **Lamon, Ward Hill**; *Recollections of Abraham Lincoln*, University of Nebraska Press, 1994
- **Lankevich,George** ; *American Metropolis: A History of New York City,* New York University Press, 1998
- **Laughlin, Clara;** *The Death of Lincoln,* New York, Doubleday, 1909
- **Lattimer, John K.;** *Kennedy and Lincoln: Medical and Ballistic Comparisons of their Assassinations,* New York , 1980
- **Leech, Margaret,** *Revcille in Washington,* Caroll&Graf, 1986
- **Leonard, Elizabeth:** *Lincoln's Avengers*, New York : W.W. Norton & Co, 1994
- **Long E.B.:** *The Civil War Day by Day*, DeCapo Press, NY.1971
- **Markle, Donald**; *Spies and Spymasters of the Civil War;* New York, Hippocrene, 1994
- **McPherson, James,** *Abraham Lincoln and the Second American Revolution,* 1991, Oxford University Press
- **McCulloch, Hugh;** Men and Measures of Half of a Century, Charles Scribner's Sons, 1888
- **McPherson, Edward**, *The Political History of the United States of America During the Period of Reconstruction* (Washington: Solomons & Chapman, 1875)
- **McKitrick, Eric L,** *Andrew Johnson and reconstruction*
- **Milton, George Fort,** *The Age of Hate;* 1930

- **Moore, Colonel W.G.**, *Notes of Colonel W.G. Moore, Private Secretary to President Johnson*, St.George L. Sioussat; *The American Historical Review, Vol.19, No 1 (October 1913), 98-132.*
- **Morcom, Richard,** *They All Loved Lucy;* American Heritage, Vol 21, No 6 (October 1970) 12-15
- **Nicolay, John and Hay, John**; *Abraham, Lincoln: A History.* 10 vols. New York: Century, 1890
- **Oates Stephen B,** With Malice Toward None, New York : Harper & Row **1977**
- **Oldroyd, Osborne**; The Assassination of Abraham Lincoln; Washington, 1901
- **Ownsbey, Betty J**.; Alias "Paine": Lewis Thorton Powell, The Mystery Man of the Lincoln Conspiracy; McFarland, 1993
- **Parker, Anna Virginia**. *The Sanders family of Grass Hills.* Madison, Ind.: Coleman Printing Co.,1966
- **Pierce, Edward Lillie**; *Memoirs and Letters of Charles Sumner* 4 vols., Boston, Roberts Brothers 1893
- **Pinkerton Alan,** *The spy of the Rebellion*, University of Nebraska Press1989
- **Pitman Benn,** *The Assassination of Lincoln and the Trial of the Conspirators*, Westport, Conn., Greenwood Press [1974, c1954]
- **Poore, Ben Perley;** *The Conspiracy Trial for the murder of the president;* Boston: Tilton& Co. 1865
- **Pratt, Fletcher**; *Stanton: Lincoln's secretary of War*; New York, Norton,**1953**
- **Raymond, Henry**; *Life and Public Services of Abraham Lincoln*, New York: Derby and Miller, 1865
- **Reck, W.Emerson,** *A. Lincoln his last 24 hours*, University of South Carolina Press, 1987
- **Rembert Patrick,** *Jefferson Davis and His Cabinet* (Baton Rouge: Louisiana State University Press, 1944),
- **Rehnquist, William,** *All the laws but one: civil liberties in wartime*; New York : Knopf
- **Ripley, Edward H,** *The Capture and Occupation of Richmond,* Putnum & Sons, 1907
- **Rhodehamel, John and Taper, Louise;** *Right or Wrong, God judge me: The writings of John Wilkes Booth*, Urbana : University of Illinois Press,1997
- **Roscoe Theodore,** *The Web of Conspiracy* , N.J., Prentice-Hall 1959
- **Rowland, Douglas (compiler),** Jefferson Davis, Constitutionalist, His Letters, Papers, and Speeches, 7 volumes, Jackson Mississippi, 1923
- **Sandburg, Carl** ; *Abraham Lincoln The War Years IV*

Bibliography

- **Seward, Frederick W.** ; *Seward at Washington*, 1846-1872, 1891
- **Schafer, Joseph** (translator/editor), *Intimate letters of Carl Schurz, 1841-1869,* Madison, Wisconsin State Historical Society of Wisconsin, 1928
- **Singer Jane**, *The Confederate Dirty War*, McFarland and Co. North Carolina, 2005
- **Smith, Gene.** *High crimes and misdemeanors : the impeachment and trial of Andrew Johnson*
- **Smith, Gene.** *American Gothic*, Simon & Schuster, 1992
- **Smith, Jean Edward:** *Grant* New York : Simon & Schuster,**2001**
- **Smith, William E.** *The Francis Preston Blair Family in Politics,* New York, Macmillan, 1933
- **Smoot, R.M.,** *The Unwritten History of the Assassination of Abraham Lincoln,* W.J. Coulter, Clinton Mass., 1908
- **Simpson, Brooks D.** *The Reconstruction presidents,* 1998
- **Stampp, Kenneth M. ,** *The era of reconstruction, 1865-1877*, New York, Vintage Books, 1965
- **Starkey, Larry.** *Wilkes Booth Came to Washington.* New York, Random House, 1976
- **Steers Edwin,** *His name is still Mudd*, Gettysburg, PA : Thomas Publications 1997
- **Steers Edwin,** *Blood on the Moon*, University of Kentucky Press, 2001
- **Stewart, William;** *Reminiscences of Senator William M. Stewart* New York, Neale Pub. Co., 1908
- **Stryker Lloyd Paul**, *Andrew Johnson, 1929*, p84
- **Stuart, Meriwether.** *Operation Sanders; where in old friends and ardent pro-southerners prove to be Union secret agents.* 1973 Virginia Historical Society
- **Styple, William B. editor;** *Generals in Bronze*, Belle Grove Publishing New Jersey 2005
- **Thomas, Benjamin & Harold Hyman;** *Stanton the Life and Times of Lincoln's secretary of War*, Knopf 1962
- **Thomas Reed Turner**, *Beware the people weeping : public opinion and the assassination of Abraham Lincoln* / Baton Rouge : Louisiana State University Press, c1982
- **Tidwell, William;** *April '65: Confederate Covert Action in the American Civil War*, Kent, Ohio : Kent State University Press, 1995
- **Tidwell William, Hall James O., Gaddy David Winfred;** *Come Retribution: the Confederate secret service and the assassination of Lincoln*, Jackson : University Press of Mississippi, 1988
- **Townsend, George Alfred**; "How Wilkes Booth crossed the Potomac", *The Century,* p. 828-829, April 1884, volume 27, Issue 6
- **Trefousse, Hans Louis**. *Impeachment of a president : Andrew Johnson, the Blacks, and Reconstruction*

- **Van Deusen, Glyndon;** *William Henry Seward*; Oxford University Press, 1967
- **Wearmouth, John M. & Roberta J.:** *Thomas A. Jones, chief agent of the Confederate Secret Service in Maryland,* Stones Throw Publishing MD. 2000
- **Welles, Gideon,** *Diary of Gideon Welles* ;Volumes 1, 2, 3: Houghton Mifflin 1911
- **Wellman, Paul,** *The House Divides* ,Garden City, N.Y.: Doubleday, 1966
- **Weichmann, Louis J.** *A True History of the Assassination of Abraham Lincoln and the Conspiracy of 1865;* (New York: Alfred A. Knopf, 1975)
- **Wilson, James H.:** *Life of John A. Rawlins,* New York, The Neale Pub. Co.,1916
- **Winkler, H. Donald;** *Lincoln and Booth,* Cumberland House, Nashville TN, 1995

Notes

Key to Abbreviations used for frequently mentioned sources:
- M-599 - refers to the sixteen reels of microfilm records stored and published by National Archives on the evidence used in the trial of the conspirators
- HRC - Hall Research Center at the Surratt House Museum
- PIT - *The Assassination of President Lincoln and the Trial of the Conspirators* (Pitman)
- LV - Laurie Verge Director of Surratt House Museum, Huntt family direct descendant.

Chapter 1: The Indispensible Man

1 Thomas & Hyman; Stanton the Life and Times of Lincoln's Secretary of War, p.41
2 Flower; Edward McMasters Stantonp.83, p.99
3 Lamon; Recollections of Lincoln, 264-265
4 Pratt; Stanton: Lincoln's Secretary of War, p. 141.
5 Diary of Gideon Welles, Vol. I, p. 61-62.
6 Flower; Op. cit.p.369
7 Diary of Gideon Welles, Vol. II, p. 16
8 Nicolay & Hay; Abraham, Lincoln: A History, p. 533

Chapter 2: Enter the Paladin

9 Clarke, Asia Booth; John Wilkes Booth A Sister's Memoir, p.35
10 Ibid p.43-44
11 Giblin, James; Good Brother, Bad Brother; p.56
12 Ibid
13 Chicago Journal, April 15, 1865
14 Clarke, Asia Booth; Op. cit p.82
15 Ibid p.83-84
16 Bakeless, John; Spies of the Confederacy, p.84
17 Some say that Van Ness' six headless horses, still make an occasional appearance and gallop around the site of the mansion.
18 Winkler, H. Donald; Lincoln and Booth p.37
19 Conrad, Thomas N., The Rebel Scout p.130
20 Tidwell, April '65: Confederate Covert Action in the American Civil War p.182-183
21 Stuart, Operation Sanders;
22 Kinchen, Confederate operations in Canada and the North, p.41
23 Ibid p. 47

24 Tidwell, April '65 p.144
25 Now called Clinton, Maryland
26 Tidwell, Come Retribution, p.24
27 Arnold, Memoirs of a Lincoln Conspirator, p.45-46
28 Gene Smith, American Gothic, p.117-118
29 Clarke, Asia Booth; Op. cit, p.86
30 Ibid p.128
31 HRC

Chapter 3: Kidnapping Lincoln

32 Headley, John W; Confederate Operations in Canada and New York,p.402 - 406
33 Douglas Frederick; The Life and Times of Frederick Douglas, p319
34 Hans Trefousse, Andrew Johnson, p. 188
35 Milton, George Fort; The Age of Hate p.147
36 Brooks, Noah; Washington in Lincoln's time, p.214
37 Charles Gautier was the premier caterer to all the celebrities in the city. Among the events he hosted was Lincoln's inaugural ball.
38 Townsend, "How Wilkes Booth crossed the Potomac", p. 827
39 Arnold, Op. cit, p.134-136
40 George J. Lankevich, American Metropolis: A History of New York City, p. 113
41 Tidwell, Come Retribution, p.462
42 Bakeless, Spies of the Confederacy, p123 - 126
43 Stringfellow ,"Letter to Jefferson Davis"; HRC
44 Ibid
45 Bakeless, Op. cit; p123 - 126
46 PIT p.44
47 Now called Hopewell, Virginia
48 Ripley, The Capture and Occupation of Richmond, p. 13
49 Flower, Op. cit; 311-312; Stanton letter to Ashley
50 Singer, The Confederate Dirty War, p.135
51 Bates, Lincoln in the Telegraph Office, p.384
52 William H. Herndon, "Letter from Lincoln's Old Partner," Religio-Philosophical Journal, December 12, 1885.
53 Lamon, Op. cit; p. 267-269
54 Hamand, pages 30-31
55 Wellman, The House Divides, p.332.
56 New York Daily Tribune, July 12, 1850
57 Taylor's body was exhumed in 1991, and a Kentucky State medical examiner announced that in his opinion at a news conference that 'Zachary Taylor had not been poisoned'. However, after examining the autopsy results Michael Parenti in his 1999 book History as Mystery says the coroner's 'opinion' is at odds with the actual levels of arsenic found in Taylor's body.

John A. Bingham principal framer of the Fourteenth Amendment was another who reportedly was certain that Taylor was assassinated.

– *New York Times*, Aug.29, 1881

Chapter 4: Setting the Stage

58 M-599, reel 6, frames 0016-0017, National Archives, (Person)
59 Thomas A. Jones: J.Wilkes Booth, p.46
   Jones asserted that Booth planned to have Stanton murdered. The attempt on Secretary Stanton's life was not made, for reasons unknown to Jones.
60 LV, Herold left his nightshirt with the Surratt laundry mark at the Huntt home. He left the house before the family woke at 6 a.m.
61 Smoot, R.M., The Unwritten History of the Assassination of Abraham Lincoln
62 Grover, "Lincoln's Interest in the Theatre," Century Magazine (April, 1909), p.943
63 After the assassination, the play had a rebirth of popularity. Clarke produced the play again in New York and was sued by Laura Keene who claimed that she had exclusive rights to produce the play in the United States.
64 IBID p.44
65 Conspirator theorists have used this incident described by Bates in 'Lincoln in the telegraph office' to imply that Stanton was involved in the plot and wanted Lincoln unprotected. Lincoln was in a playful mood that day. It's highly likely that the same result would have occurred if Eckert was sitting in Rathbone's chair.
66 Chaconas; The long missing confession of George Atzerodt, HRC at Surratt House Museum.
67 Lamon, Op Cit; p 279
68 Bates, Op Cit; p.307 - 308
69 Ibid p.384-385
70 Ownsbey, Betty J.; Alias "Paine": Lewis Thorton Powell, The Mystery Man of the Lincoln Conspiracy, p.139
71 Judiciary House Committee, House of Representatives: The Impeachment Committee Investigation (Washington, D.C.: Government Printing Office, 1867) Testimony of Major Thomas T. Eckert, pp.673-675
72 John Surratt, New York Times, February 7, 1909 p.SM3
73 PIT; p. 47
74 Atzerodt statement to Reverend Butler.
75 PIT;   p145
76 Ibid p.154 - 157
77 PIT; p.75, Testimony of Mary Jane Anderson
78 Ibid
79 Bryan, The Great American Myth; p.182
80 Fred Peterson, New York Times; Feb 9, 1913 - Matthews had recently moved from his old residence in the Peterson's House. Lincoln died in his old room.
81 Bishop Jim, The Day Lincoln was Shot p.241
82 James Tanner, Letter to Henry F. Waich, April 17, 1865
83 PIT; p. 152
84 Styple, Generals in Bronze p.288
85 Pierce, Memoirs and Letters of Charles Sumner 4: 241; Letter to John Bright, May 1,1865

86 Storey Moorfield, The Atlantic Monthly; April 1930; p.463 - 465
87 Tanner, Letter to Hadley H. Walch, April 17,1865
88 Dixon, "Mrs. Elizabeth Dixon's letter to her sister, Mrs Louisa Wood," Lincoln Lore,# 1587, May 1950
89 Oldroyd, Osborne; The Assassination of Abraham Lincoln, p.35
90 Leale, Lincoln's last hours, Harpers Weekly, February 13, 1909
91 Dixon, Op Cit;
92 It was later purchased by Henry Ford (Founder of Ford Motor Company) and is part of The Henry Ford collection at the Greenfield Village museum in Dearborn Michigan.
93 Stewart, William; Reminiscences of Senator William M. Stewart p194-195
William Morris Stewart was Nevada's first Senator elected in 1864. He succeeded in establishing the University of Nevada. In 1888 he introduced a Senate bill to establish the Carson Indian Training School and obtained funding from the U.S. Bureau of Indian Affairs. He served in the Senate until 1875 when he decided to retire and practice law. Elected to the Senate again in 1887 and reelected in 1893 and 1899. He finally retired from the Senate in 1905. He died in Washington D.C. four years later at the age of 82.
94 Chase, Samuel P.; The Civil War Diaries of Samuel P. Chase, p268-267
95 New York Times, April 15, 1865
96 New York Times, February 14, 1897

Chapter 5: The Great Manhunt

97 Roscoe Theodore, The Web of Conspiracy p.190 – 191
98 PIT; p. 84
99 As quoted by Roscoe p.194
100 Bishop Op Cit; p.255 -257
101 PIT; p.144
102 Fletcher made a claim for a portion of the reward money stating that he identified the saddle and bridle of the one-eyed Bay horse abandoned by Lewis Payne as belonging to Atzerodt that night. However, his identification was not enough to link Atzerodt to any of the shootings at that time since no one had identified the rider of the horse as Seward's attacker.
103 The reader could equate the events of September 11, 2001 as a modern parallel of government reaction. Even though all of America saw the planes hitting the Twin Towers of New York, it took the government hours to assess the extent of the threat.
104 Bryan Op Cit; p.199
105 PIT; p. 84
106 For a more extensive debunking of this myth see Michael Kauffman's, American Brutus, p.272, 273
107 Good, We Saw Lincoln Shot; p.19
108 Poore; vol. 1, 227
109 Some people believe that the theatrical good luck wish to "Break a leg" was derived from Booth's last successful stage appearance.
110 Starkey, Larry: Wilkes Booth Came to Washington, p 126. Starkey was the first to espouse this 'alternate route' theory.

111 Weichmann, Louis J.: A True History of the Assassination of Abraham Lincoln and the Conspiracy of 1865 p. 172
112 LV, Learning of the assassination the next day Joseph Huntt was warned that if he told the soldiers anything he'd be hung higher than a Georgia pine.
113 New York Times, February 7, 1909, Sunday Magazine p.SM3
114 Kauffman, American Brutus p.268 , p.454
115 Doster, Episodes of the Civil War p.269
116 Townsend, Op Cit;, p. 828-829
117 Surratt Courier Aug 1996
118 Oldroyd, Op Cit; p269 – 270
119 Roscoe; Web of Conspiracy, p.257
120 Surratt Courier, "The Pursuit and Death of John Wilkes Booth, Sept-Nov 1989
121 New York Times, July 30, 1896
122 Ibid
123 Ibid
124 Ibid
125 Lattimer; Kennedy and Lincoln: Lattimer concluded that the direction of the bullet would have made it almost impossible for Booth to shoot himself.

Chapter 6: The Secrets of Mars

126 National Archives, War Dept Records – Later reports corrected the farmer's name from John Garther to William Gaither.
127 PIT; p.152
128 Ownsbey Op Cit; p.139
129 M-599 Reel 3, Frames 0596 thru 0602
130 Surratt Courier ; Oct 1988
131 Basler Roy; Collected Works of Abraham Lincoln VIII p.410
132 Pratt, Op Cit; p.405-407
133 Basler Roy; Op Cit; p.410
134 Kauffman Op Cit; p.344-345
135 Long Bridge was the exception. It connected Washington to Alexandria Virginia. Alexandria was considered secure from Rebel activity. Long Bridge was open for free travel a few days before the general order went out to the other bridges surrounding Washington.
136 Surratt Courier, Sept 1996
137 Early American History Auctions; Item Number: 96628
138 Howard, Civil War Echoes p. 84
139 John I. Davenport; "Recollections", New York Journal, January 14, 1896.
140 Michael Burlingame, editor, Walter B. Stevens, A Reporter's Lincoln, p. 156
141 Flower, Op Cit; p.312
142 H. Draper Hunt, Hannibal Hamlin: Lincoln's First Vice President, p. 197-198.
143 Trefousse, Hans Louis. Andrew Johnson : a biography p. 180
144 McCulloch, Hugh; Men and Measures of Half of a Century p.373

145 Cotton, N.S. The familial incidence of alcoholism: A review. Journal of Studies

on Alcohol 40:89-116, 1979.
146 Mary Todd Lincoln, letter to Sally Orme (15th March, 1866)
    147 Welles, Vol II p454
    148 Ibid p.461
    149 Crook, Through Five Administrations p.92

Chapter 7: Trial and Cover-up

150 Tidwell, April '65 p.150-154
151 Poore vol. 1, p 111
152 Poore vol. 1, 242-243
153 Rhodehamel, Right or Wrong, God Judge Me, p. 146
154 Poore vol. 1; 150-151
155 The interrogatory with Cobb is found in M-599, starting at reel 4, frame 171
156. Ibid
157. Ibid
158 Surratt Courier Sept.1996
159 Doster, Op Cit; p 274 – 275
160 PIT; p.151
161 Doster, Op Cit; p 274 – 275
162 Laughlin, p.329
163 Ibid 279
164 The National Intelligencer reported that they could state on the 'highest authority' that there was a conspiracy to assassinate every member of the cabinet. 'Booth, it is said, sent his card up to the Vice-President, but Mr. Johnson could not conveniently see him." The New York Times, April 18, 1865
165 Roscoe Op Cit; p.183
166 Howard Op Cit; p.84
167 M-599, Reel 3, Frames 0596 - 0602
168 The New York Times, April 18, 1865
169 Bishop Op Cit; p 227
170 Roscoe Op Cit; p316
171 National Archives, war department Records
172 Ibid
173 Doster, Op Cit; p.275-276
174 Smith, Gene: American Gothic, p.216-217
175 Cox, Politics, Principle, and Prejudice 1865-1866 p.58
176 Leonard Op Cit;184-185
177 Craven Avery, The Coming of the Civil War p. 202

Chapter 8: A Critical Rupture -1865

178 Hendrick, Burton J. Lincoln's War Cabinet p.387
179 Smith, Gene. High Crimes and Misdemeanors p123,124
180 Quoted by Cox, Politics, Principle, and Prejudice, p.56
181 Congressional Globe, 28th Congress, 1st session (1844), pp. 96-97

182 Leonard, Op Cit; 202,206
183 Smith, Jean. Grant p.418
184 Stampp, Kenneth M. , The Era of Reconstruction, 1865-1877 p.68
185 McKitrick, Eric L, Andrew Johnson and Reconstruction p.52
186 Thomas, Op Cit; 457
187 Ibid: 456

Chapter 9: A Counter-Revolution Begins 1866

188 Castel, Albert; The Presidency of Andrew Johnson p. 77
189 Flower Op Cit; 307
190 Jean Edward Smith; Grant p 424, 425
191 Van Deusen, William Henry Seward P.451
192 McPherson, Abraham Lincoln and the Second American Revolution, p.17
193 Smith, The Blair Family - p365
194 Gorham, George C.: Life and Public Services of Edwin M. Stanton, Vol. 2 p.316 – 317
195 Schafer, Intimate letters of Carl Schurz, 1841-1869 p.365
196 Gorham, Op Cit; Vol. 2 p.427
197 Rutherford B. Hayes to Guy M. Bryan, October 1, 1866, in Charles R. Williams (ed.), Diary and Letters of Rutherford Birchard Hayes (5 vols., Columbus, Ohio, 1922-1926), III, 32, 33.
198 Jean E Smith; Grant p.428
199 Wilson, Life of John A. Rawlins. P.330
200 Ibid   428,429
201 Boutwell, Reminiscences, xi, 108-109 "Johnson's Plot," 572-574;
202 Gorham Op Cit; 331, 332
203 Nation (New York, 1865-), III (November 15, 1866), 390.
204 Boutwell, "The Usurpation," Atlantic Monthly, Oct., 1866, 506
205 Welles II 638

Chapter 10: Implosion! 1867

206 Roscoe Op Cit; p.509
207 Welles III p.46
208 Moore, Colonel W.G., Notes of Colonel W.G. Moore 2/14/1867
209 Beauregard; "Secretary Stanton and Congressman Bingham" Lincoln Herald, Winter 1989
210 Flower Op Cit; 316-319
211 Tidwell, Come Retribution, p.417
212 Leonard Op Cit; p.270-271
213 Castel Op Cit; p.137
214 Hall, Surratt Courier, August 1990
215 Thomas, Op Cit; 553
216 Church, Ulysses S. Grant, P347
217 Smith, The Blair Family, p388

8 New York Herald, August 31, 1867.
9 Van Deusen, Op Cit; p.476, 477
220 Moore Op Cit; p.115
221 Gorham Op Cit; 396
222 Hesseltine, Ulysses S. Grant, Politician p. 77—79;

Chapter 11: Aftermath

223 Trefousse Op Cit; p. 333
224 Smith, William, The Blair Family, p.394
225 McPherson, The Political History of the United States During Reconstruction, Washington: Solomons & Chapman, 1875, pp. 381-82.
226 Crook Op Cit 151, 152
227 Castel Op Cit; 210
228 Hendrick, Statesmen of the Lost Cause, p.158
229 Dunbar, Jefferson Davis, VIII, 356
230 Higham, Charles. Murdering Mr. Lincoln p245
231 Ibid
232 Thomas Op Cit; p. 601
233 Styple: Op Cit; p.41
234 Thomas p. 612-613
235 His testimony in the trial gave Johnson the cover that the president needed, but after the trial, he became a man who officially never existed. His military records are missing even though local records show him as being born in Holliston Ma and volunteering to serve in Company F, 3rd Regt. Mass. Heavy Artillery on July 15, 1863. A small newspaper article detailing the soldiers from Holliston, lists his death as occurring in Grand Haven Mi. with burial in Holliston. However, no death certificate could be found in State records as to the cause.
236 Weichmann Op Cit; p. 191
237 Ownsbey, Op Cit; ", p137-139
238 Smoot Op Cit; p.4-5
239 Weichmann Op Cit; p. 166
240 Laughlin p.333
241 Burnett; Assassination of President Lincoln
242 Beauregard, "Secretary Stanton and Congressman Bingham", Lincoln Herald, Winter 1989
243 Bone Beverly, "Edwin Stanton in the Wake of the Lincoln Assassination" Lincoln Herald, Winter 1980
244 Quoted by Doris Kearns Goodwin, Lyndon Johnson and the American Dream, p.148
245 Ambrose, Eisenhower Soldier and President p.440-442

Index

Abbott, Ezra Dr., 146
Anderson, Robert, 24, 25
Antonelli, Cardinal, 315, 316
Aquidneck Hotel, 248
Arnold, Sam, 49, 70, 71, 75, 89, 90, 91, 92, 94, 98, 99, 197, 199, 200, 203, 207, 218, 234, 245, 359
Arthur, Chester, 373
Ashley, James, 319, 337
Atzerodt, George, 10, 72, 89, 93, 94, 122, 124, 128, 129, 134, 170, 179, 180, 193, 194, 195, 196, 197, 231, 236, 240, 242, 377
  Assassination Night, 133, 134
  Statement of, 100, 196, 201, 202, 203, 205
  Trial, 218, 231, 232, 233, 234
Atzerodt, John, 193, 196
Augur, Christopher, 142, 143, 153, 154, 157, 161, 231
Bainbridge, A.R., 183, 185
Baird, Absalom, 302, 303, 304
Baker, Lafayette, 157, 182, 183, 189, 257, 258, 331, 333
Baker, Luther, 183, 187, 188
Baltimore, 47, 48, 49, 51, 70, 73, 92, 94, 99, 128, 143, 154, 168, 171, 193, 199, 200
Banks, Nathanial, 322
Barlow, Samuel, 257
Barnes, Dr. Joseph K., 199, 249
Bell, William, 135, 136, 171
Benjamin, Judah, 60, 65, 73, 79, 95, 96, 237, 274, 275, 364, 365
Bingham, John A., 217, 234, 323, 383, 385
Bishop, Jim, 158, 159
Black Codes, 280
Blaine, James, 280

Blair, Francis jr.,, 359
Blair, Francis Sr, 79, 260, 262, 292
Blair, Frank jr, 260, 261, 292, 298, 324, 325, 358
Blair, Montgomery, 29, 43, 141, 154, 257, 260, 261, 262, 263, 266, 267, 271, 281, 299, 334, 339, 342
Booth, Asia, 50, 57, 77, 372
Booth, Edwin, 50, 51, 56, 70, 98, 207, 247, 336, 372
Booth, John Wikes
  CSA Agent, 58, 67, 69
Booth, John Wilkes, 8, 10, 14, 47, 48, 49, 50, 51, 53, 56, 57, 60, 69, 75, 76, 77, 87, 89, 98, 100, 111, 119, 120, 121, 122, 123, 124, 125, 126, 128, 129, 133, 137, 138, 139, 155, 156, 161, 164, 165, 166, 167, 168, 169, 170, 171, 172, 176, 177, 178, 179, 180, 181, 182, 183, 184, 185, 186, 188, 193, 195, 196, 197, 198, 199, 200, 201, 202, 203, 204, 205, 206, 237, 238, 239, 240, 241, 242, 243, 244, 245, 247, 248, 275, 338, 372, 373, 374, 375, 378, 379, 384, 394
  Assassination Night, 133, 134, 135, 137, 139, 140, 141
  CSA Agent, 66
  Death of, 187, 188, 189
  Diary, 240, 331, 332, 333
  Engagement, 98, 100
  in New York, 93, 98, 99, 100
  Kidnap plot, 89, 90, 91, 92, 93, 94, 95, 96, 98
  Loves, 74, 75, 76, 77
  Navy Yard Bridge, 159, 161, 164, 170
  Recruiting team, 70, 71, 72, 73

Index

Stage Career, 51, 52, 55, 56
Torpedo Plot, 100, 130
Trial, 218, 220, 222, 223, 224, 227, 228, 229, 230
Booth, John Wilkes", 50, 364
Booth, Junius Jr, 69, 77
Booth, Junius Sr., 47
Boutwell, George, 255, 311, 313, 345
Bridges
　Bennings, 92, 171
　Navy Yard, 134, 136, 154, 156, 157, 161, 164, 169, 170, 196, 204, 224
Briscoe, Washington, 134
Brooks, Noah, 87
Brown, John, 52, 53, 54, 55, 165
Brownell Herbert, 391
Browning, William, 57, 222, 223, 224, 239, 240, 370
Brownlow, Parson, 300
Bryan, Guy M, 307
Bryant, William, 180, 181
Bryantown, 154, 167, 172, 176
Buchanan, James, 24, 25, 26, 27, 32, 62, 217, 237, 271
Burnett, Henry, 217, 383
Burrough, Joseph "Johnny Peanuts", 137, 139, 165, 166
Butler, Benjamin, 26, 166, 211, 263, 330, 331, 332, 333, 337, 338
Cameron, Simon, 31, 32
Campbell, John Judge, 104
Cartter, Chief Justice, 142, 143
Chandler, William Eaton, 373
Chase, Salmon, 22, 27, 32, 33, 43, 86, 87, 143, 148, 149, 254, 261, 263, 334, 358, 362, 363, 368
Chester, Samuel, 99, 100, 125, 203
Clampitt, John, 171
Clarke, John Sleeper, 51, 122
Clay, Clement, 64, 65, 218, 237, 365
Clay, Henry, 115
Clendenin, David T., 217
Cobb, Lucy, 258
Cobb, Silas, 164, 227, 228, 229, 230, 231, 370
Colburn, Nettie, 117
Colfax, Schuyler, 253, 314
Conger, Everton, 183, 186, 187, 188
Conover, Sanford, 219, 220, 337, 338, 359, 362
Conrad, Thomas Nelson, 59, 60, 61, 73
Cook, Col. Roger E., 201
Copperheads, 64, 65, 66, 189, 217, 256, 264, 266, 286, 290, 343, 358
Corbett, Thomas 'Boston', 186, 187, 188, 189
Cottingham, George, 378
Couch, Darius General, 308
Cox, Samuel, 172, 173, 177, 178
Cox, Samuel jr, 178
Crook, William, 216, 359, 360
Cushing, Caleb, 265
Dahlgren, John A,, 38
Dana, Charles, 143, 155, 212, 214, 263
Dana, David, 155, 167, 172
Davis, Charles,Winter, 26, 255
Davis, Jefferson, 53, 60, 62, 64, 79, 82, 85, 95, 103, 116, 131, 169, 218, 237, 238, 259, 268, 288, 359, 362, 363, 364, 365, 369
Davis, Thomas, 166
Dawes, Henry, 34, 253
Deery, John, 119
Dennison, William, 297
Devlin, Mary, 55
Dewitt, David Miller, 150

Index

Dix, John General, 142
Dixon, Elizabeth, 146, 147
Doherty, Edward, 183, 185
Donaldson, James, 128, 129, 197, 242
Donaldson, William. See Donaldson, James
Doster, William E., 10, 130, 201, 202, 231, 232, 233, 236, 246
Douglas, Adele., 235, 382, 385
Douglas, Stephen A., 24, 62, 235, 308
Douglass, Fredrick, 84
Dramatic Oil Company, 57
Dunham, Charles. See Conover, Sanford
Dunn, Alphonso, 119
Early, Jubal, 58, 59, 153, 154
Eckert, Thomas, 126, 127, 129, 332, 384
Eisenhower, Dwight D., 388, 389, 390, 391, 392
Ekin, James A., 217
Evarts, William, 355, 356
Evarts, William", 356
Farragut, David G, 308, 322
Farwell, Leonard, 144, 232, 244
Faubus, Orval, 390
Fessenden, William, 356
Fillmore, Millard, 51, 115
Fletcher, John, 125, 155, 157, 227, 230
Foote, Solomon, 148, 149
Forbes, Charles, 137
Ford, Henry, 57, 122, 123
Ford's Theater, 89, 119, 122, 123, 125, 133, 137, 141, 142, 144
Fort Moultrie, 24
Fort Sumter, 24, 25, 26, 93, 119
Foster, Albert S., 217

Fox, Gustavus, 384
Freedmen Bureau, 283
Freemont, John C, 262
Gardiner, George, 172
Garfield, James, 319, 357, 374
Garrett, Richard, 182, 184, 185, 186
Gourlay, Jeannie, 139
Grant, U.S., 58, 59, 68, 69, 71, 80, 90, 94, 96, 102, 105, 106, 107, 120, 122, 123, 126, 128, 129, 143, 153, 194, 213, 218, 219, 262, 265, 269, 272, 280, 290, 305, 309, 310, 311, 313, 314, 320, 321, 322, 324, 325, 326, 327, 329, 330, 333, 349, 350, 352, 355, 356, 357, 358, 360, 367, 368, 369, 388
Interim War Secretary, 339, 340, 341, 342, 348, 349
Grant, U.S.", 106
Greeley, Horace, 65
Greene, Thomas, 60
Grimes, James, 356
Gustavus Spencer. See Howell, Augustus
Hahn, George, 272
Hale John, 98
Hale, John Parker, 75, 76, 248, 249, 372
Hale, Lucy, 74, 75, 76, 77, 87, 98, 122, 185, 188, 248, 372, 373
Hamlin, Hannibal, 85, 86, 211
Hampton, Wade, 59
Hancock, Winfield Scott, 182, 183, 235
Hansell, Emerick, 136
Harbin, Thomas, 72, 180, 181
Harding, George, 33
Harlan, James, 253, 297, 374
Harney, Thomas, 96, 97
Harris, Thomas M., 217, 377

Index

Hawk, Harry, 123, 138, 144
Hay, John, 40, 57, 76, 113, 122
Hayes, Rutherford B, 307
Hays, Rutherford B, 387
Heintzelman, Samuel, 204
Herndon House, 122, 124, 128, 133
Herndon William, 113
Herold, Davy, 14, 73, 89, 92, 121, 125, 129, 135, 155, 157, 164, 166, 167, 172, 177, 179, 180, 182, 183, 185, 195, 196, 198, 200, 218, 224, 227, 228, 229, 230, 234
  Assassination Night, 133, 134, 135
Hess, Dwight, 119
Holmes, Oliver Wendell, 75
Holt, Joseph, 25, 217, 219, 222, 234, 237, 271, 274, 335, 336, 338, 360, 381, 382, 383
Hooker, Joseph, 244, 263, 368
Howard, Hamilton, 242
Howard, Jacob Senator, 242
Howe, Albion P., 217
Howell, Augustus, 94, 197
Hunter, David, 217
Huntt, Joseph Eli, 121, 378
Huntt, Laura Beasten, 169
Hutchison, Ellen Stanton, 23, 40
Jackson, Andrew, 32, 209, 210, 260, 271
Jett, Willie, 183, 184, 185, 186, 375

Johnson, Andrew, 10, 14, 15, 57, 59, 143, 147, 149, 161, 162, 195, 199, 203, 205, 206, 208, 209, 210, 211, 212, 213, 214, 215, 216, 217, 218, 219, 222, 223, 224, 231, 232, 234, 235, 236, 237, 238, 239, 240, 241, 242, 243, 244, 247, 253, 260, 262, 263, 264, 267, 274, 275, 277, 281, 284, 292, 293, 294, 303, 308, 310, 314, 316, 319, 321, 326, 329, 331, 332, 335, 336, 337, 338, 341, 350, 355, 356, 357, 358, 359, 360, 361, 362, 363, 364, 366, 367, 368, 369, 370, 381, 382, 384, 392
  Assassination Night, 144, 145, 146, 149, 150, 162
  Conflicts with Congress, 276, 277, 278, 280, 281, 282, 283, 284, 285, 286, 287, 288, 289, 294, 312, 313, 314, 319, 320, 322, 324, 325, 330, 345, 346, 348, 350, 351, 352
  Conflicts with Grant, 290, 309, 310, 311, 340, 341, 348, 349, 350
  Conflicts with Stanton, 259, 265, 272, 282, 292, 293, 299, 300, 301, 302, 303, 304, 310, 319, 320, 321, 322, 328, 329, 333, 336, 337, 339, 350
  New Orleans Riot, 302, 303, 304, 305, 307
  Pardons, 254, 257, 258, 266, 269, 270
  Petition for clemency, 234, 235, 335, 382, 383, 385
  Political Maneuvers, 256, 257, 266, 267, 268, 269, 270, 288, 294, 296, 297, 298, 301, 307, 308, 325, 326, 327, 340, 350, 351
  Reconstruction, 251, 253, 254, 255, 256, 278, 279

Index

Tenure Act, 322, 323, 324, 334
Vice President, 84, 85, 86, 95, 124, 128, 129, 143
Johnson, Bradly Col, 59
Johnson, Charles, 215
Johnson, Eliza, 208, 216
Johnson, Lyndon, 389, 390, 392, 393
Johnson, Reverdy, 366
Johnson, Robert, 215, 258
Johnston, Joseph, 102, 263
Jones, Robert R., 158, 222
Jones, Thomas, 173, 176, 177, 179, 180
Julian, George, 40, 211
Kate Brown. *See* Slater, Sarah
Kate Thompson. See Sarah Slater
Kautz, Augustus, 217
Keene, Laura, 50, 122, 123, 137
Kimmel House, 134, 193
King, Martin Luther., 392
King, Preston, 235
King, Rufus, 315, 317
Kirkwood Hotel, 95, 122, 124, 133, 148, 195, 198, 203, 222, 223, 224, 239
Knox, Kilburn, 120, 121
Ku Klux Klan, 291, 352
Lamon, Ward Hill, 114, 115, 128, 413
Lamson, Mary Stanton, 22
Lane, James, 235
Laurie Family Spiritualists, 117
Leale, Charles Dr., 147
Lee, John, 69, 158, 159
Lee, John", 58
Lee, Robert E., 58, 68, 69, 80, 82, 93, 94, 102, 103, 105, 141, 182, 213, 263, 269

Lincoln, Abraham, 31, 39, 40, 41, 42, 43, 44, 45, 53, 57, 59, 60, 65, 68, 69, 70, 71, 75, 76, 90, 91, 92, 94, 95, 98, 108, 109, 110, 111, 119, 120, 122, 123, 126, 127, 138, 147, 148, 182, 203, 204, 210, 211, 212, 213, 214, 217, 218, 219, 221, 229, 233, 237, 239, 260, 262, 263, 270, 285, 294, 360, 363, 370, 374, 375, 376, 394, 410, 411, 412
  Advisors, 31, 32, 33, 34, 35, 38, 41, 276, 292, 370
  Assassination, 8, 245, 262, 268, 275, 277, 319, 331, 359, 362, 374
  Assassination Night, 137, 138, 141, 143, 156, 162, 203, 204
  Black Suffrage, 111, 272, 360
  Campaign Decisions, 211, 212, 261, 262
  Death, 147, 148, 263
  Hampton Roads, 79, 80, 82
  in Richmond, 102, 103, 104, 105
  Kidnap Plot, 59, 71, 75, 89, 90, 92, 93, 94
  President Elect, 27, 28, 29
  Reconstruction, 251, 252, 253, 254, 257, 264, 294
  Second Inaugural, 84, 86, 87
  Torpedo Plot, 104, 105
  Warnings, 113, 114, 115, 118
Lincoln, Mary, 40, 44, 117, 122, 127, 203, 215, 372
  Assassination Night, 139, 145, 146, 147
Lincoln, Robert, 76, 146, 147, 372, 374, 376
Lincoln, Tad, 103, 119, 372
Lincoln, Willie, 116

Index

Lloyd, John, 72, 166, 167, 202, 377, 378
Lowell, James Russel, 309
Lucas, William, 181
Maddox, Joseph E., 264
Marble, Manton, 264
Matthews, John, 125, 126, 140, 207
  Assassination Night, 140
Maximilian, 267
McClellan, George, 36, 42, 58, 263, 368
McCullough, Hugh, 209, 213, 251, 253, 257, 300
McGowan, Theodore, 137
McPhail, James, 196, 197, 205, 233, 332
McPherson, Edward, 277
Meigs, Montgomery, 141
Merrick, R.T, 334
Merritt, James, 206, 219, 220
Milton, George Fort, 48, 49, 150
Monroe, Capt. Frank, 195, 233
Montauk, 195, 248
Montgomery, Richard, 219
Moore, W.S., 294, 335, 336, 337, 346, 348, 382
Morton, Oliver, 288
Mosby, John, 60, 61, 73, 79, 94, 96, 109, 172, 182, 183
  Torpedo Plot, 96
Mosby's Rangers, 61, 73
Mudd, Dr. Samuel, 71, 155, 166, 169, 172, 198, 218, 234, 359
Mussey, R.D, 232, 235, 382
Napoleon III, 63, 267, 271
Napoleon, Louis. *See* Napoleon III
National Hotel, 74, 75, 207, 244
Nelson, Samuel, 86
Nicolay, John, 44
Nothey, John, 124, 377
O'Beirne, James, 145, 182
O'Laughlin, Michael, 70, 71, 89, 94, 98, 121, 197, 199, 200, 203, 218, 234
Oldroyd, Osborne, 155, 177
Ord, Edward, 324, 346
Orr, James L., 308
Parker House, 58
Parker, John F., 138, 156, 157
Payne, Lewis. See Powell, Lewis
Person, Edward, 120
Peterson House, 142, 144, 148, 161, 162
Pickett, George, 102, 104
Pickett, Lasalle Mrs., 104
Pierce, Franklin, 62, 281
Pierrepont, Edward, 335
Polk, James Knox, 22, 260
Pomeroy, Samuel, 216
Pope Pius IX, 315
Pope, John, 305, 324, 325, 346
Powell, Lewis Thorton, 10, 73, 89, 93, 111, 122, 124, 129, 135, 136, 155, 168, 171, 172, 196, 200, 218, 234, 235, 376, 377, 379
  Assassination Night, 133, 135, 136
Quesenberry, Elizabeth., 180
Rathbone, Henry, 127, 138, 374
Raybold, Thomas, 122, 123
Rhett, Robert Barnwell, 21
Richards, Major A.C., 156, 157
Richter, Harmon, 194, 201
Ripley, Edward, 104, 105
Robinson, George, 136
Ruggles, Mortimer.B., 183, 184, 185
Russell Richard B, 389, 391
Sainte Marie, Henri Beaumont, 315
Sanders, George Nicholas, 61, 62, 63, 64, 65, 66, 219, 220, 221, 237, 238, 240, 365

Index

Sanders, Reid, 64
Schofield, John, 324, 356
Schurz, Carl, 280, 282, 304, 305, 411
Scott, General Winfield, 26, 27, 29, 33
Seddon, James, 60
Seward, Augustus, 136
Seward, Fanny, 135, 373
Seward, Frances, 373
Seward, Fredrick, 135, 141, 154, 373
Seward, William, 26, 33, 35, 53, 79, 80, 85, 105, 120, 135, 155, 167, 200, 218, 251, 253, 256, 261, 262, 267, 271, 274, 293, 298, 308, 312, 315, 317, 321, 322, 323, 324, 329, 334, 340, 345, 366, 373, 383
  Assassination Night, 135, 136, 141, 142
Seymour, Horatio, 358
Sharpe, George, 237, 365
Sheridan, Philip, 59, 102, 153, 304, 324, 325, 326, 340, 350
Sherman, John, 298, 321
Sherman, William Tecumseh, 69, 263, 310, 311, 348, 350
Sickles, Dan, 324, 325, 329, 340, 350
Singleton, James, 203
Slater, Sarah, 94, 95, 96, 200
Smith, John, 196, 197, 332
Smoot, Richard, 72, 180, 198, 379
Soule, Pierre, 63
Spangler, Ed, 218, 234, 359
  Assassination Night, 133, 137
Speed, Joshua, 85, 217, 235, 253, 268, 297, 362
St. Lawrence Hall, 58

Stanberry, Henry, 309, 326, 327, 328, 329, 330, 341, 356, 362, 363
Stanton, Edwin, 22, 23, 33, 34, 35, 36, 37, 38, 39, 40, 41, 42, 43, 44, 85, 86, 102, 108, 109, 120, 121, 126, 127, 141, 142, 153, 161, 182, 204, 206, 212, 217, 222, 227, 228, 229, 230, 240, 241, 248, 249, 251, 252, 253, 256, 257, 259, 261, 262, 263, 264, 268, 271, 272, 273, 274, 275, 280, 282, 284, 289, 292, 293, 297, 298, 299, 300, 310, 312, 313, 319, 320, 321, 322, 326, 327, 328, 329, 330, 333, 334, 335, 336, 340, 348, 349, 350, 351, 360, 362, 363, 367, 368, 369, 370, 381, 383, 384
  Assassination Night, 141, 142, 143, 144, 145, 146, 147, 159, 161
  Attorney General, 21, 24, 25, 26, 27, 29
  Firing, 351
  New Orleans Riot, 301, 302, 303, 304, 305
  Suspension, 336, 337, 339, 340, 341, 342, 346
  Tenure Act, 323, 334
Stephens, Alexander, 82, 259
Stevens, Thaddeus, 31, 32, 255, 267, 268, 277, 278, 279, 280, 284, 286, 289, 307, 309, 321, 353, 391, 394
Stewart, Joseph B., 139
Stewart, William, 148, 149, 150, 162
Stone, Judge Fredrick, 173
Stringfellow, Franklin, 80, 82, 95, 96, 97, 169
Stuart, Richard Dr., 177, 181
Sumner, Charles, 94, 145, 147, 253, 255, 261, 272, 276, 277, 280, 284, 285, 288, 307, 351, 355, 391

Index

Surratt, Anne, 235, 382, 385
Surratt, John, 71, 72, 73, 75, 79, 89, 92, 94, 95, 96, 129, 130, 135, 167, 169, 172, 180, 193, 197, 198, 199, 200, 218, 237, 315, 379
  Capture, 315, 316, 317
  Escape to Europe, 274, 275
  Trial, 334
Surratt, Mary, 71, 72, 92, 94, 96, 124, 167, 168, 171, 198, 202, 218, 234, 235, 275, 333, 360, 377, 378
Secret, 377, 378, 379, 381, 383, 384
Surrattsville, 71, 73, 94, 96, 124, 154, 164, 167, 168, 198, 377
Swann, Oswald, 173
T.B., 92, 167, 168
Tanner, James, 142, 143
Taylor, Zachary, 115, 116
Thomas, George General, 300
Thomas, Lorenzo, 351
Thompson, Jacob, 25, 26, 64, 65, 66, 95, 218, 219, 237
Tilden, Samuel, 387
Tompkins, C.H., 217
Torpedo Plot, 97, 99, 100, 104, 110, 130, 131, 182
Townsend, George Alfred, 173, 349
Trefousse, Hans, 214, 361
Trenholm, George Alfred, 64, 365
Trumbull, Lyman, 216, 283, 287, 288, 349, 356
Tucker, Beverly, 237, 238, 239, 240, 242, 268, 365
Turner, Ella Starr, 74, 207, 243, 244, 247, 248
Vallandigham, Clement C., 65, 358
Van Ness mansion, 60
Verdi, Tullio Dr., 135, 141
Wade, Benjamin, 59, 255, 356, 357, 367
Wallace George., 392
Wallace, Lewis, 217
Wallace, Watson, 219
Walter, Father, 235
Weed, Thurlow, 26, 340, 345
Weichmann, Louis, 92, 97, 124, 168, 198, 200, 218, 377, 378, 381
Welles, Gideon, 36, 37, 38, 43, 85, 141, 153, 216, 249, 251, 252, 253, 271, 281, 287, 294, 299, 321, 322, 323, 334, 341, 351, 355, 368, 369, 384
Welles, Gideon", 252
Willards Hotel, 74, 125, 126, 183
Williams, William, 179
Wilson, James F., 353
Winthrop, William, 317
Wirz, Henry, 238
Wise, Henry, 53
Withers, William, 123, 137, 139
Wood, Fernando, 93
Woodland, Henry, 177, 179
Wylie, Andrew, 235, 385
Zekiah Swamp, 176

Made in the USA
Lexington, KY
17 June 2014